PETRO ECONOMICS

PETRO ECONOMICS

R.K. Singh

RANDOM PUBLICATIONS

NEW DELHI - 110 002 (INDIA)

Petro Economics

ISBN 978-93-51116-70-7

Published in 2015 in India by

RANDOM PUBLICATIONS

4376-A/4B, Gali Murari Lal, Ansari Road
New Delhi-110 002
Phone: +9111-43580356, 23289044
E-mail: randomexports@gmail.com; sales@randompublications.com;
info@randompublications.com

Reprinted 2024

Type Setting by: Friends Media, Delhi-110089
Digitally Printed at: Replika Press Pvt. Ltd.

Preface

Petroleum economics is a complicated series of political and economic interactions pertaining to the oil industry. While economics in general is a complex subject, in the case of oil, political concerns add a new layer to the study of economics. People who study petroleum economics need to be familiar with economics generally, but also geopolitical history and the history of the oil industry as a whole. Experts in this field can work for government agencies, oil companies, and private companies interested in the economics of oil production, transport, and refining. As with economics in general, there are a number of approaches to petroleum economics. Many experts boil down economic activities to a balance between supply and demand. In this case, supply and demand are both influenced by political concerns. Political events can have an impact on oil supply as well as demand, and in turn, oil supply and demand can influence politics.

Economics drives the entire oil/gas producing industry. Almost every decision is made on the basis of an economic evaluation. Economic evaluations are also performed to determine reserves and the "standardized measure of value" for reporting purposes for publicly held companies. In many cases, the goal of the company is to make decisions that have the best chance of maximizing the present day profit. There are a number of theories to describe economic phenomena in the oil industry, as well as to explore political relationships and social phenomena. This branch of economics also includes a broad number of connected fields, including international shipping, agriculture, manufacturing, transport, and so forth. Understanding of these fields is important, as all of these industries are involved in the global demand for oil. Strategic or geopolitical dimensions, international nature, economic and financial issues, technological adventures, challenges of sustainable development: these are a few facets of the world of energy. To ensure their development and to penetrate new markets, the companies in the energy sector need professionals with a global vision. Petroleum politics have been an increasingly important aspect of diplomacy since the rise of the petroleum industry in the Middle East in the early 20th century. As competition grows for an increasingly scarce but vital resource, the strategic calculations of major and minor countries alike place more prominent emphasis on the pumping, refining, transport and use of petroleum products. People interested in this subject study a wide variety of topics, from theories about global oil availability in the future to the environmental costs associated with oil and gas production. They can apply their studies to shaping oil and gas policy, assisting companies with the development of new oil fields, and educating people interested in the economies and politics of oil-producing nations. Alternative energy is also a topic of study for some people in this field, as they are interested in the political push for the development of alternatives to oil, as well as the economic impacts of shifting energy supplies.

This book will be of great value to petroleum engineers, students in business and economics, policy makers, and anyone else interested in the future of petroleum production.

I thank all members of my team who have helped in the preparation of the book. My special thanks go to "Random Publications" who have published the book.

— R.K. Singh

Contents

Chapter 1

Economics of Petrodollar and Euro

Petrodollar or Petroeuro? A new Source of Global Conflict

The current political and economic rift between the US and the European Union has been called a clash of civilizations. Its major cause is a struggle over the gains to be had from producing the world's leading currency. No observer of the lead-up to the war in Iraq and its aftermath could have failed to notice that the level of cooperation between Europe and America was extremely low. France and Germany were very strong opponents of the US/UK invasion and even after the war was declared over, disagreements persisted over the lifting of sanctions and how Iraq should be run.

So was this just a one-off tiff or was it a symptom of deeper flaws in the relationship? I believe that the war on Iraq illustrated for the first time that continental Europe, led by France and Germany, no longer wishes to follow the Americans politically, although what has been termed a 'clash of civilisation is probably better viewed as a 'clash of economies'.

While disagreements over the US trade barriers on steel imports or the European restrictions on imports of American genetically modified crops have attracted widespread comment, the most intense economic rivalry of all has received far less media attention than it perhaps should: this is the rivalry between the dollar and the euro for the position of world reserve currency, a privileged status that has been held by the dollar ever since the Bretton Woods agreement nearly 60 years ago.

At present, approximately two thirds of world trade is conducted in dollars and two thirds of central banks' currency reserves are held in the American currency which remains the sole currency used by international institutions such as the IMF. This confers on the US a major economic advantage: the ability to run a trade deficit year after year. It can do this because foreign countries need dollars to repay their debts to the IMF, to conduct international trade and to build up their currency reserves. The US provides the world with these dollars by buying goods and services produced by foreign countries, but since it does not have a corresponding need for foreign currency, it sells far fewer goods and services in return, i.e. the US always spends more than it earns, whereas the rest of the world always earns more than it spends. This US trade deficit has now reached extraordinary levels, with the US importing 50% more goods and services than it exports. So long as the dollar remains the dominant international currency the US can continue consuming more than it produces and, for example, build up its military strength while simultaneously affording tax cuts.

Getting a share of this economic free lunch has been one of the motivations, and perhaps the main motivation, behind setting up the euro. Were the euro to become a reserve currency equal to, or perhaps even instead of, the dollar, countries would reduce their dollar holdings while building up their euro savings. Another way of putting this would be to say that Eurozone countries would be able to reduce their subsidy to American consumption and would find that other countries were now subsidising Eurozone consumption instead.

A move away from the dollar towards the euro could, on the other hand, have a disastrous effect on the US economy as the US would no longer be able to spend beyond its means. Worse still, the US would have to become a net currency importer as foreigners would probably seek to spend back in the US a large proportion of the estimated three trillion dollars which they currently own. In other words, the US would have to run a trade surplus, providing the rest of the world with more goods and services than it was receiving in return. A rapid and wholesale move to the euro might even lead to a dollar crash as everyone sought to get rid of some, or all, of their dollars at the same time. But that is an outcome that no-one, not even France or Germany, is seeking because of the huge effect it would have on the world economy. Europe would much prefer to see a gradual move to a euro-dollar world, or even a euro-dominated one.

It turns out that there is a small group of countries which is playing the arbiter in this global contest. These are the world's oil exporters, in particular OPEC and Russia. Ever since the days when the US dominated world oil production, sales of oil and natural gas on international markets have been exclusively denominated in dollars. This was partly a natural state of affairs since, up until the early 1950s, the US accounted for half or more of the world's annual oil production. The tendency to price in dollars was additionally reinforced by the Bretton Woods agreement which established the IMF and World Bank and adopted the dollar as the currency for international loans.

The vast majority of the world's countries are oil importers and, since oil is such a crucial commodity, the need to pay for it in dollars encourages these countries keep the majority of their foreign currency reserves in dollars not only to be able to buy oil directly but also to protect the value of their own currencies from falling against the dollar. Because a sudden devaluation of a country's currency against the dollar would lead to a jump in oil prices and a possible economic crisis, every country's central bank needs dollar reserves so as to be able to buy its own currency on the foreign exchange markets when its value needs to be supported.

The fact that oil sales and loans from the IMF are dollar-denominated also encourages poorer countries to denominate their exports in dollars as this minimises the risk of losses through any fluctuations in the value of the dollar. The knock-on effect of this is that, since many of these exports are essential raw materials which richer countries need to import, their denomination in dollars reinforces the need for rich countries to keep their own currency reserves in dollars.

While the denomination of oil sales is not a subject which is frequently discussed in the media, its importance is certainly well understood by governments. For example, when in 1971 President Nixon took the US off the gold standard, OPEC did consider moving away from dollar oil pricing, as dollars no longer had the guaranteed value they once did. The US response was to do various secret deals with Saudi Arabia in the 1970s to ensure that the world's most important oil exporter stuck with the dollar. What the Saudis did, OPEC followed. More recently, in June 2003, the Prime Minister of Malaysia publicly encouraged his country's oil and gas exporters to move from the dollar to the euro. The European and American reactions were polar opposites: the EU's Energy Commissioner, Loyola de Palacio, welcomed the suggestion, saying that 'in the future the euro is [going to be] taking a place in the international markets in general as the money of exchange' and that this was 'a matter of realism'. Her counterpart in the US, the director of the Energy Information

Administration, Guy Caruso, said that he couldn't see 'any particular merit' in the move and that over the long run 'the dollar's always won out'. Either way, Malaysia is only a relatively minor oil exporter, so what it does can only have a very limited effect. A switch by a major oil exporter would be of far greater significance.

The first country to actually make the switch was a very important oil exporter indeed: Iraq, in November 2000,. Before the war in Iraq began, some observers, myself included, argued that this might well be a major reason for the US desire to invade and the strong Franco-German opposition to the invasion,. Corroborating evidence included the apparent influence which loyalty (or lack thereof) to the dollar seemed to have on the US attitude towards other OPEC members. Iran had been talking of selling its own oil for euros, and was subsequently included in George Bush's 'axis of evil'. Venezuela, another important oil exporter, had started bartering some of its oil, thus avoiding the use of the dollar, and was encouraging OPEC to do likewise- and the US was widely suspected in having played a part in the attempted coup against the Venezuelan president, Hugo Chavez.

Semi-official confirmation that petro-currency rivalry was at the heart of the split between France and Germany, on the one hand, and the US, on the other, was provided by Howard Fineman, the chief political correspondent for Newsweek, in an article he wrote in April 2003, in the aftermath of the war. The Europeans and Americans were then arguing over whether the UN's oil-for-food programme in Iraq should remain in place or not. Using the term 'clash of civilisations' to describe the divide which was developing, Fineman explained that the disagreement had little to do with the French calls for the search for weapons of mass destruction to resume and for sanctions to remain in place until the search was complete. Instead, Fineman said, it was mainly about the dollar vs the euro. Citing White House officials and a presidential aide, he explained that the dispute between the two continents was really about 'who gets to sell - and buy - Iraqi oil, and what form of currency will be used to denominate the value of the sales. That decision, in turn, will help decide who controls Iraq, which, in turn, will represent yet another skirmish in a growing global economic conflict. We want a secular, American-influenced pan-ethnic entity of some kind to control the massive oil fields (Iraq's vast but only real source of wealth). We want that entity to be permitted to sell the oil to whomever it wants, denominated in dollars.' Fineman concluded his article by confidently predicting that future Iraqi oil sales would be switched back to dollars.

Fineman's White House sources would appear to have been reliable as that is precisely what has happened: when Iraqi oil exports resumed in June of last year, it was announced that payment would be in dollars only . It was also decided that the billions of Iraqi euros which were being held in a euro account, controlled by the UN under the oil-for-food programme, were to be transferred into the Development Fund for Iraq, a dollar account controlled by the US .

Furthermore, Youssef Ibrahim, a former senior Middle East correspondent for the New York Times and energy editor on the Wall Street Journal, who is a member of the influential Council on Foreign Relations, has called Iraq's switch to the euro 'another reason' for the war, saying that a general move by oil producers to the euro would be a 'catastrophe' for the US.

America's willingness to use violence to defend its economic interests does not seem to have reduced the number of oil exporters considering switching to the euro as they recognise that their use of the dollar enables the US to build up its military strength. In addition to Malaysia, Indonesia has the switch under consideration while Iran has been shifting its currency reserves into euros. Moreover, according to the Vice-President of the Iranian central bank, it has actually sold some of its oil to Europe for euros and is encouraging members of an Asian trade organisation, the Asian Clearing Union, to pay for Iranian oil in the European currency. Along with Malaysia, it is also at the forefront of efforts to establish a new gold-backed currency, the Islamic Gold Dinar, to be used in international trade amongst Muslim countries instead of both the dollar and the euro. In a further development, in June 2004, Iran announced that it had plans to establish an oil-trading market for Middle Eastern and OPEC producers which could threaten the dominance of London's International Petroleum Exchange and New York's Nymex. Such a move could help remove some of the technical difficulties that exist with a switch away from dollar-denomination of oil sales.

It is therefore not surprising to find that, just as with Iraq, the European Union and the US are dealing with Iran in very different ways. While the EU has been holding trade negotiations with Iran21 and involved in dialogue about its nuclear programme, the US has refused to get involved in direct talks with the Iranian government which it views as 'evil'. The American Enterprise Institute, a highly influential American 'think tank', has in fact been actively calling for 'regime change' and, although this policy has yet to be officially endorsed by the Bush administration, in July 2004 it was claimed in the British press that a senior official of the Bush administration had indicated that, if re-elected, Bush would intervene in the internal affairs of Iran in an attempt to overturn the Iranian government .

European enthusiasm for the 'petroeuro' also appears undampened by the US takeover of Iraq. Since the war, the European Union has been actively encouraging Russia, another opponent of the US invasion, to move to euro oil and gas sales. In October 2003, during a joint press conference with Germany's Prime Minister Gerhard Schroeder, the Russian President Vladimir Putin declared that Russia was thinking about selling its oil for euros. A few days later, the European Commission President, Romano Prodi, said, after a summit between Russia and the European Union, that Russia was now drawn to having its imports and exports denominated in euros.

In December 2003, speculation about the future roles of the dollar and the euro increased when OPEC Secretary General Alvaro Silva, a former Venezuelan oil minister, said that the organisation was now considering trading in euros or in a basket of currencies other than the dollar, as the US currency was declining in value. Although a few days later the Saudi oil minister Ali al-Naimi said that OPEC would not be discussing a switch to the euro at its next meeting (comments reinforced by the Qatari President of OPEC and the Algerian oil minister), articles discussing a possible move continued to appear in the media and the euro's value against the dollar soared. Despite the speculation, no decision to move to the euro was taken at OPEC's meeting in early February 2004 and thereafter the euro's value fell back again.

In fact, close inspection of the dollar-euro exchange rate shows that since the euro's introduction in January 1999, petro-currency rivalry appears to have played an important part in swinging the rate one way or the other. The markets, it seems, have noticed the importance of what is happening. On the other hand, the lack of an open discussion of the issues suggests that politicians and bankers are keen to move ahead with their plans with little or no explanation to the general public.

1) January 1999: launch of the euro.
2) January 1999 - Oct 2000: euro in "bear market[2] versus the dollar.
3) November 2000: Iraq switches oil sales to euro. Euro's fall versus the dollar is halted.
4) April 2002: senior OPEC representative gives speech in which he states that OPEC would consider possibility of selling oil in euros.

5) April 2002 to May 2003: euro in "bull market" versus the dollar.
6) June 2003: US switches Iraqi oil sales back to dollar.
7) June 2003 to September 2003: euro falls versus dollar.
8) October 2003 to early February 2004: statements by Russian and OPEC politicians/officials that switch to euro for oil sales is being considered. Euro's value versus the dollar increases.
9) 10 February 2004: OPEC meets and no decision to switch to euro is taken.
10) February 2004 to May 2004: euro falls versus the dollar.
11) June 2004: Iran announces intention to establish oil-trading market to rival those of London and New York.
12) June 2004: euro's value versus the dollar begins to increase again.

Should we not, however, be debating more openly what kind (or kinds) of international financial structure(s) we want to adopt, since the question has potentially huge implications for the stability of the world economy and for peace and stability in oil-exporting countries? A good starting point for such a debate would be the recognition that no country or countries should be allowed to dominate the system by controlling the issuance of the currency or currencies used. Similarly fundamental would be to prevent any country from running a persistent trade surplus or deficit so as to avoid the build up of unjust subsidies, unpayable debts and economic instability. At Bretton Woods, John Maynard Keynes, who understood how important these two conditions were, proposed a system which would have met them, but his proposal was rejected in favour of the dollar.

The dollar, though, is no longer a stable, reliable currency: the IMF has warned that the US trade deficit is so bad that its currency could collapse at any time. Will we really have to wait for a full-blown dollar crisis before a public debate about creating a just and sustainable trading system can begin?

The Beginning of the End of the Petrodollar: What Connects Iraq to Iran

Throughout history, empires and their civilisations have come and gone. During the first part of the last century, the US quietly built its empire, first in the North and Central Americas and in South America. Soon after the Second World War, the US worked to maximise the advantages it gained, and the power it assumed, between 1943 and 1945, from its victory over Germany and Japan, and as a consequence of massive Soviet casualties, and large British debt and financial burden caused by the war. The USA assumed the leading role in the Western world by, on one hand, containing the Soviet Union and preventing the spread of communist revolution beyond the borders of the Soviet bloc; and on the other hand, ensuring uncontested American supremacy within the Western world.

During the Cold War years, there was little or no challenge to the dominant position of the US in the Western world. However, with the end of the Soviet Union in 1991, the knot tying the basic objectives of the US global strategy together began to come unravelled. Once the communist danger was off the table, American supremacy ceased to be an automatic requirement of the Western system.

Since 20 September 2002, the US government has abandoned its former multilateral approach to global affairs, and adopted an imperial posture known as the so-called Bush doctrine. This new agenda is based on militarist and imperial values with some theocratic overtones. This current agenda looks much like what some people see in US foreign policy at the end of the 19th century, and the beginning of the 20th, when the US actively sought to dominate the entire Caribbean basin, Central America and even the western Pacific.

Six months after the Bush doctrine was announced, the new American doctrine was applied as a justification for an unprovoked war against Iraq by the neo-conservative administration of the US government. Toppling Saddam Hussein's regime without the support of the UN, and in the face of strong opposition from traditional US allies, was a clear presentation of a new unilateralist American foreign policy. The "regime change" in Baghdad was not an isolated event, but only an opening salvo in a much broader neo-conservative agenda. The neo-conservatives 'advocate a paradigm shift in which the United States spreads American values by asserting American power-by force, if necessary'. This agenda seeks to reshape American hegemonic practices according to old imperial doctrines, but with new post-colonial political and military tools.

Since 2005, there is a looming crisis brewing over Iran. In the media the phantom of Iran "threat" is being amplified across the world. In order to justify a military operation against Iran, the neo-conservative rulers of the US have started a demonization campaign against this country, presenting the latest incarnation of America's enemy, in much the same way Saddam Hussein was in the run-up to the invasion of Iraq.

They have put a lot of effort into making people believe that Iran is ruled by dangerously crazy people who are trying to make a nuclear bomb, and that they would not hesitate to bomb one or more US cities. In view of such a danger, the only answer is to wage a preventive war. Speculations about possible U.S.-Israel attacks on Iran have reached a stage of war propaganda by Western media. A recent report by the Oxford Research Group revealed that any bombing of Iran by U.S. forces, or by their Israeli allies, would result in the unnecessary death of many innocent lives.

Many observers view the US neo-conservative clique and its agenda as a conspiracy. This article, however, is based on the premise that they are merely part of a larger equation of global economic and political conditions. This view is rooted in an understanding that vested interests representing the energy, electronics, weapons, and influential segments of the media and communications industries in the US are always entrenched in key sectors of government. These interests are concerned with maintaining their privileged position. And key elements of the US economic and political elite are now responding directly to changes in global conditions that have arisen since the end of the Cold War. This is not a conspiracy. It is only business as usual.

Since the end of the Cold War, the US has waged four wars – two in Iraq, one in the former-Yugoslavia, and one in Afghanistan- and is threatening more. All this aggression is not the result of a paranoid theory, but simply a convergence of political and economic interests, travelling under the rubric of "war on terror". This argument is not based on the image of a few evil people, conspiring in secret, against the people for their evil aims. However, diverging from conspiracy theory does not ignore the fact that indeed there are real conspiracies, criminal or otherwise. In particular, the US political landscape is littered with examples of illegal political, corporate and government conspiracies, such as Watergate, and the Iran-Contra scandal. Having said that I generally consider the belief in conspiracy theories a pointless diversion of focus, and waste of energy. While real conspiracies have existed throughout history, history itself is not a conspiracy.

Since the end of the Cold War, the power of the United States is in decline. Particularly its share of world trade and manufacturing is substantially less than it was just prior to the end of the Cold War, and its relative economic strength measured against the EU and the East Asian economic group of Japan, China and Southeast Asia is similarly in retreat. The persistent use of US military power can be viewed as a reaction to its declining economic power and not merely as a response to the post-Cold War geopolitical picture. The American neo-conservative leaders see the military power of the US 'as a trump card that can be employed to prevail over all its rivals', and thus stop this decline. This is what the Bush administration is trying to achieve: to create a militarised world in which the strength of the US military forces can change and re-define the rules of the game.

This is a clear goal, a specific agenda, which does not constitute a conspiracy. It is merely the way in which the system currently works, and the US is taking advantage of existing structural opportunities. This article is an attempt to provide primarily a macroeconomic explanation to the origins of and motivations behind the recent US policies shaped by the neo-conservative Bush administration.

American "Dollar" Imperialism

Since the US emerged as the dominant global superpower at the end of the Second World War, US hegemony rested on three unchallengeable pillars: 1) overwhelming US military superiority over all its rivals; 2) the superiority of American production methods and the relative strength of the US economy; 3) control over global economic markets, with the US dollar acting as the global reserve currency.

Of these three, the role of the dollar may be the greatest among equals. As a result of this situation, today America borrows from practically the entire world without keeping the reserves of any other currency. Because the dollar is the de facto global reserve currency, US currency accounts for approximately two-thirds of all official exchange reserves. America does not have to compete with other currencies in interest rates, and even at low interest rates capital flies to the dollar. The more dollars are circulated outside the US, the more the rest of the world has had to provide the US with goods and services in exchange for these dollars. The US even has the luxury of having its debts denominated in its own currency.

How does this work?

- The United States runs a balance of payments deficit by spending more money in other countries (buying their products, investing in them, or giving them dollars) than they spend in the United States.
- The extra dollars are held by the countries' central banks. The banks do not ask the United States to redeem them for gold or another currency. As long as foreign banks accept and hold dollars as if they were gold, the dollars act as reserves.

The US economy began to dominate the world economy in the early 20th century. The US dollar was then tied to gold, so that the value of the dollar neither increased nor decreased, but remained the same amount of gold. Most money was paper, as it is now, but governments were required, if requested, to redeem that paper for gold. This "convertibility" put an upper limit on the amount of paper currency governments could print in order to prevent inflation. This link between paper money and gold was a product of law as well as custom. The Federal Reserve had to ensure that every dollar of paper money was backed by at least forty cents of gold. There was no tradition (as there is today) of continuous inflation. The large levels of inflation and astronomic levels of government deficits during the Great Depression, 1929-1931, rendered the support of US dollars by gold impossible. This led the US President Roosevelt to decouple the dollar from gold in 1932. Until this point, the US may well have been a dominant power in the world economy, but from an economics point of view, it was not an empire. The fixed value of the dollar did not allow the US government to extract economic benefits from other countries by supplying them with dollars convertible to gold.

The American Empire was born, in a real economics sense of the term, with Bretton Woods in 1945. After 1945, the dollar was not fully convertible to gold, but was made convertible to gold only to foreign governments. As a result of this, the dollar established itself as the global reserve currency. No one planned this development. It came directly from the fact that the US was the dominant world power: well over half of all international money transactions were financed in terms of dollar; the US produced more than half the world output; the US also owned a large section of the gold reserves in the world. This became possible because during the Second World War, the US had supplied its allies with provisions, demanding gold as payment, thus accumulating significant portions of the world's gold reserves. By 1945, the US had accumulated 80 percent of the world's gold, and 40 percent of the world's production.

The aggressive policies of the 1960s, however, put an increasing pressure on the US dollar. The US economy experienced a cumulative reserve deficit. In particular, the dollar supply was relentlessly increased to finance America's war in Vietnam. The US printed and spent more money than their gold reserves allowed. By 1963, the US gold reserve at Manhattan barely covered liabilities to foreign central banks, and by 1970 the gold coverage had fallen to 55%, by 1971 22%. Before the Vietnam War, the US had $30 billion in gold reserves, but it spent more than $500 billion on the war alone. By this time, the post-war reconstruction period had come to an end, and the European and Japanese economies had improved their economic position relative to the US, which had increased pressure on the US dollar. The situation reached a crisis point in 1970-71 when foreign central banks tried to convert their dollar reserves into gold. In response to a massive flight from the dollar, the US government defaulted on its payment on 15 August 1971 by cutting the link between the dollar and gold. Because it was clear that the US government would not be able to buy back its dollars in gold. If governments and foreign central banks tried to convert even a quarter of their holdings at one time, the United States would not be able to honour its obligations.

This was a serious crisis inspired by a significant loss of confidence in dollar. As a result, the dollar was left 'floated' in the international monetary market, which weakened the position of the dollar as the hegemonic currency. From that point on, the US had to find a way convincing the rest of the world to continue to accept every devalued dollars in exchange for economic goods the US needed to get from others. It had to find an economic reason for the rest of the world to hold US dollars: oil provided that reason, and the term petrodollar became the crucial link in this.

A petrodollar is a dollar earned by a country through the sale of oil. In 1972-74 the US government concluded a series of agreements with Saudi Arabia to support the power of the House of Saud in exchange for accepting only US dollars for its oil. Saudi Arabia has been the largest oil producer and the leader of OPEC. It is also the only member of the cartel that does not have an allotted production quota. It is the 'swing producer', meaning that it can increase or decrease oil production to bring oil draught or glut in the world market.

As a result of this situation, Saudi Arabia practically determines oil prices. Soon after the agreement with Saudi government, an OPEC agreement accepted this, and since then all oil has been traded in US dollars. Why is this important? Oil is not just the most important commodity traded internationally. It is the lifeblood of all modern economies. If you don't have oil, you have to buy it, and if you want to buy it on the world markets, you commonly have to purchase it with dollars.

Other countries buy and hold dollars like they buy and hold gold because they cannot purchase oil without dollars. This system of the US dollar acting as global reserve currency in oil trade keeps the demand for the dollar 'artificial' high. This enables the US to carry out printing dollars at the price of nothing to fund increased military spending and consumer spending on imports. As long as the US has no serious challengers and the other states have confidence in the US dollar the system functions.

This has been the situation and the essential basis for the US economic hegemony since the 1970s. Needless to say, this system enables the US administration to effectively control the world oil market. So long as OPEC oil was priced in U.S. dollars, and so long as OPEC invested the dollars in U.S. government instruments, the U.S. government enjoyed a double loan. The first part of the loan was for oil. The government could print dollars to pay for oil, and the American economy did not have to produce goods and services in exchange for the oil until OPEC used the dollars for goods and services. Obviously, the strategy could not work if dollars were not a means of exchange for oil. The second part of the loan was from all other economies that had to pay dollars for oil but could not print currency. Those economies had to trade their goods and services for dollars in order to pay OPEC.

While this has produced undeniable benefits for the US political and economic elites, it has left the US economy intimately tied to the dollar's role as global reserve currency.

With the creation of the euro in late 1999, an entirely new element was added to the global financial system. In just a few years after this, the euro has emerged as a real alternative, establishing itself as the second most important currency in the world's financial markets. If a significant part of petroleum trade were to use euros instead of dollars, many more countries would have to keep a greater part of their currency reserves in euros. According to a June 2003 HSBC report, even a modest shift away from dollars, or a change in the flow, would create significant changes. The dollar would then have to directly compete with the euro for global capital. Not only would Europe not need dollars anymore, but also Japan, which imports more than 80 percent of its oil from the Middle East, would have to convert most of its dollar assets to euros. The US, too, being the world's largest oil importer, would have to hold a significant amount of euro reserves. This would be disastrous for American attempts at monetary management.

Today Americans spend 700 billion dollar a year more than they produce, so they have to borrow that 700 billion. This means that in average each US citizen enjoys $3,000 more imported products than he/ she earns. They get this large amount of money from the Central Banks of China, Japan and European countries, because they keep dollar reserves. So the rest of the world are sellers, the Japanese, the

Chinese, the EU. The rest of the world invests, produces, exports to the US, and they lend more and more to the US. The increasing fragility of the US economy is underlined by the 2005 report from the IMF. This report pointed out that the US economy is increasingly being supported by what the IMF report called "unprecedented borrowing" from foreigners. The report went on to saying that the US deficit is unsustainable in long-term.

What does all of this have to do with Iraq and Iran?

The 2003 Invasion of Iraq : The interplay between the reserve currency role of the dollar and link with the oil producing countries can be observed in the recent conflict in Iraq. On 6 November 2000, while Americans were distracted by the controversial Florida presidential vote count, the Iraqi government announced that it would revalue its considerable petroleum reserves from dollars to euros – hence launching the so-called 'secret weapon' of Iraq. This was the first time an OPEC country dared violate the dollar-price rule. And since then, the value of the euro has increased and the value of the dollar has steadily declined. Libya has been urging for some time that oil be priced in euros rather than dollars, and Iran, Venezuela, and other countries have indicated that they would like to denominate their petroleum in euros. Since the oil trade is a central factor underpinning the dollar's hegemony, all these are potentially very significant threats to the strength of the US economy, and US global hegemony.

The US, in alliance with Britain, intervened in Iraq militarily in March 2003, and installed its own authority to run the country. The invasion and subsequent occupation of Iraq may well be remembered as the first oil currency war. There is now a wealth of evidence to suggest that the invasion of Iraq had less to do with any threat from Saddam's WMD programme and certainly less to do with fighting international terrorism than it has to do with gaining control over Iraq's oil reserves and in doing so maintaining the US dollar as the dominant currency for the international oil market. To preserve the U.S. dollar as the leading oil trading currency was a leading motive of the U.S. in the Iraq war — perhaps the fundamental underlying motive, even more than the control of the oil itself.

Two months after the invasion, the Iraqi euro accounts were switched back to dollars, and it was announced that payments for Iraqi oil would be once again in US dollars only. Global dollar supremacy was once again restored. But the story does not end there. Paradoxically, despite all these military and political advances and the rapidly increasing grip of US military power in Eurasia, for a variety of economic and political reasons, a growing number of oil producers in the Middle East, South America, and Russia are talking about openly trading oil for euros instead of dollars, or trading oil in a "basket of currencies". To do so would accelerate the US dollar's fall, and boost the euro's claim to become the world's second reserve currency. If a nation's economy is only as good as its currency, and the dollar continues to lose value, the US economy would be headed for a steep fall under these conditions. Superior military forces of the US and other Western states may take but cannot hold Iraq's (and Iran's) oil. Far from staving off the downfall of the US dollar, their aggression and arrogance may instead compel OPEC to "go euro" en masse. In the meantime, many people will be hurt and killed.

In Iraq, for instance, 'the civilian death toll has risen inexorably for the entire duration of the US-led military presence ... following the initial invasion'. Those who have hoped that a U.S. military victory in Iraq would somehow bring about a more peaceful world must be in for a rude awakening. Figures released by the Iraq Body Count project (IBC) on 9 March 2006 show that the total number of civilians reported killed has risen year-on-year since May 1st 2003 (the date that President Bush announced 'major combat operations have ended').

Déjà vu – the search for Weapons of Mass Destruction (this time in Iran)

As I write these sentences, there is a growing sense of déjà vu: in the past few months media reports have speculated that Washington is thinking an aggressive, pre-emptive nuclear bombardment of Iran to destroy the deep underground Iranian nuclear facilities. Iran may be attempting to acquire nuclear weapons, and it is undeniably clear that Iran's newly-elected President Ahmadinejad, with his extreme nationalist demagogy, has a more confrontational policy than his predecessors, but the Iranian regime is not suicidal, considering the riches Iran sits on. And so far there is no evidence that they have come close to building nuclear weapons. Tehran has declared that it is interested solely in a nuclear power industry and insisted on its right as a Nuclear Non-Proliferation Treaty signatory to develop all aspects of the nuclear fuel cycle. On 3 October 2004, Mohammed el-Baradei, the head of the International Atomic Energy Agency (IAEA) declared that 'Iran has no nuclear weapons programme ... So far I see nothing that could be called an imminent danger. I have seen no nuclear weapons programme in Iran. What I have seen is that Iran is trying to gain access to nuclear enrichment technology, and so far there is no danger in Iran'. American officials later accused the IAEA of irresponsibility and having a lenient approach and Iran of deceit. In a provocative speech to an influential pro-Israeli lobby group — the American Israel Public Affairs Committee (AIPAC) — on 5 March 2006, US ambassador to the United Nations, John Bolton, bluntly threatened Iran with "painful consequences" if it failed to accede completely to Washington's demands.

Similar to the war against Iraq, possible military operations against Iran have nothing to do with the Tehran regime's imaginary Weapons of Mass Destruction, but relate to the macroeconomics of petrodollar and the unpublicised but real challenge to US dollar supremacy from the euro as an alternative oil transaction currency. Iran is about to commit a far greater offence than Saddam Hussein's conversion to the euro for Iraq's oil exports in 2000. The plan is not just to sell oil for euros, but also to create an exchange market for all interested parties, oil producers as well as those customers, to trade oil for euros. Iranian authorities announced, in June 2004, that they were planning to begin, in March 2006, competing with the two existing exchanges — New York's NYMEX and London's IPE — with respect to international oil trades, where an euro-based international oil trading mechanism will be used. The NYMEX and IPE (both owned by American companies) are the places where world oil prices are fixed (in US dollars). The macroeconomic implications of an Iranian oil bourse are significant. If Iranian initiative becomes a successful alternative for global oil trade, the first international exchange since 1945 where buyers and sellers of oil can conduct their oil transactions using a currency other than the US dollar, it would seriously challenge the monopoly currently enjoyed by the financial centres in both London (IPE) and New York (NYMEX). This alternative oil bourse will consolidate the euro (petroeuro) as an alternative oil transaction currency, which will end the petrodollar's hegemonic status as the only global oil currency.

Iran is the second largest OPEC oil producer next to Saudi Arabia. It is fourth largest in the world, after Russia, Saudi Arabia and the US. Geographically, Iran is well located for this initiative: close proximity to major oil resources of the Middle East and the Caspian Sea regions and being not far from the major oil importers such as China, India and European Union countries. Economically, Iran's move to a euro-based system of oil transactions makes perfect sense: Iran sells 30 percent of its oil production to Europe and the rest mainly to India and China. The bourse may also lead to greater levels of foreign direct investment in Iran's oil sector. As a result, if the decline in the dollar against euro continues, more states will increase the percentage of euros vis-à-vis the dollar they hold in reserve, which would further benefit Iran as according to a member of Iran's Parliament Development Commission, Mohammad Abasspour, more than half of the country's assets in the Forex Reserve Fund are now euros.

What is important for this initiative is that much demand for oil now comes from the East, most significantly from China. The real impact for global currency reserves will be felt when the immense foreign currency reserves of the People's Bank of China will one day be switched away from the dollars. Once the PBOC makes a decisive move, other central banks worldwide would follow the suit, magnifying the effects on the currency markets. Looking ahead there are a lot of reasons why countries within the eurozone and Russia would prefer to trade oil in euros over dollars. The volatility in the US dollar and the cost of converting currencies could make petroeuros particularly attractive. Of course there are many political barriers that need to be overcome, but oil priced in both dollars and euros appears likely over time.

One hundred years ago, the British pound was the world's number-one currency. The pound achieved its ascendancy because Great Britain was the first modern industrialised country. The greater productivity of its industries enabled its products to displace those of the rest of the world in terms of price and quantity, and because elsewhere industrialised production was only beginning to take hold. The whole world was selling raw materials to Britain, and Britain - as the famous expression had it - was "the workshop of the world". Britain's military, particularly naval, strength, and its accumulation of colonial possessions reinforced the supremacy of the pound and the position of London as the world's financial centre. However this did not last forever: the development of industrial production in other countries began to undermine the supremacy of British economy, and its competitors began to overtake it in terms of productivity, and the new conditions of world economy revealed by the First World War signalled the death knell for the British pound. As a result of Britain's soaring indebtedness during and after the First World War, the US dollar emerged first as an alternative currency and then the dominant currency. Once the dollar usurped the pound the turnaround was rapid. It seems the fundamental forces, that will drive the downfall of the dollar hegemony, have been building for decades, but only now may the circumstances be right for their stark manifestation.

The Power Shift to the East

A very different world is emerging. It is perhaps too soon to tell whether the US and the EU will head down toward geopolitical rivalry, but the warning signs are certainly present. The rise of euro and the resulting competition with the American dollar will have geopolitical consequences. In the near future, the US and Europe are likely to engage in more intense competition over trade and finance. A more assertive Europe and a less competitive American economy do make it likely that trade disputes will become more politicised.

None of these political-economic trends could plausibly lead to armed conflict between the US and Europe, of course. But any one of them could result in a dramatically different world than the one we live in today.

In 20 years time, however, by 2025, America and Europe may both be spending much more time worrying about the rise of Asia than about each other. Even without a collapse of the dollar hegemony, there seems to be satisfactory evidence for a great and rapid shift of wealth and power to China and India. The transfer of power from the West to the East is gathering pace since the late 1990s, and Washington think-tanks have been publishing thick white papers charting Asia's, and China's in particular, rapid progress in microelectronics, nanotech, and aerospace, and printing dark scenarios about what it means for America's global leadership. The American administration considers China as a potential "strategic competitor" and has exerted enormous pressure on it since the early 1990s. One flash point with the US is China's fast growing demands for oil. China was the world's second largest consumer of petroleum products in 2004, having surpassed Japan for the first time in 2003, with total demand of 6.5 million barrels per day (bbl/d). China's oil demand is projected by EIA to reach 14.2 million bbl/d by 2025, with net imports of 10.9 million bbl/d.

The opening up of China's economy to global forces was part of US Cold War policy, with the intention of reaching a rapprochement with Mao Zedong in the 1970s against the Soviet bloc. How ironic that now, three decades later, the US increasingly regards a fast expanding market economy in China as a serious threat to US global hegemony. The uncertainty of the US economy and the decline of US technological leadership indicate that the time has come for the US to rethink its strategic economic options. All this may soon dramatically change the context for dealing with global economic challenges.

Today, China is the most obvious power on the rise. But it is not alone. India and other Asian states now boast growth rates that could outstrip those of major Western countries for decades to come. China is currently the world's sixth largest economy with an annual economic growth of more than nine percent. India's annual growth rate is eight percent. China's economy is expected to overtake France and Britain this year, be double the size of Germany's by 2010, and to overtake Japan's, currently the world's second largest, by 2020. Due to its one-child policy, China's working-age population will peak at 1 billion in 2015 and then shrink steadily. India has nearly 500 million people under age 19 and higher fertility rates. By mid-century, India is expected to have 1.6 billion people – and 220 million more workers than China. Of course, this could be a source for instability. But a great advantage for growth if the government can provide education and opportunity for India's masses. The experience of the last 10 years provides more optimism than problems for India in near future.

China has become the engine driving the recovery of other Asian economies from the setbacks of the 1990s. Japan, for example, has become the largest beneficiary of China's economic growth, and its leading economic indicators have improved as a result. Thanks to increased exports to China, Japan is finally emerging from a decade of economic crisis.

After China, India is emerging as an economic superpower. From outside and with just a touristic observation it is hard to tell that India is emerging as an economic giant. Jolting signs of extreme poverty abound even in the business capitals. A lack of subways, and badly designed road system, and terrible traffic. But visit the office towers and research and development centres emerging everywhere in India, and you'll see the miracle. Indians are today playing invaluable roles in the global innovation chain. Motorola, Hewlett-Packard, Cisco Systems, and many other high-tech giants now rely on their teams in India to devise software platforms and dazzling multimedia features for next-generation devices. Intel has 2000 electrical engineers with PhDs in Bangalore designing absolutely the latest ships. Indian engineering houses use 3-D computer simulations to produce sophisticated designs of everything from car engines and forklifts to aircraft wings for clients like General Motors and Boeing Corp. The post-war era witnessed economic miracles in Japan and South Korea. But neither was populous enough to power worldwide growth, or change the global game in a complete spectrum of industries. China and India, by contrast, possess the weight and dynamism to transform the 21st century global economy. The closest parallel to their emergence is the saga of the 19th century America: a huge continental economy with a young driven force that grabbed the lead in agriculture, apparel, and the high technologies of the era, such as steam engines, the telegraph, and electric lights. But in a way, even America's rise falls short in comparison to what's happening today. Never has the world seen the simultaneous, sustained takeoffs of two countries that together account for one-third of the world's population.

What makes the two Asian giants especially powerful is that they complement each other's strengths. China will stay dominant in mass manufacturing, and is one of the few countries building multibillion-dollar electronics and heavy industrial plants. The Chinese not only make textiles and cheap toys. They also make semiconductors and very advanced technology. India is a rising power in software, design, services, and precision industry. If Chinese and Indian industries truly collaborate, they would take over the world high-tech industry. These immense workforces are already converging. Thanks to the Internet and the collapse in the telecommunication costs, multinationals are having their goods built in China with software and circuitry designed in India.

One obvious reason to this shift in the balance of power in many technologies is that China and India graduate a combined more than half a million engineers and scientists a year. The total number of graduates in America is only 60.000. In three years' time, the total number of young researchers will rise to 1.6 million in India and China together. Because these two countries can throw more brains at technical problems, their contribution to innovation is increasing fast.

Western business isn't just shifting research work to Asia, because Indian and Chinese brains are young, cheap and plentiful. In many cases, the Asian engineers are better educated and they combine complex skills: mastery of latest software tools, a knack for complex mathematical algorithms, and fluency in new multimedia technologies. That's true that many Western companies came to India and China for the low cost. But they are staying for the quality, and they are investing for the innovation.

What is driving innovation in Asia, however, is not the Western demand, but fast rising homegrown consumer class. China is currently the world's third largest travel market, with 120 million air passengers in 2004. China's passenger car market also is already third largest in the world. For instance, Volkswagen is producing more cars in China than in Germany. China has the world's biggest base of mobile-phone subscribers – 350 million — and that is expected to rise 600 million by 2009. With over 100 million Internet users this year, China is a dominant presence in the Internet world. In two years, China should overtake the US in homes connected to broadband. The rapid growth of Chinese Internet market has turned the country into a promised land for many Internet giants, like Yahoo, Google, MSN and eBay.

Recent studies show that the attitudes and aspirations of today's Chinese and Indians resemble those of Americans a few decades ago. Surveys of thousands of young adults in both countries found that they are overwhelmingly optimistic about the future and believe success is in their hands.

The last 10 to 12 years have witnessed 3 billion people entering into what we call the global economy. From the past examples, we're accustomed to thinking of newcomers as countries that concentrate on doing unskilled, labour-intensive tasks. What is interesting about these 3 billion people is that, while, on average, they are poor and while most of them are unskilled, there are such a large number of them, and a small percentage of 3 billion is still a lot of people. A small percentage of these 3 billion, 300 million of them are highly skilled and very well educated and ready to produce everything with the latest scientific methods. These 300 million, still a large number, as large as the US, larger than Japan, and any European country, makes a big impact on the global economy. All these have already dramatically changed the pattern of world economy.

Asia's rise is just beginning, and if the big regional powers can remain stable while improving their policies, rapid growth could continue for decades. In the coming decades, how these Asian giants integrate with the rest of the world will largely shape the 21st century global order. All these powerful trends may soon be followed by increasing geopolitical strength in Asia as well. All this should not be really surprising. Asia, and especially East Asia, was already dominant for most of human history and remained so until very recently, that is less than two centuries ago. Only then, for a number of reasons, Asian economies lost their position to the West, but it seems only temporarily. Leadership of the world system has been temporarily centred in the West, Europe and America. That shift happened in the 19th century, and another shift appears to be happening again at the beginning of the 21st, as the centre of the world economy seems to be shifting back to the East.

The world today is too complicated for any single power to dominate it, and the US is trying to maintain its hegemony by relying on diminishing assets. As I mentioned at the start, hegemonic powers come and then eventually go, but the whole process of growth and decline is lengthy. History demonstrates that all global powers experience a long period of growth, followed by an equally long period of contraction. At this latter stage, they tend to become progressively more aggressive and unstable.

British imperial hegemony was over by the end of the 19th century, but it still remained an important military and economic power to be reckoned with. US power has been in decline since the 1970s, essentially because it lost some economic power in relation to others who have gained some significant influence particularly over the last 15 years. The fact, however, remains that the US is still by far the most powerful country on military political fronts and will continue to be so for some years yet. Equipped with advanced precision-guided munitions, high-performance aircraft, and intercontinental-range missiles, the American armed forces can unquestionably deliver death and destruction to any target on earth and expect little in the way of retaliation. But US reliance on this, the only remaining asset, strategy of military political blackmail can also lead to US to bankruptcy as the failing dollar pillar fails to support it as well. The 'American Century' is ending, if it ever existed, and clinging to it as an icon is both unnecessary and dangerous: confrontation in the name of Empire only encourages conflict.

The Demise of the Dollar

The new world order, Arab states have launched secret moves with China, Russia and France to stop using the US currency for oil trading. In the most profound financial change in recent Middle East history, Gulf Arabs are planning – along with China, Russia, Japan and France – to end dollar dealings for oil, moving instead to a basket of currencies including the Japanese yen and Chinese yuan, the euro, gold and a new, unified currency planned for nations in the Gulf Co-operation Council, including Saudi Arabia, Abu Dhabi, Kuwait and Qatar.

Secret meetings have already been held by finance ministers and central bank governors in Russia, China, Japan and Brazil to work on the scheme, which will mean that oil will no longer be priced in dollars.

The plans, confirmed to The Independent by both Gulf Arab and Chinese banking sources in Hong Kong, may help to explain the sudden rise in gold prices, but it also augurs an extraordinary transition from dollar markets within nine years.

The Americans, who are aware the meetings have taken place – although they have not discovered the details – are sure to fight this international cabal which will include hitherto loyal allies Japan and the Gulf Arabs. Against the background to these currency meetings, Sun Bigan, China's former special envoy to the Middle East, has warned there is a risk of deepening divisions between China and the US over influence and oil in the Middle East. "Bilateral quarrels and clashes are unavoidable," he told the Asia and Africa Review. "We cannot lower vigilance against hostility in the Middle East over energy interests and security." This sounds like a dangerous prediction of a future economic war between the US and China over Middle East oil – yet again turning the region's conflicts into a battle for great power supremacy. China uses more oil incrementally than the US because its growth is less energy efficient. The transitional currency in the move away from dollars, according to Chinese banking sources, may well be gold. An indication of the huge amounts involved can be gained from the wealth of Abu Dhabi, Saudi Arabia, Kuwait and Qatar who together hold an estimated $2.1 trillion in dollar reserves.

The decline of American economic power linked to the current global recession was implicitly acknowledged by the World Bank president Robert Zoellick. "One of the legacies of this crisis may be a recognition of changed economic power relations," he said in Istanbul ahead of meetings this week of the IMF and World Bank. But it is China's extraordinary new financial power – along with past anger among oil-producing and oil-consuming nations at America's power to interfere in the international financial system – which has prompted the latest discussions involving the Gulf states.

Brazil has shown interest in collaborating in non-dollar oil payments, along with India. Indeed, China appears to be the most enthusiastic of all the financial powers involved, not least because of its enormous trade with the Middle East.

China imports 60 per cent of its oil, much of it from the Middle East and Russia. The Chinese have oil production concessions in Iraq – blocked by the US until this year – and since 2008 have held an $8bn agreement with Iran to develop refining capacity and gas resources. China has oil deals in Sudan (where it has substituted for US interests) and has been negotiating for oil concessions with Libya, where all such contracts are joint ventures.

Furthermore, Chinese exports to the region now account for no fewer than 10 per cent of the imports of every country in the Middle East, including a huge range of products from cars to weapon systems, food, clothes, even dolls. In a clear sign of China's growing financial muscle, the president of the European Central Bank, Jean-Claude Trichet, yesterday pleaded with Beijing to let the yuan appreciate against a sliding dollar and, by extension, loosen China's reliance on US monetary policy, to help rebalance the world economy and ease upward pressure on the euro. Ever since the Bretton Woods agreements – the accords after the Second World War which bequeathed the architecture for the modern international financial system – America's trading partners have been left to cope with the impact of Washington's control and, in more recent years, the hegemony of the dollar as the dominant global reserve currency.

The Chinese believe, for example, that the Americans persuaded Britain to stay out of the euro in order to prevent an earlier move away from the dollar. But Chinese banking sources say their discussions have gone too far to be blocked now. "The Russians will eventually bring in the rouble to the basket of currencies," a prominent Hong Kong broker told The Independent. "The Brits are stuck in the middle and will come into the euro. They have no choice because they won't be able to use the US dollar." Chinese financial sources believe President Barack Obama is too busy fixing the US economy to concentrate on the extraordinary implications of the transition from the dollar in nine years' time. The current deadline for the currency transition is 2018.

The US discussed the trend briefly at the G20 summit in Pittsburgh; the Chinese Central Bank governor and other officials have been worrying aloud about the dollar for years. Their problem is that much of their national wealth is tied up in dollar assets.

"These plans will change the face of international financial transactions," one Chinese banker said. "America and Britain must be very worried. You will know how worried by the thunder of denials this news will generate."

Iran announced late last month that its foreign currency reserves would henceforth be held in euros rather than dollars. Bankers remember, of course, what happened to the last Middle East oil producer to sell its oil in euros rather than dollars. A few months after Saddam Hussein trumpeted his decision, the Americans and British invaded Iraq.

Petrodollar

A petrodollar is a United States dollar earned by a country through the sale of petroleum. The term was coined by Ibrahim Oweiss, a professor of economics at Georgetown University, in 1973. Oweiss felt there was a need for a word to describe the situation then occurring in oil producing, OPEC countries which were earning large amounts of money, in dollars, from oil production.

The term should not be confused with *petrocurrency* which refers to the currencies of petroleum exporting nations. However Canada's currency, the Canadian dollar, is sometimes referred to as a *petrodollar* in this context, as Canada is the largest oil net exporter to use the term "dollar" for its currency.

Petrodollar Recycling

Petrodollar recycling refers to the phenomenon of major oil-producing states mainly from OPEC earning more money from the export of oil than they could usefully invest in their own economies. It was a phenomenon of the late 1970s and early 1980s with the peak years for petrodollar surpluses. During this period, states such as Saudi Arabia, Kuwait and Qatar amassed large surpluses of petrodollars which they could not invest in their own countries. This was due to small populations or being at early stages of industrialization. These petrodollar surpluses can be defined as net US dollars earned by those nations which were in excess of the internal development needs of those nations.

These surpluses could be profitably invested in other nations. Alternatively, the world economy would have contracted if that money was withdrawn from the world economy while the exporting nations needed to be able to profitably invest to preserve their wealth for the future. While recycling petrodollars reduced the recessionary impact of the oil crisis, it caused problems especially for oil-importing countries that were paying much greater prices for oil and incurring debts. The International Monetary Fund (IMF) estimates that the foreign debts of 100 developing countries increased by 150% between 1973 and 1977. Johannes Witteveen, the Managing Director of the IMF, said in 1974, "the international monetary system is facing its most difficult period since the 1930s."

From 1974 to the end of 1981, total current account surpluses for all members of OPEC amounted to $450.5 billion. Ninety percent of this surplus was accumulated by the Arab countries of the Persian Gulf and Libya with Iran also accumulating oil surpluses prior to the revolution in 1979. The petrodollars were invested by commercial banks in the US and Europe. As the recessionary condition of the world economy made investment in corporations less attractive, bankers lent the money to developing countries especially in Central and South America such as Brazil, Argentina and Mexico as well as other developing countries like Turkey.

The 1973 OPEC crisis had created a vast dollar shortage in these countries, however, they still needed to finance their oil imports. In 1977, Turkish Prime Minister Suleyman Demirel summarized this shortage as "We're even in need of 70 cent." In subsequent decades, some of these nations have had difficulty in repaying these debts, leading to charges by anti-globalisation activists that it was a form of neocolonialism. This process also contributed to the growth of the

Euromoney market as a rival to US monetary markets. In an alternative view of petrodollar recycling, based on balance of payments and banking data from the 1970s and 1980s, David Spiro shows that a large portion of Arab petrodollars were invested directly in US government securities, and in the financial markets of the largest five economies. OPEC countries were net lenders to commercial banks, but this was not the primary channel for petrodollar recycling.

Arab oil-exporting countries also used their surpluses to fund foreign aid programs, with Arab nations being one of the largest donors of foreign aid since 1973. The IMF also introduced a new lending facility during this period called the Oil Facility. Funded by oil-exporting nations and other lenders, it was available to nations suffering from problems with their Balance of trade due to the rise in oil prices.

Currencies used to Trade Oil

Since the agreements of 1971 and 1973, OPEC oil is exclusively quoted in US dollars. This created a permanent demand for dollars on the international exchange markets. As of 2005, OPEC continues to trade in US Dollars, but some OPEC members (such as Iran and Venezuela) have been pushing for a switch to the euro.

Since the beginning of 2003, Iran has required euro in payment of exports toward Asia and Europe, though prices are still expressed in US dollars. Iran is planning to open an International Oil Bourse (IOB, exchange), on the free trade zone on the island of Kish, for the express purpose of trading oil priced in other currencies, including euros.

Oil Producers' Trading Surpluses

With the large rise in oil prices in the 1970s, there was concern that the world economy might contract if the oil producers extracted money and failed to recycle it back to oil consumers. With a similar rise in prices at the start of the 21st century, more of these oil surpluses have been reinvested through sovereign wealth funds. Two early examples were the Kuwait Investment Authority and the Petroleum Fund of Norway.

Currencies Correlated with Oil Prices

The pound sterling has sometimes been regarded as a petrocurrency thanks to North Sea oil exports.

The Dutch guilder was regarded as a petrocurrency thanks to its large quantities of natural gas and North Sea oil exports. This caused the Dutch Guilder to strengthen severely in the 1970s when the OPEC started their price hikes. As a result of this strengthening industrial manufacturing and services were crowded out and became non-competitive on world markets, a phenomenon that is often referred to in economics literature as Dutch disease.

The Canadian dollar is increasingly viewed as a petrocurrency. As the price of oil rises, oil-related export revenues rise, and thus constitute a larger component of Canadian exports. Thus, the movements of the Canadian dollar have become increasingly correlated with the price of oil. For example, the exchange rate of Canadian dollars for Japanese yen (99% of Japan's oil is imported) is 85% correlated with crude prices.

Petrodollar Theories of the War

A small but significant number of observers consider the issues around which the newspaper discussions of the Iraq war revolve to be nothing but a screen that hides other causes fuelling the present conflict — causes that require some knowledge of economics to grasp. According to this view, a leading motive of the U.S. in the Iraq war — perhaps the fundamental underlying motive, even more than the control of the oil itself — is an attempt to preserve the U.S. dollar as the leading oil trading currency, on the view that the institution of petrodollars, as these have developed since the early 1970s, is fundamental to well-being of the U.S. economy.

A corollary of this view is that the real underlying antagonism in the conflict is not a military or geopolitical or national-security issue between the U.S. and Iraq, but rather an economic struggle between the U.S. and Europe. Below are three such arguments and a link to a fourth. The first two pieces are by Canadians and the third is by an Australian. (Following these pieces is a link to a less expert analysis by an American who is a self-confessed novice in analyzing international affairs.)

America's War Against Europe

There are many reasons for George Bush's single-minded drive toward Baghdad. In other articles I have written for YellowTimes.org I hinted that a not so obvious reason for the drive against Iraq is Bush's war against Europe. In fact, I have now come to believe that is the primary reason for his Iraqophenia. Whenever a nation decides to go to war, there are plans made for who is going to win and who is going to lose; no one goes to war expecting to lose but it isn't always the obvious target of the aggression that is the real thrust behind the war. Sometimes, it isn't a case of what you expect to win from a war but rather a case of what you hope someone else loses; and it doesn't have to be your stated enemy who you hope will sustain the losses. In this case, Bush's hoped-for victim is the European economy. It is robust, and is likely to become much stronger in the easily foreseeable future. Britain's entry into the European Union is inevitable; Scandinavia will join sooner rather than later. Already, even without those countries, there will be 10 new member nations in May 2004 which will swell the GDP of the E.U. to about $9.6 billion with 450 million people as against $10.5 billion and 280 million people in the United States. This represents a formidable competing block for the United States but the situation is significantly more complex than what is revealed just by those numbers. And much of it hinges on the future of Iraq.

I have written before, as have many others, that this upcoming war is about oil. To be sure there are other reasons, but oil is the single most impelling force. Not in the way you might expect, however. It isn't so much that there are believed to be huge untapped oil reserves in Iraq, untapped only due to outdated technology; it isn't so much an American desire to get its grubby hands on that oil; it is much more a question of whose grubby hands the Americans want to keep it out of. What precipitated all of this was not September 11, nor a sudden realization that Saddam was still a nasty guy, nor just the change in leadership in the United States. What precipitated it was Iraq's November 6, 2000 switch to the euro as the currency for its oil transactions.

At the time of the switch, it might have seemed daft that Iraq was giving up such a lot of oil revenue to make a political statement. But that political statement has been made and the steady depreciation of the dollar against the euro since then means that Iraq has derived good profits from switching its reserve and transaction currencies. The euro has gained about 17 percent against the dollar since that time, which also applies to the $10 billion held in Iraq's United Nations "oil for food" reserve fund. So the question arises, as it did for George Bush, what happens if OPEC makes a sudden switch to euros? In a nutshell, all hell breaks loose.

At the end of World War II, an agreement was reached at the Bretton Woods Conference which pegged the value of gold at $35 per ounce and that became the international standard against which currency was measured. But in 1971, Richard Nixon took the dollar off the gold standard and ever since the dollar has been the most important global monetary instrument, and only the United States can produce them. The dollar, now a fiat currency [i.e., "money that is made legal tender by the decree, or fiat, of the government but that is not covered by a specie reserve" (*Columbia Encyclopedia*, 6th ed.)], is at a 16-year trade-weighted high despite record U.S. current-account deficits and the status of the U.S. as the leading debtor nation. The U.S. national debt as of April 4, 2002 was $6.021 trillion against GDP of $9 trillion.

Trade between nations has become a cycle in which the U.S. produces dollars and the rest of the world produces things that dollars can buy. Nations no longer trade to capture comparative advantage but rather to capture needed dollars to service dollar-denominated foreign debts and to accumulate dollar reserves in order to sustain the exchange value of their domestic currencies. In an effort to prevent speculative and potentially harmful attacks on their currencies, those nations' central banks must acquire and hold dollar reserves in amounts corresponding to their own currencies in circulation. This creates a built-in support for a strong dollar that in turn forces the world's central banks to acquire and hold even more dollar reserves, making the dollar stronger still.

This phenomenon is known as "dollar hegemony," which is created by the geopolitically constructed peculiarity that critical commodities, most notably oil, are denominated in dollars. Everyone accepts dollars because dollars can buy oil.

The reality is that the strength of the dollar since 1945 rests on being the international reserve currency for global oil transactions (i.e., "petro-dollar"). The U.S. prints hundreds of billions of these fiat petro-dollars, which are then used by nation states to purchase oil and energy from OPEC producers (except presently Iraq and, to some degree, Venezuela). These petro-dollars are then re-cycled from OPEC back into the U.S. via Treasury Bills or other dollar-denominated assets such as U.S. stocks, real estate, etc. The recycling of petro-dollars is the price the U.S. has extracted since 1973 from oil-producing countries for U.S. tolerance of the oil-exporting cartel.

Dollar reserves must be invested in U.S. assets which produces a capital-accounts surplus for the U.S. economy. Despite poor market performance during the past year, U.S. stock valuation is still at a 25-year high and trading at a 56 percent premium compared with emerging markets. The U.S. capital-account surplus finances the U.S. trade deficit. Since it is the U.S. that prints the petro-dollars, they control the flow of oil. Period. When oil is denominated in dollars through U.S. state action and the dollar is the only fiat currency for trading in oil, an argument can be made that the U.S. essentially owns the world's oil for free.

So what happens if OPEC as a group decides to follow Iraq's lead and suddenly begins trading oil on the euro standard? Economic meltdown. Oil-consuming nations would have to flush dollars out of their central bank reserves and replace them with euros. The dollar would crash in value and the consequences would be those one could expect from any currency collapse and massive inflation (think of Argentina for an easy example). Foreign funds would stream out of U.S. stock markets and dollar denominated assets, there would be a run on the banks much like the 1930s, the current account deficit would become unserviceable, the budget deficit would go into default, and so on.

And that's just in the United States. Japan would be particularly hard hit because of total dependence on foreign oil and incredible sensitivity to the U.S. dollar. If Japan's economy tumbles, so does that of many other countries, especially the United States in a crescendo of dominos. Now this is the potential effect of a "sudden" switch to euros. A more gradual shift might be manageable but even that would change the financial and political balance of the world. Given the size of the European market, its population, its need for oil (it actually imports more oil than the U.S.), it may be rapidly approaching that the euro will become the de facto monetary standard for the world.

There are some good reasons for OPEC as a group to follow Iraq and begin to value oil in euros. There seems little doubt that they would relish the opportunity to make a political statement after years of having to kowtow to the U.S., but there are solid economic reasons as well. The mighty dollar has reigned supreme since 1945, and in the last few years has gained even more ground with the economic dominance of the United States. By the late 1990s, more than four-fifths of all foreign exchange transactions, and half of all world exports, were denominated in dollars. In addition, U.S. currency accounts for about two thirds of all official exchange reserves. The world's dependency on U.S. dollars to pay for trade has seen countries bound to dollar reserves, which are disproportionately higher than America's share of global output.

It is important to note that the euro is not at any disadvantage versus the dollar when one compares the relative sizes of the economies involved, especially given the E.U. enlargement plans. Moreover, the E.U. has a bigger share of global trade than the U.S. and while the U.S. has a huge current account deficit, the E.U. has a more balanced external accounts position. One of the more compelling arguments for keeping oil pricing and payments in dollars has been that the U.S. remains a large importer of oil, despite being a substantial producer itself. But the EU is an even larger importer of oil and petroleum products than the U.S., and represents for OPEC a more attractive market, closer and less domineering.

The point of Bush's war against Iraq, therefore, is to secure control of those oil fields and revert their valuation to dollars. Then to increase production exponentially and force prices to drop. Finally, to threaten significant action against any of the oil producers who would switch to the euro. In the long run, then, it is not really Saddam who is the target; it is the euro and, therefore, Europe. There is no way the United States will sit by idly and let those upstart Europeans take charge of their own fate, let alone of the world's finances.

Of course, all of this depends on Bush's insane plan not becoming the trigger for a Third World War, as it so readily might.

[Paul Harris is self-employed as a consultant providing Canadian businesses with the tools and expertise to successfully reintegrate their sick or injured employees into the workplace. He has travelled extensively in what we arrogant North Americans refer to as "the Third World," and he believes that life is very much like a sewer: what you get out of it depends on what you put into it. Paul lives in Canada, and often writes for YellowTimes.org, an international news and opinion publication. YellowTimes.org encourages its material to be reproduced, reprinted, or broadcast provided that any such reproduction identifies the original source.]

Bush's Deep Reasons for War on Iraq: Oil, Petrodollars, and the Opec Euro Question

As the United States made preparations for war with Iraq, White House Press Secretary Ari Fleischer, on 2/6/03, again denied to US journalists that the projected war had "anything to do with oil." He echoed Defence Minister Donald Rumsfeld, who on 11/14/02 told CBS News that "It has nothing to do with oil, literally nothing to do with oil."

Speaking to British MPs, Prime Minister Tony Blair was just as explicit: "Let me deal with the conspiracy theory idea that this is somehow to do with oil. There is no way whatever if oil were the issue that it would not be infinitely simpler to cut a deal with Saddam...." (London Times 1/15/03)

Nor did Bush's State of the Union Message, or Colin Powell's address to the United Nations Security Council, once mention the word "oil." Instead the talk was (in the president's words) of "Iraq's illegal weapons programs, its attempts to hide those weapons from inspectors, and its links to terrorist groups." However our leaders are not being candid with us. Oil has been a major US concern about Iraq in internal and unpublicized documents, since the start of this Administration, and indeed earlier. As Michael Renner has written in Foreign Policy in Focus, February 14, 2003, "Washington's War on Iraq is the Lynchpin to Controlling Persian Gulf Oil."

But the need to dominate oil from Iraq is also deeply intertwined with the defense of the dollar. Its current strength is supported by OPEC's requirement (secured by a secret agreement between the US and Saudi Arabia) that all OPEC oil sales be denominated in dollars. This requirement is currently threatened by the desire of some OPEC countries to allow OPEC oil sales to be paid in euros.

The Internally Stated US Goal of Securing the Flow of Oil from the Middle East

As early as April 1997, a report from the James A. Baker Institute of Public Policy at Rice University addressed the problem of "energy security" for the United States, and noted that the US was increasingly threatened by oil shortages in the face of the inability of oil supplies to keep up with world demand. In particular the report addressed "The Threat of Iraq and Iran" to the free flow of oil out of the Middle East. It concluded that Saddam Hussein was still a threat to Middle Eastern security and still had the military capability to exercise force beyond Iraq's borders.

The Bush Administration returned to this theme as soon as it took office in 2001, by adopting, some say commissioning, a second report from the same Institute. (This Task Force Report was co-sponsored by the Council on Foreign Relations in New York, another group historically concerned about US access to overseas oil resources.)

As reported by the Scotland Sunday Herald (10/6/02),

"President Bush's Cabinet agreed in April 2001 that `Iraq remains a destabilising influence to the flow of oil to international markets from the Middle East' and because this is an unacceptable risk to the US `military intervention' is necessary.

"Vice-president Dick Cheney, who chairs the White House Energy Policy Development Group, commissioned a report on `energy security' from the Baker Institute for Public Policy, a think-tank set up by James Baker, the former US secretary of state under George Bush Snr.

"The report, Strategic Energy Policy Challenges For The 21st Century, concludes: `The United States remains a prisoner of its energy dilemma. Iraq remains a destabilising influence to ... the flow of oil to international markets from the Middle East. Saddam Hussein has also demonstrated a willingness to threaten to use the oil weapon and to use his own export programme to manipulate oil markets. Therefore the US should conduct an immediate policy review toward Iraq including military, energy, economic and political/ diplomatic assessments. 'The United States should then develop an integrated strategy with key allies in Europe and Asia, and with key countries in the Middle East, to restate goals with respect to Iraqi policy and to restore a cohesive coalition of key allies.'

"Baker who delivered the recommendations to Cheney, the former chief executive of Texas oil firm Halliburton, was advised by Kenneth Lay, the disgraced former chief executive of Enron, the US energy giant which went bankrupt after carrying out massive accountancy fraud."

[The Sunday Herald did not mention that the report begins with references to "recent energy price spikes" and "electricity outages in California," which we now know were engineered by Enron market manipulations for which two Enron energy traders have since pleaded guilty to conspiracy charges (Forbes, 2/5/03).]

The Unstated US Goals of Increasing the Flow of Oil from the Middle East, and US Dominance of the Area

Behind the acknowledged concern about the "free flow" of Persian Gulf oil are other motives. Following the recommendations of the Task Force Report, the Bush administration wishes to increase international (which may well turn out to mean US) investment in the under-developed Iraq oilfields. On 1/16/03 the Wall Street Journal reported that officials from the White House, State Department, and Department of Defense have been meeting informally with executives from Halliburton, Schlumberger, ExxonMobil, ChevronTexaco and ConocoPhillips to plan the post-war expansion of oil production from Iraq (whose oilfields were largely held by US companies prior to their nationalization). The Journal story has since been denied by Administration officials; but, as the Guardian noted on 1/27/03, "It stretches credulity somewhat to imagine that the subject has never been broached."

It is worth pointing out that Saddam Hussein already has offered exploratory concessions (which remained inactive because of the UN sanctions) to France, China, Russia, Brazil, Italy, and Malaysia. If Saddam is replaced by a new client regime, it seems likely that these concessions will be superseded, although there are reports that the US has offered France, Russia and China a share of post-war Iraqi oil, as an inducement to get their support in the Security Council. Last September former CIA Chief Woolsey threatened in the Washington Post (9/15/02) that the price for participation by France and Russia in the post-war Iraq oil bonanza should be their support for "regime change." It would not take much of such menacing talk from official sources to turn the Bush campaign against Iraq into a campaign against Europe.

Iraq's proven oil reserves are 113 billion barrels, the second largest in the world after Saudi Arabia, and eleven percent of the world's total. The total reserves could be 200 million barrels or more, all of it relatively easy and cheap to extract.

Thus increasing Iraqi oil production will diminish the market pressure on oil-importing countries like the US. It will also weaken the power of OPEC to influence oil markets by decisions to restrict output. Indeed, were Iraqi oil production to expand to near its capacity, the quotas established by OPEC would cease to be honored in today's market.

But the US is not just interested in oil from Iraq, it is concerned to maintain political dominance over all the oil-producing countries of the region. Secretary of State Colin Powell gave a glimpse of US intentions when he told the Senate Foreign Relations Committee on February 6 that success in the Iraq war "could fundamentally reshape that region in a powerful, positive way that will enhance U.S. interests." In conceding that it will be necessary to station US troops in occupied Iraq for the foreseeable future, the US is serving notice to Iran and to Saudi Arabia (both of which were once secure bases for US troops but are so no longer) that the US will reassert its presence as the dominant military power in the region.

The Unstated US Goal of Preserving Dollar Hegemony Over the Global Oil Market

Dominance of Middle Eastern oil will mean in effect maintaining dollar hegemony over the world oil economy. Given its present strategies, the US is constrained to demand no less. As I explain in this extract from my book, Drugs, Oil, and War, the present value of the US dollar, unjustified on purely economic grounds, is maintained by political arrangements, one of the chief of which is to ensure that all OPEC oil purchases will continue to be denominated in US dollars. (This commitment of OPEC to dollar oil sales was secured in the 1970s by a secret agreement between the US and Saudi Arabia, before the two countries began to drift apart over Israel and other issues.)

The chief reason why dollars are more than pieces of green paper is that countries all over the world need them for purchases, principally of oil. This requires them in addition to maintain dollar reserves to protect their own currency; and these reserves, when invested, help maintain the current high levels of the US securities markets. As Henry Liu has written vividly in the online Asian Times (4/11/02),

> *"World trade is now a game in which the US produces dollars and the rest of the world produces things that dollars can buy. The world's interlinked economies no longer trade to capture a comparative advantage; they compete in exports to capture needed dollars to service dollar-denominated foreign debts and to accumulate dollar reserves to sustain the exchange value of their domestic currencies. To prevent speculative and manipulative attacks on their currencies, the world's central banks must acquire and hold dollar reserves in corresponding amounts to their currencies in circulation. The higher the market pressure to devalue a particular currency, the more dollar reserves its central bank must hold. This creates a built-in support for a strong dollar that in turn forces the world's central banks to acquire and hold more dollar reserves, making it stronger. This phenomenon is known as dollar hegemony, which is created by the geopolitically constructed peculiarity that critical commodities, most notably oil, are denominated in dollars. Everyone accepts dollars because dollars can buy oil. The recycling of petro-dollars is the price the US has extracted from oil-producing countries for US tolerance of the oil-exporting cartel since 1973.*
>
> *"By definition, dollar reserves must be invested in US assets, creating a capital-accounts surplus for the US economy. Even after a year of sharp correction, US stock valuation is still at a 25-year high and trading at a 56 percent premium compared with emerging markets."*

But central bankers around the world do not expect either the US dollar or the US stock markets to sustain their current levels. As William Greider in The Nation (9/23/02) has pointed out:

> *"US economy's net foreign indebtedness—the accumulation of two decades of running larger and larger trade deficits—will reach nearly 25 percent of US GDP this year, or roughly $2.5 trillion. Fifteen years ago, it*

> *was zero. Before America's net balance of foreign assets turned negative, in 1988, the United States was a creditor nation itself, investing and lending vast capital to others, always more than it borrowed. Now the trend line looks most alarming. If the deficits persist around the current level of $400 billion a year or grow larger, the total US indebtedness should reach $3.5 trillion in three years or so. Within a decade, it would total 50 percent of GDP."*

There is also a major potential threat to the overpriced dollar in Japan's unresolved deflationary crisis. As observers like Lawrence A. Joyce have commented, the dollar would take a major pummeling if the Japanese government (as seems quite possible) were suddenly required to fulfil its legal obligations to bail out failed Japanese banks (which could easily happen if a sustained scarcity of oil were to keep oil prices at $40 a barrel or higher):

> *"There is only one place where the Japanese government can get enough money to bail out its banking system: The Japanese government owns about 15% of our U.S. Treasury securities. And it would have to start selling them if it found itself facing a major banking crisis.*
>
> *"That would send the already ailing dollar down even further. And the initiation of a sale of our Treasury securities by Japan, of course, would immediately trigger a worldwide stampede to do the same before the securities become worth only a fraction of what they were purchased for. At the same time, interest rates in the U.S. would immediately go through the roof."*

Washington is of course aware of these problems, and believes that overwhelming military strength and the will to use it supply the answer, persuading or forcing other countries to support the dollar at its artificial level as the key to their own security. In an article entitled "Asia: the Military-Market Link," and published by the U.S. Naval Institute in January 2002, Professor Thomas Barnett of the US Naval War College, wrote: "We trade little pieces of paper (our currency, in the form of a trade deficit) for Asia's amazing array of products and services. We are smart enough to know this is a patently unfair deal unless we offer something of great value along with those little pieces of paper. That product is a strong US Pacific Fleet, which squares the transaction nicely."

There is some merit to this argument with respect to friendly countries like Japan, whose defense costs have been lowered by the

US presence in Asia. But of course the Islamic countries of the world are less likely to appreciate the "great value" of a threatening US presence.

Instead they are more likely to follow the example of Malaysian Prime Minister Mahathir Mohamad, and turn to the Islamic gold dinar as a way to diminish dollar hegemony in world markets and increase the power of Islamic nations to challenge US policies.

The United States has at present little reason to fear a challenge to the dollar from Malaysia. But Malaysia is an Islamic country; and the US has every reason to fear a similar challenge from the Islamic nations in OPEC, were they to force OPEC to cease OPEC oil sales in dollars, and denominate them instead in euros.

The Unstated US Goal of Preserving Dollar Hegemony Against Competition from the Euro

As noted in a recent article by W. Clark, "The Real But Unspoken Reasons for the Iraq War", the OPEC underpinning for the US dollar has shown signs of erosion in recent years. Iraq was one of the first OPEC countries, in 2000, to convert its reserves from dollars to euros. At the time a commentator for Radio Free Europe/Radio Liberty predicted that Saddam's political act "will cost Iraq millions in lost revenue." In fact Iraq has profited handsomely from the 17 percent gain in the value of the euro against the dollar in that time.

Other countries have gradually been climbing on to the euro bandwagon. An article in the Iran Financial News, 8/25/02, revealed that more than half of Iran's Forex Reserve Fund assets had been converted from dollars to euros. In 2002 China began diversifying its currency reserves away from dollars into euros. According to Business Week (2/17/03) Russia's Central Bank in the past year has doubled its euro holdings to 20 percent of its $48 billion foreign exchange reserves. And for a very good reason, according to its First Deputy Chairman Oleg Vyugin: "Returns on dollar instruments are very low now. Other currency instruments pay more."

Business Week continues:

> *'The story is the same across the globe. Money traders say that institutions as diverse as Bank of Canada, People's Bank of China, and Central Bank of Taiwan are giving more weight to the European currency. By the end of this year, they predict, the euro could account for 20% of global foreign currency reserves, which today amount to a cool $2.4 trillion. Little more than a year*

ago, the euro made up just 10%. "No one is saying that the euro's going to replace the dollar as the premier reserve currency," says Michael Klawitter, a currency strategist at WestLB Research in London. "But it will increase in importance for many central banks."...

'The shift to the euro has big implications for the foreign exchange markets and the U.S. and European economies. Currency specialists say the yawning U.S. current account deficit, now at 5%, is bound to drive the dollar down further, and the euro still higher, over the next two to four years. Although the greenback may stage a short-term recovery once the looming war with Iraq is over, predictions are that it will then continue its downward trend, and that central banks will play their part in the descent. "Even if central banks increase their euro holdings by just a few percent, it will have a major impact in the markets," says Klawitter. "We're talking many billions of dollars."'

If not deterred, OPEC could follow suit. Libya has been urging for some time that oil be priced in euros rather than dollars. Javad Yarjani, an Iranian senior OPEC official, told a European Union seminar in April 2002 that, despite the problems raised by such a conversion, "I believe that OPEC will not discount entirely the possibility of adopting euro pricing and payments in the future."

Meanwhile Hugo Chavez has been taking Venezuelan oil out of the petrodollar economy by bartering oil directly for commodities from thirteen other third world countries. Although this has not yet qualified Venezuela for official membership in Bush's "axis of evil," the heavy hand of the Bush Administration in the recent coup attempt against Chavez was only too obvious.

To conclude, the Bush administration is not threatening Iraq out of pique or whim. The recent policies of both parties have indeed made the US vulnerable to foreign oil and petrodollar pressures. But hopefully decent Americans will protest the notion that it is appropriate to rain missiles and bombs upon civilians of another country, who have had little or nothing to do with this crisis of America's own making. Some in addition will continue to explore avenues whereby America's oil and financial vulnerabilities can be diminished without continuing down the road to Armageddon.

These problems are serious, but economists have put forward proposals for diminishing them peacefully and multilaterally. With respect to oil, Ralph Nader has just written, "The demand is simple: Stop this war before it starts and immediately establish a sane national energy security strategy." In fact one key ingredient of such a strategy, restriction of demand, can be found in saner parts of the Baker Institute reports that the Bush administration has so far chosen to ignore.

But an energy strategy for the United States must be addressed in the larger context of an economic and financial restructuring of global institutions and currency flows. With respect to the more esoteric financial problems of the dollar, the economist and futurist Hazel Henderson has written that "My recommendations for reforming current international institutions, revitalizing the UN and expanding civic society are summarized in Beyond Globalization (1999). A more balanced world order must center on reforming global finance, taxing currency exchange and reducing the dollar's unsustainable role as the world's de facto reserve currency (which is destructive for all countries — even the US itself). I favour a global reserve currency regime based on the parity of the US dollar and the euro. The fundamentals in the USA and the EU suggest that the G-8 has an opportunity to peg the dollar and the euro into a trading band. This, together with the new issue of SDR's [Special Drawing Rights]. Proposed by all the IMF country members, promoted by George Soros and opposed only by the USA, would lend to more stable currency markets."

Without endorsing these specific proposals, I wish to second two rather obvious principles:

1) The problems of global financial instability must be addressed. As George Soros, famed as the man who broke the British pound in 1992, wrote later in the Financial Times,ýÿ "To argue that financial markets in general, and international lending in particular, need to be regulated is likely to outrage the financial community. Yet the evidence for just that is overwhelming."
2) A multilateral approach to these core problems is the only way to proceed. The US is strong enough to dominate the world militarily. Economically it is in decline, less and less competitive, and increasingly in debt. The Bush peoples' intention appears to be to override economic realities with military ones, as if there were no risk of economic retribution. They should be mindful of Britain's humiliating retreat from Suez in 1956, a retreat forced on it by the United States as a condition for propping up the failing British pound.

America's influence in the world has up to now been based largely on good will generated by its willingness to resolve matters multilaterally. This legacy of good will is being squandered recklessly, as US officials insult European leaders and steer NATO towards irreconcilable disagreement.

The assumption seems to be that America does not need Europe and can afford to break up an entente that has endured since World War II. The risks of such arrogance are explored in a separate Postscript.

It's Not about Oil or Iraq: It's about the U.S. and Europe Going Head-to-head on World Economic Dominance

America's Bush administration has been caught in outright lies, gross exaggerations and incredible inaccuracies as it trotted out its litany of paper thin excuses for making war on Iraq. Along with its two supporters, Britain and Australia, it has shifted its ground and reversed its position with a barefaced contempt for its audience. It has manipulated information, deceived by commission and omission and frantically "bought" UN votes with billion dollar bribes.

Faced with the failure of gaining UN Security Council support for invading Iraq, the USA has threatened to invade without authorisation. It would act in breach of the UN's very constitution to allegedly enforced UN resolutions.

It is plain bizarre. Where does this desperation for war come from?

There are many things driving President Bush and his administration to invade Iraq, unseat Saddam Hussein and take over the country. But the biggest one is hidden and very, very simple. It is about the currency used to trade oil and consequently, who will dominate the world economically, in the foreseeable future — the USA or the European Union.

Iraq is a European Union beachhead in that confrontation. America had a monopoly on the oil trade, with the US dollar being the fiat currency, but Iraq broke ranks in 1999, started to trade oil in the EU's euros, and profited. If America invades Iraq and takes over, it will hurl the EU and its euro back into the sea and make America's position as the dominant economic power in the world all but impregnable.

It is the biggest grab for world power in modern times.

America's allies in the invasion, Britain and Australia, are betting America will win and that they will get some trickle-down benefits for jumping on to the US bandwagon.

France and Germany are the spearhead of the European force — Russia would like to go European but possibly can still be bought off.

Presumably, China would like to see the Europeans build a share of international trade currency ownership at this point while it continues to grow its international trading presence to the point where it, too, can share the leadership rewards.

Debate Building on the Internet

Oddly, little or nothing is appearing in the general media about this issue, although key people are becoming aware of it — note the recent slide in the value of the US dollar. Are traders afraid of war? They are more likely to be afraid there will not be war.

But despite the silence in the general media, a major world discussion is developing around this issue, particularly on the internet. Among the many articles: Henry Liu, in the 'Asia Times' last June, it has been a hot topic on the Feasta forum, an Irish-based group exploring sustainable economics, and W. Clark's "The Real Reasons for the Upcoming War with Iraq: A Macroeconomic and Geostrategic Analysis of the Unspoken Truth" has been published by the 'Sierra Times', 'Indymedia.org', and 'ratical.org'.

This debate is not about whether America would suffer from losing the US dollar monopoly on oil trading — that is a given — rather it is about exactly how hard the USA would be hit. The smart money seems to be saying the impact would be in the range from severe to catastrophic. The USA could collapse economically.

Oil Dollars

The key to it all is the fiat currency for trading oil. Under an OPEC agreement, all oil has been traded in US dollars since 1971 (after the dropping of the gold standard) which makes the US dollar the de facto major international trading currency. If other nations have to hoard dollars to buy oil, then they want to use that hoard for other trading too. This fact gives America a huge trading advantage and helps make it the dominant economy in the world.

As an economic bloc, the European Union is the only challenger to the USA's economic position, and it created the euro to challenge the dollar in international markets. However, the EU is not yet united behind the euro — there is a lot of jingoistic national politics involved, not least in Britain — and in any case, so long as nations throughout the world must hoard dollars to buy oil, the euro can make only very limited inroads into the dollar's dominance. In 1999, Iraq, with the world's second largest oil reserves, switched to trading its oil in euros. American analysts fell about laughing; Iraq had just made a mistake that was going to beggar the nation. But two years on, alarm bells were sounding; the euro was rising against the dollar, Iraq had given itself a huge economic free kick by switching.

Iran started thinking about switching too; Venezuela, the 4th largest oil producer, began looking at it and has been cutting out the dollar by bartering oil with several nations including America's bete noir, Cuba. Russia is seeking to ramp up oil production with Europe (trading in euros) an obvious market. The greenback's grip on oil trading and consequently on world trade in general, was under serious threat. If America did not stamp on this immediately, this economic brushfire could rapidly be fanned into a wildfire capable of consuming the US's economy and its dominance of world trade.

How Does the US Get its Dollar Advantage?

Imagine this: you are deep in debt but every day you write cheques for millions of dollars you don't have — another luxury car, a holiday home at the beach, the world trip of a lifetime.

Your cheques should be worthless but they keep buying stuff because those cheques you write never reach the bank! You have an agreement with the owners of one thing everyone wants, call it petrol/gas, that they will accept only your cheques as payment. This means everyone must hoard your cheques so they can buy petrol/gas. Since they have to keep a stock of your cheques, they use them to buy other stuff too. You write a cheque to buy a TV, the TV shop owner swaps your cheque for petrol/gas, that seller buys some vegetables at the fruit shop, the fruiterer passes it on to buy bread, the baker buys some flour with it, and on it goes, round and round — but never back to the bank.

You have a debt on your books, but so long as your cheque never reaches the bank, you don't have to pay. In effect, you have received your TV free.

This is the position the USA has enjoyed for 30 years — it has been getting a free world trade ride for all that time. It has been receiving a huge subsidy from everyone else in the world. As it debt has been growing, it has printed more money (written more cheques) to keep trading. No wonder it is an economic powerhouse!

Then one day, one petrol seller says he is going to accept another person's cheques, a couple of others think that might be a good idea. If this spreads, people are going to stop hoarding your cheques and they will come flying home to the bank. Since you don't have enough in the bank to cover all the cheques, very nasty stuff is going to hit the fan! But you are big, tough and very aggressive. You don't scare the other guy who can write cheques, he's pretty big too, but given a 'legitimate' excuse, you can beat the tripes out of the lone gas seller and scare him and his mates into submission.

And that, in a nutshell, is what the USA is doing right now with Iraq.

America's Precarious Economic Position

America is so eager to attack Iraq now because of the speed with which the euro fire could spread. If Iran, Venezuela and Russia join Iraq and sell large quantities of oil for euros, the euro would have the leverage it needs to become a powerful force in general international trade. Other nations would have to start swapping some of their dollars for euros. The dollars the USA has printed, the 'cheques' it has written, would start to fly home, stripping away the illusion of value behind them. The USA's real economic condition is about as bad as it could be; it is the most debt-ridden nation on earth, owing about US$12,000 for every single one of it's 280 million men, women and children. It is worse than the position of Indonesia when it imploded economically a few years ago, or more recently, that of Argentina.

Even if OPEC did not switch to euros wholesale (and that would make a very nice non-oil profit for the OPEC countries, including minimising the various contrived debts America has forced on some of them), the US's difficulties would build. Even if only a small part of the oil trade went euro, that would do two things immediately:

- Increase the attractiveness to EU members of joining the 'eurozone', which in turn would make the euro stronger and make it more attractive to oil nations as a trading currency and to other nations as a general trading currency.
- Start the US dollars flying home demanding value when there isn't enough in the bank to cover them.
- The markets would over-react as usual and in no time, the US dollar's value would be spiralling down.

The US Solution

America's response to the euro threat was predictable. It has come out fighting.

It aims to achieve four primary things by going to war with Iraq:

- Safeguard the American economy by returning Iraq to trading oil in US dollars, so the greenback is once again the exclusive oil currency.
- Send a very clear message to any other oil producers just what will happen to them if they do not stay in the dollar circle. Iran

has already received one message — remember how puzzled you were that in the midst of moderation and secularization, Iran was named as a member of the axis of evil?

- Place the second largest reserves of oil in the world under direct American control.
- Provide a secular, subject state where the US can maintain a huge force (perhaps with nominal elements from allies such as Britain and Australia) to dominate the Middle East and its vital oil. This would enable the US to avoid using what it sees as the unreliable Turkey, the politically impossible Israel and surely the next state in its sights, Saudi Arabia, the birthplace of al Qaeda and a hotbed of anti-American sentiment.
- Severe setback the European Union and its euro, the only trading bloc and currency strong enough to attack the USA's dominance of world trade through the dollar.
- Provide cover for the US to run a covert operation to overturn the democratically elected government of Venezuela and replace it with an America-friendly military supported junta — and put Venezuala's oil into American hands. Locking the world back into dollar oil trading would consolidate America's current position and make it all but impregnable as the dominant world power — economically and militarily. A splintered Europe (the US is working hard to split Europe; Britain was easy, but other Europeans have offered support in terms of UN votes) and its euro would suffer a serious setback and might take decades to recover. It is the boldest grab for absolute power the world has seen in modern times. America is hardly likely to allow the possible slaughter of a few hundred thousand Iraqis stand between it and world domination.

President Bush did promise to protect the American way of life. This is what he meant.

Justifying War

Obviously, the US could not simply invade Iraq, so it began casting around for a 'legitimate' reason to attack. That search has been one of increasing desperation as each rationalization has crumbled. First Iraq was a threat because of alleged links to al Qaeda; then it was proposed Iraq might supply al Qaeda with weapons; then Iraq's military threat to its neighbours was raised; then the need to deliver Iraqis from Saddam Hussein's horrendously inhumane rule; finally there is the question of compliance with UN weapons inspection.

The USA's justifications for invading Iraq are looking less impressive by the day. The US's statements that it would invade Iraq unilaterally without UN support and in defiance of the UN make a total nonsense of any American claim that it is concerned about the world body's strength and standing.

The UN weapons inspectors have come up with minimal infringements of the UN weapons limitations — the final one being low tech rockets which exceed the range allowed by about 20 percent. But there is no sign of the so-called weapons of mass destruction (WMD) the US has so confidently asserted are to be found. Colin Powell named a certain north Iraqi village as a threat. It was not. He later admitted it was the wrong village.

'Newsweek' (24/2) has reported that while Bush officials have been trumpeting the fact that key Iraqi defector, Lt. Gen. Hussein Kamel, told the US in 1995 that Iraq had manufactured tonnes of nerve gas and anthrax (Colin Powell's 5 February presentation to the UN was just one example) they neglected to mention that Kamel had also told the US that these weapons had been destroyed.

Parts of the US and particularly the British secret 'evidence' have been shown to come from a student's masters thesis.

America's expressed concern about the Iraqi people's human rights and the country's lack of democracy are simply not supported by the USA's history of intervention in other states nor by its current actions. Think Guatemala, the Congo, Chile and Nicaragua as examples of a much larger pool of US actions to tear down legitimate, democratically elected governments and replace them with war, disruption, starvation, poverty, corruption, dictatorships, torture, rape and murder for its own economic ends. The most recent, Afghanistan, is not looking good; in fact that reinstalled a murderous group of warlords which America had earlier installed, then deposed, in favour of the now hated Taliban.

Saddam Hussein was just as repressive, corrupt and murderous 15 years ago when he used chemical weapons, supplied by the US, against the Kurds. The current US Secretary for Defence, Donald Rumsfeld, so vehement against Iraq now, was on hand personally to turn aside condemnation of Iraq and blame Iran. At that time, of course, the US thought Saddam Hussein was their man — they were using him against the perceived threat of Iran's Islamic fundamentalism.

Right now, as 'The Independent' writer, Robert Fisk, has noted, the US's efforts to buy Algeria's UN vote includes promises of rearming the military which has a decade long history of repression, torture, rape and murder Saddam Hussein himself would envy. It is estimated 200,000 people have died, and countless others been left maimed by the activities of these monsters. What price the US's humanitarian concerns for Iraqis? (Of course, the French are also wooing Algeria, their former north African territory, for all they are worth, but at least they are not pretending to be driven by humanitarian concerns.) Indonesia is another nation with a vote and influence as the largest Muslim nation in the world. Its repressive, murderous military is regaining strength on the back of the US's so-called anti-terror campaign and is receiving promises of open and covert support — including intelligence sharing.

And Venezuela

While the world's attention is focused on Iraq, America is both openly and covertly supporting the "coup of the rich" in Venezuela, which grabbed power briefly in April last year before being intimidated by massive public displays of support by the poor for democratically-elected President Chavez Frias. The coup leaders continue to use their control of the private media, much of industry and the ear of the American Government and its oily intimates to cause disruption and disturbance.

Venezuela's state-owned oil resources would make rich pickings for American oil companies and provide the US with an important oil source in its own backyard. Many writers have noted the contradiction between America's alleged desire to establish democracy in Iraq while at the same time, actively undermining the democratically-elected government in Venezuela. Above the line, America rushed to recognise the coup last April; more recently, President Bush has called for "early elections", ignoring the fact that President Chavez Frias has won three elections and two referendums and, in any case, early elections would be unconstitutional.

One element of the USA's covert action against Venezuela is the behaviour of American transnational businesses, which have locked out employees in support of "national strike" action. Imagine them doing that in the USA! There is no question that a covert operation is in process to overturn the legitimate Venezuelan government. Uruguayan congressman, Jose Nayardi, made it public when he revealed that the Bush administration had asked for Uruguay's support for Venezuelan white collar executives and trade union activists "to break down levels of intransigence within the Chavez Frias administration". The process, he noted, was a shocking reminder of the CIA's 1973 intervention in Chile which saw General Pinochet lead his military coup to take over President Allende's democratically elected government in a bloodbath. President Chavez Frias is desperately clinging to government, but with the might of the USA aligned with his opponents, how long can he last?

The Cost of War

Some have claimed that an American invasion of Iraq would cost so many billions of dollars that oil returns would never justify such an action. But when the invasion is placed in the context of the protection of the entire US economy for now and into the future, the balance of the argument changes.

Further, there are three other vital factors:

First, America will be asking others to help pay for the war because it is protecting their interests. Japan and Saudi Arabia made serious contributions to the cost of the 1991 Gulf war.

Second — in reality, war will cost the USA very little — or at least, very little over and above normal expenditure. This war is already paid for! All the munitions and equipment have been bought and paid for. The USA would have to spend hardly a cent on new hardware to prosecute this war — the expenditure will come later when munitions and equipment have to be replaced after the war. But amunitions, hardware and so on are being replaced all the time — contracts are out. Some contracts will simply be brought forward and some others will be ramped up a bit, but spread over a few years, the cost will not be great. And what is the real extra cost of an army at war compared with maintaining the standing army around the world, running exercises and so on? It is there, but it is a relatively small sum.

Third — lots of the extra costs involved in the war are dollars spent outside America, not least in the purchase of fuel. Guess how America will pay for these? By printing dollars it is going to war to protect. The same happens when production begins to replace hardware components, minerals, etc. are bought in with dollars that go overseas and exploit America's trading advantage.

The cost of war is not nearly as big as it is made out to be. The cost of not going to war would be horrendous for the USA — unless there were another way of protecting the greenback's world trade dominance.

America's Two Active Allies

Why are Australia and Britain supporting America in its transparent Iraqi war ploy?

Australia, of course, has significant US dollar reserves and trades widely in dollars and extensively with America. A fall in the US dollar would reduce Australia's debt, perhaps, but would do nothing for the Australian dollar's value against other currencies. John Howard, the Prime Minister, has long cherished the dream of a free trade agreement with the USA in the hope that Australia can jump on the back of the free ride America gets in trade through the dollar's position as the major trading medium. That would look much less attractive if the euro took over a significant part of the oil trade.

Britain has yet to adopt the euro. If the US takes over Iraq and blocks the euro's incursion into oil trading, Tony Blair will have given his French and German counterparts a bloody nose, and gained more room to manouevre on the issue — perhaps years more room.

Britain would be in a position to demand a better deal from its EU partners for entering the "eurozone" if the new currency could not make the huge value gains guaranteed by a significant role in world oil trading. It might even be in a position to withdraw from Europe and link with America against continental Europe.

On the other hand, if the US cannot maintain the oil trade dollar monopoly, the euro will rapidly go from strength to strength, and Britain could be left begging to be allowed into the club.

The Opposition

Some of the reasons for opposition to the American plan are obvious — America is already the strongest nation on earth and dominates world trade through its dollar. If it had control of the Iraqi oil and a base for its forces in the Middle East, it would not add to, but would multiply its power.

The oil-producing nations, particularly the Arab ones, can see the writing on the wall and are quaking in their boots.

France and Germany are the EU leaders with the vision of a resurgent, united Europe taking its rightful place in the world and using its euro currency as a world trading reserve currency and thus gaining some of the free ride the United States enjoys now. They are the ones who initiated the euro oil trade with Iraq.

Russia is in deep economic trouble and knows it will get worse the day America starts exploiting its take-over of Afghanistan by running a pipeline southwards via Afghanistan from the giant southern Caspian oil fields. Currently, that oil is piped northwards — where Russia has control. Russia is in the process of ramping up oil production with the possibility of trading some of it for euros and selling some to the US itself. Russia already has enough problems with the fact that oil is traded in US dollars; if the US has control of Iraqi oil, it could distort the market to Russia's enormous disadvantage. In addition, Russia has interests in Iraqi oil; an American take over could see them lost. Already on its knees, Russia could be beggared before a mile of the Afghanistan pipeline is laid.

Another Solution?

The scenario clarifies the seriousness of America's position and explains its frantic drive for war. It also suggests that solutions other than war are possible.

Could America agree to share the trading goodies by allowing Europe to have a negotiated part of it? Not very likely, but it is just possible Europe can stare down the USA and force such an outcome. Time will tell. What about Europe taking the statesmanlike, humanitarian and long view, and withdrawing, leaving the oil to the US, with appropriate safeguards for ordinary Iraqis and democracy in Venezuela?

Europe might then be forced to adopt a smarter approach — perhaps accelerating the development of alternative energy technologies which would reduce the EU's reliance on oil for energy and produce goods it could trade for euros — shifting the world trade balance.

Now that would be a very positive outcome for everyone.

[Geoffrey Heard is an Australian who lives in Melbourne and says he holds a degree in psychology and a diploma in Marketing. In 1993 he started his own marketing and PR firm called MarketNOW. Before that he was public relations manager for a number of institutes of technology, principal information officer for the Papua New Guinea Government during self-government and leading up to independence, and senior editorial officer for the Queensland Health Education Council. His telephone number is 03 9583 0788 in Australia.]

Chapter 2

International Energy Outlook

Liquid Fuels

Consumption of petroleum and other liquid fuels increases from 85.7 million barrels per day in 2008 to 112.2 million barrels per day in 2035 in the *IEO2011* Reference case. Although world liquids consumption actually declined in 2009 (to 83.9 million barrels per day), it recovered in 2010 to an estimated 86.0 million barrels per day and is expected to continue increasing in 2011 and beyond as economic growth strengthens, especially among the developing non-OECD nations.

In the long term, world liquids consumption increases despite world oil prices that rise to $125 per barrel (real 2009 dollars) by 2035. More than 75 percent of the increase in total liquids consumption is projected for the nations of non-OECD Asia and the Middle East, where strong economic growth and, in the case of the Middle East, access to ample and relatively inexpensive domestic resources drive the increase in demand.

To satisfy the increase in world liquids demand in the Reference case, liquids production increases by 26.6 million barrels per day from 2008 to 2035, including the production of both conventional liquid supplies (crude oil and lease condensate, natural gas plant liquids, and refinery gain) and unconventional supplies (biofuels, oil sands, extra-heavy oil, coal-to-liquids [CTL], gas-to-liquids [GTL], and shale oil). In the Reference case, sustained high world oil prices allow for the economical development of unconventional resources and the use of enhanced oil recovery (EOR) technologies to increase production of conventional resources. High world oil prices also incentivize the development of additional conventional resources through technically difficult, high-risk, and very expensive projects, including wells in ultra-deep water and the Arctic. The most significant non-OPEC contributors to production growth are Russia, the United States, Brazil, and Canada. Total non-OPEC liquids production in 2035 is 15.3 million barrels per day higher than in 2008, representing 57 percent of the total world increase.

OPEC producers are assumed to restrict investment in incremental production capacity in the Reference case, below the levels justified by high prices. As a result, OPEC provides roughly 42 percent of the world's total liquids supply over the 2008-2035 period, consistent with its share over the past 15 years.

Unconventional resources from both OPEC and non-OPEC sources become increasingly competitive in the *IEO2011* Reference case, although unconventional petroleum liquids production development faces some difficulties, such as environmental concerns for Canada's oil sands projects and investment restrictions for Venezuela's extra-heavy oil projects. Production of nonpetrolium unconventional liquids, such as biofuels, CTL, and GTL, is spurred by sustained high prices in the Reference case. However, their development also depends on country-specific programs or mandates. World production of unconventional liquids, which in 2008 totaled only 3.9 million barrels per day or about 5 percent of total world liquids production, increases in the Reference case to 13.1 million barrels per day in 2035, when it accounts for 12 percent of total world liquids production.

World Oil Prices

The impacts of world oil prices on energy demand are a considerable source of uncertainty in the *IEO2011* projections. Prices have been exceptionally volatile over the past several years, reaching a high of $145 in July 2008 (daily spot price in nominal dollars) and a low of $30 in December 2008, as the global recession substantially dampened demand and thus prices. Improving economic circumstances, especially in the developing economies, strengthened liquids demand, and prices rose in 2009 and 2010.

More recently, growing demand and unrest in many oil-supplying nations of the Middle East and North Africa have supported price increases into 2011. Prices rose from an average $62 per barrel in 2009 to $79 per barrel in 2010, and they are expected to average about $100 per barrel in 2011. In the *IEO2011* Reference case, world oil prices continue increasing, to $108 per barrel in 2020 and $125 per barrel in 2035.

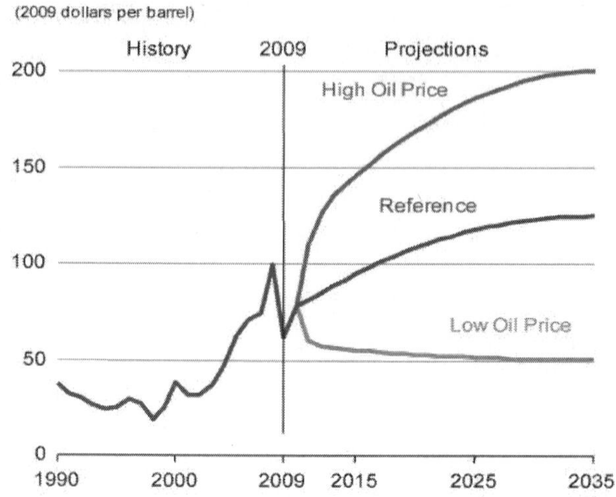

Figure : *World oil prices in three cases, 1990-2035*

In addition to the Reference case prices, *IEO2011* includes analyses of high and low world oil price paths. The three alternative price paths, which are consistent with those presented in EIA's *Annual Energy Outlook 2011*, are used to develop five price scenarios that can be used to illustrate the range of uncertainty associated with prices in world liquids markets. The high and low oil price paths and resulting scenarios illustrate price uncertainty, but they do not span the complete range of possible price paths.

In past editions of the IEO, high and low oil price scenarios typically have examined the impacts of changes in liquids supplies relative to the Reference case, based on different assumptions about OPEC decisionmaking and access to non-OPEC resources and their impacts on world liquids supply. In the *IEO2011* Traditional Low Oil Price case, as in past IEOs, the available supply is higher at all price levels; and in the Traditional High Oil Price case, the available supply is lower at all price levels, reflecting shifts in the liquids supply curve. The traditional oil price cases assume that demand curves are constant, with changes in demand resulting only from movement along the demand curves as prices rise or fall.

In contrast, the Low Oil Price and High Oil Price cases in *IEO2011* assume that changes in demand growth, resulting in different levels of demand, also affect prices. Thus, the Low Oil Price and High Oil Price cases incorporate alternative assumptions about economic growth and other structural factors in non-OECD countries that shift the "demand schedule" for liquids fuels while also continuing to maintain a portion of the change in "supply schedules" that drive the Traditional High Oil Price and Traditional Low Oil Price cases.

The *IEO2011* Low Oil Price case assumes that liquids demand in the non-OECD countries (where most of the world's demand uncertainty lies) at any given price level is lower than in the Reference case, and that total liquids supply available at any price point is higher than in the Reference case.

It also assumes that the shifts in demand and supply schedules lead to changes in the liquids quantities, resulting in price levels that are the same as those in the Traditional Low Oil Price case. That is, the only change is in the amount of oil consumed in the world market. Similarly, the *IEO2011* High Oil Price case assumes that liquids demand in the non-OECD countries at any given price level is higher than in the Reference case, and that the total liquids supply available at any price point is lower than in the Reference case, with the shifts in demand and supply schedules leading to changes in the quantities of liquids available, so that price levels that are the same as those in the Traditional High Oil Price case. Again, the only change is in the amount of oil consumed in the market.

In the Reference case, world oil prices are $95 per barrel in 2015 (real 2009 dollars), increasing slowly to $125 per barrel in 2035 ($200 per day in nominal terms). The Reference case represents EIA's current best judgment regarding exploration and development costs and accessibility of oil resources outside the United States. It also assumes that OPEC producers will choose to maintain their share of the market and will schedule investments in incremental production capacity so that OPEC's conventional oil production represents about 42 percent of the world's total liquids production. To retain that share, OPEC would have to increase production by 11.3 million barrels per day from 2008 to 2035, or 43 percent of the projected total increase in world liquids supply. Non-OPEC conventional supplies—including production from high-cost projects and from countries with unattractive fiscal or political regimes—account for an increase of 7.1 million barrels per day over the projection, and non-OPEC production of unconventional liquid fuels provides the remaining 8.2 million barrels per day of the increase.

In the High Oil Price case, world oil prices are about $200 per barrel in 2035 ($320 per barrel in nominal terms), with the higher prices resulting from the combination of an outward shift (greater demand at every price level) in the "demand schedule" for liquid fuels in the non-OECD nations and a downward shift (reduced supply at every price level) in the "supply schedule." The shift in the demand schedule is driven by higher economic growth relative to the Reference case in the non-OECD region, with non-OECD growth rates raised by 1.0 percentage point relative to the Reference case in each projection year starting with 2015.

The downward shift in the supply schedule is a result of the assumption that several non-OPEC producers further restrict access to, or increase taxes on, production from prospective areas, and that the OPEC member countries reduce their production substantially below current levels. High oil prices encourage the expansion of unconventional production relative to the Reference case.

In the Traditional High Oil Price case, OPEC countries are assumed to reduce their production from the current rate, sacrificing market share, and oil resources outside the United States are assumed to be less accessible and/or more costly to produce than in the Reference case. As in the High Oil Price case, higher oil prices allow unconventional resources to become more economically attractive, and their production increases above the levels in the Reference case. Oil consumption is lower solely due to the higher prices (which are the same as in the High Oil Price case), reflecting a movement upward and to the left along the demand curve.

In the Low Oil Price case, world crude prices are $50 per barrel in 2035 ($82 per barrel in nominal terms), compared with $125 per barrel in the Reference case. The low prices result from the combination of a shift to lower demand at every price level in the demand schedule and a shift to increased supply at every price level in the supply schedule. The shift in demand is driven by lower economic growth in the non-OECD region relative to the Reference case, with non-OECD growth rates lowered by 1.5 percentage points relative to the Reference case in each projection year starting with 2015. The upward shift in the supply schedule in this case results from greater access and more attractive fiscal regimes in prospective non-OECD areas, as well as higher levels of production from OPEC members. However, the lower prices make it uneconomical to expand production of unconventional resources. In the Traditional Low Oil Price case, the OPEC countries increase their conventional oil production to obtain a 52-percent share of total world liquids production, and oil resources are more accessible and/or less costly to produce (as a result of technology advances, more attractive fiscal regimes, or both) than in the Reference case. With these assumptions, conventional oil production is higher in the Traditional Low Oil Price case than in the Reference case, but low prices constraint the expansion of unconventional resources. Oil consumption is higher solely as a result of the lower prices (which are the same as in the Low Oil Price case), reflecting a movement downward and to the right along the demand curve.

World Liquids Consumption

World liquids consumption in the *IEO2011* Reference case increases from 85.7 million barrels per day in 2008 to 97.6 million barrels per day in 2020 and 112.2 million barrels per day (225 quadrillion Btu) in 2035. World GDP is a key driver of demand, growing by an average 3.6 percent per year from 2008 to 2020 and 3.2 percent per year from 2020 to 2035. Developing non-OECD nations, particularly in Asia and the Middle East, experience strong economic growth in the Reference case, which is accompanied by increasing demand for liquids in the transportation and industrial sectors.

Rising prices for liquids increase the cost-competitiveness of other fuels, leading many users of liquids outside the transportation sector to switch to substitute sources of energy when possible. As a result, the transportation share of total liquid fuels consumption increases, accounting for about 80 percent of the overall increase in liquids consumption in all sectors over the projection period. In 2035, the transportation sector consumes 60 percent of total liquids supplied, as compared with 54 percent in 2008.

Strong expansion of liquids use is projected for non-OECD countries, fuelled by a return to robust economic growth, burgeoning industrial activity, and rapidly expanding transportation use. The largest increase in regional non-OECD consumption from 2008 to 2035 is projected for non-OECD Asia, at 17.3 million barrels per day. Within non-OECD Asia, the largest increases in demand come from China (9.1 million barrels per day) and India (4.6Â million barrels per day), with the increase from China being the largest for any single country worldwide. Large consumption increases are also expected in the Middle East (2.9 million barrels per day), followed by Central and South America (2.5Â million barrels per day). Liquids consumption in OECD regions generally grows more slowly over the next 25 years, reflecting slowly growing or declining populations and relatively low economic growth as compared with non-OECD nations. In addition, growth in demand for liquids in many OECD countries is slowed by government policies and legislation aimed at improving the efficiency of personal motor vehicles. This includes increased automobile efficiency standards and government incentives introduced in many nations during the recession, such as the U.S. "cash for clunkers" program, designed to encourage consumers to trade in older, less efficient cars for newer ones that are more fuel-efficient. In Japan and OECD Europe, liquids consumption declines by average annual rates of 0.4 percent (0.5 million barrels per day) and 0.2 percent (0.7 million barrels per day), respectively, from 2008 to 2035.

As a result of the different growth trends for the non-OECD and OECD regions, non-OECD liquids consumption in 2020 exceeds OECD consumption. The difference widens considerably over time, and in 2035 non-OECD consumption is 23 percent greater than OECD consumption. Although China's demand for liquids increases by 3.5 percent per year over the projection, its consumption in 2035 still is 5.0 million barrels per day less than U.S. liquids consumption. In the Low Oil Price case, non-OECD consumption and OECD consumption are nearly identical, at 57.0 and 56.3 million barrels per day in 2035, respectively. OECD consumption is higher than in the Reference case, because low prices discourage conservation and allow consumers to continue to use liquid fuels without economic impact. Most of the increase in OECD consumption in the Low Oil Price case occurs in the Americas and in Asia.

In contrast to the OECD, non-OECD consumption is 4.8 million barrels per day lower in the Low Oil Price case than in the Reference Case. In this case, slower growth in demand for liquids among the developing nations keeps world oil prices low—in contrast to the Traditional Low Oil Price case, where low prices encourage increased consumption worldwide. Although OECD liquids consumption levels in 2035 are similar in the Low Oil Price and Traditional Low Oil Price cases, non-OECD consumption grows to a total of 74.4 million barrels per day in 2035 in the Traditional Low Oil Price case—17.4 million barrels per day higher than in the Low Oil Price case and 12.6 million barrels higher than in the Reference case. In the High Oil Price case, where high oil prices are a result of strong growth in non-OECD demand for liquids, non-OECD liquids consumption represents 61 percent of the world total in 2035. China's consumption of liquids grows by an average of 3.8 percent per year (from 7.8 million barrels per day in 2008 to 21.2 million barrels per day in 2035), as compared with 3.5 percent per year in the Reference case. India and the Middle East also increase consumption by an average of more than 2.0 percent per year. OECD consumption declines slightly through the mid-term and increases only slightly in the longer term, with high world oil prices encouraging consumers to conserve fuel and turn to alternatives fuels whenever possible. OECD liquid fuel use in the High Oil Price case remains below the 2008 level of 48.0 million barrels per day through 2035.

Non-OECD demand, which is higher in the High Oil Price case than in the Reference case, provides support for higher world oil prices. For example, in the High Oil Price case China's liquids consumption in 2035 is equal to U.S. consumption. In contrast, in the Traditional High Oil Price case, demand for liquids in all regions is affected only by price, with high prices dampening liquids demand and encouraging conservation and fuel switching.

As a result, liquids consumption in the Traditional High Oil Price case is lower than in the Reference case in every *IEO2011* region. In the Traditional High Oil Price case, non-OECD liquids consumption totals 59.4 million barrels per day in 2035, as compared with 74.2 million barrels per day in the High Oil Price case and 61.8 million barrels per day in the Reference case. OECD liquids consumption in 2035 in the Traditional High Oil Price case is almost the same as in the High Oil Price case.

Recent Market Trends

In 2010, world oil prices responded primarily to expectations about demand, with producers, consumers, and traders looking for some indication as to when the world's economy would recover, what shape the recovery would take, and how strong the corresponding increase in oil demand would be. While stronger than expected regional growth led many market players to expect a buoyant return of global liquids demand and an increase in oil prices, the financial crises in several European nations served as a caution about the still fragile global economy and the potential negative impact of higher oil prices on demand.

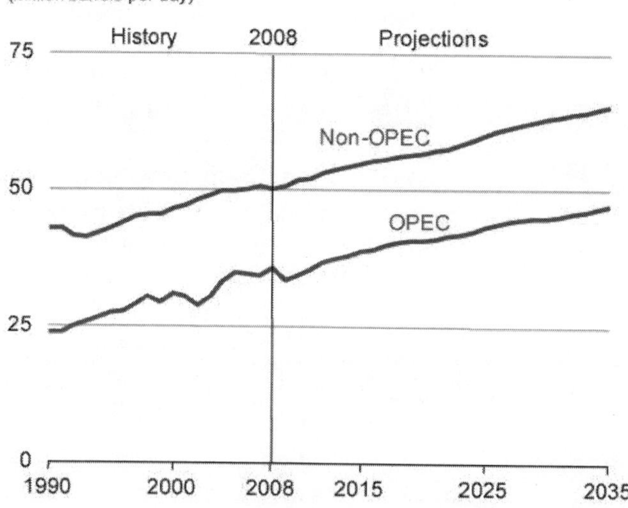

***Figure :** World total liquid fuels production, 1990-2035*

In addition, 2010 was an eventful year for supply factors that shape long-term pricing. The Deepwater Horizon oil spill in the U.S. Gulf of Mexico may have consequences for future U.S. production that are not yet fully understood. In addition, new discoveries and development in Africa's frontier exploration regions have increased production expectations for the continent and expanded the range of countries with future production potential, which not so long ago was generally limited to a few established producers relying on EOR and deepwater production in Angola and Nigeria.

In addition, although OPEC compliance with its 2008 production quotas has held relatively steady, averaging under 60 percent for the year, the recent decision by OPEC not to increase official production targets despite rising oil prices, along with public statements by members calling for $80 to $100 per barrel as the new "fair" oil price, has drawn into question the organization's concern for world economic recovery.

Iraq, the only OPEC member not subject to a production quota, has seen initial production gains at the individual fields included in its two 2009 bid rounds; however, those gains have only compensated for other declines and have not lead to an increase in total production. Although foreign companies in Iraq have been able to establish operations and achieve initial production gains in relatively short order despite ongoing security risks and political uncertainty, most industry analysts still do not expect Iraq to reach its production target of 9.5 million barrels per day—almost four times the country's current production level—within the next decade.

World Liquids Production

In the *IEO2011* Reference case, world liquids production in 2035 exceeds the 2008 level by 26.6 million barrels per day, with production increases expected for both OPEC and non-OPEC producers. Overall, 57 percent of the total increase is expected to come from non-OPEC areas, including 31 percent from non-OPEC unconventional liquids production alone. OPEC produces 46.9 million barrels per day in 2035 in the Reference case, and non-OPEC producers provide 65.3 million barrels per day.

The Reference case assumes that OPEC producers will choose to maintain their market share of world liquids supply and will invest in incremental production capacity so that their liquids production represents approximately 40 percent of total global liquids production throughout the projection. Increasing volumes of conventional liquids (crude oil and lease condensate, natural gas plant liquids [NGPL], and refinery gain) from OPEC members contribute 10.3 million barrels per day to the total increase in world liquids production from 2008 to 2035, and conventional liquids supplied from non-OPEC nations contribute 7.1 million barrels per day.

Unconventional liquids production increases by about 5 percent annually on average over the projection period, because sustained high oil prices make unconventional liquids more competitive, and "above-ground" factors limit the production of economically competitive conventional liquids. Unconventional fuels account for 35 percent (9.2 million barrels per day) of the increase in total liquids production in the Reference case, and 8.2 million barrels per day of the increase in unconventional supply comes from non-OPEC sources. High oil prices, improvements in exploration and extraction technologies, emphasis on recovery efficiency, and the emergence and continued growth of unconventional resource production are the primary factors supporting the growth of non-OPEC liquids production in the *IEO2011* Reference case.

Liquids Production Modelling Approach

The *IEO2011* projections for liquids production are based on a two-stage analytical approach. Production projections before 2015 are based largely on a project-by-project assessment of production volumes and associated scheduling timelines, with consideration given to the decline rates of active projects, planned exploration and development activity, and country-specific geopolitical situations and fiscal regimes. There are often lengthy delays between the point at which supply projects are announced and when they begin producing. The extensive and detailed information available about such projects, including project scheduling and the investment and development plans of companies and countries, makes it possible to take a detailed approach to the modelling of mid-term supply.

Although some projects are publicized more than 7 to 10 years before their first production, others can come on line within 3 years. For that reason, project-by-project analyses are unlikely to provide a complete representation of company or country production plans and achievable production volumes beyond 3 years into the future. Instead, production decisions made after the mid-term, or 2015, are assumed to be based predominantly on resource availability and the resulting economic viability of production.

In view of the residual effects of previous government policies and the unavoidable lag time between changes in policy and any potential production changes, however, most country-level changes in production trends are noticeable only in 2020 and beyond. Geopolitical and other above-ground constraints are not assumed to disappear entirely after 2015, however. Longstanding above-ground factors for which there are no indications of significant future changes—for instance, the government-imposed investment conditions currently in place in Iran, or OPEC adherence to production quotas—are expected to continue affecting world supplies long after 2015. Even if above-ground constraints were relaxed, the expansion of production capacity could be delayed, depending on the technical difficulty and typical development schedules of the projects likely to be developed in a particular country.

For some resource-rich countries it is assumed that current political barriers to production increases will not continue after 2015. For instance, both Mexico and Venezuela currently have laws that restrict foreign ownership of hydrocarbon resources. Their resource policies have discouraged investment—both foreign and domestic—and hindered their ability to increase or even maintain historical production levels. In the Reference case, both Mexico and Venezuela ease restrictions at some point after 2015, allowing some additional foreign involvement in their oil sectors that facilitates increases in liquids production, including from deepwater prospects in Mexico and extra-heavy oils in Venezuela's Orinoco belt.

Iraq is another resource-rich country where currently there are significant impediments to investment in the upstream hydrocarbon sector. Liquids production in Iraq dropped substantially after the U.S.-led invasion in 2003. From 2002 to 2003 production declined from 2.0 million barrels per day to 1.3 million barrels per day, and since then it has achieved only inconsistent and slow growth. Although Iraq's production levels are not expected to increase substantially in the near term, it is assumed that political and legal uncertainty eventually will subside, and that renewed investment and development activity will ensue, resulting in significant growth in production from 2015 to 2035.

Non-OPEC Production

The return to sustained high oil prices projected in the *IEO2011* Reference case encourages producers in non-OPEC nations to continue investment in conventional liquids production capacity and increase investment in EOR projects and unconventional liquids production. Non-OPEC production increases steadily in the projection, from 50.0 million barrels per day in 2008 to 65.3 million barrels per day in 2035, as high prices attract investment in areas previously considered uneconomical, and fears of supply restrictions encourage some net consuming nations to expand unconventional liquids production from domestic resources, such as coal and crops.

Despite the maturity of most non-OPEC producing basins, conventional liquids production in the Reference case increases from 46.8 million barrels per day in 2008 to 53.9 million barrels per day in 2035. The overall increase results primarily from production increases in four countries: Brazil, Russia, Kazakhstan, and the United States. Among non-OPEC producers, the near absence of prospects for new, large conventional petroleum liquids projects, along with declines in production from existing conventional fields, results in heavy investment in the development of smaller fields. Producers are expected to concentrate their efforts on more efficient exploitation of fields already in production, either through the use of more advanced technology for primary recovery efforts or through EOR. Those efforts are expected to allow most established non-OPEC producers to maintain or slow production declines but not to raise production volumes.

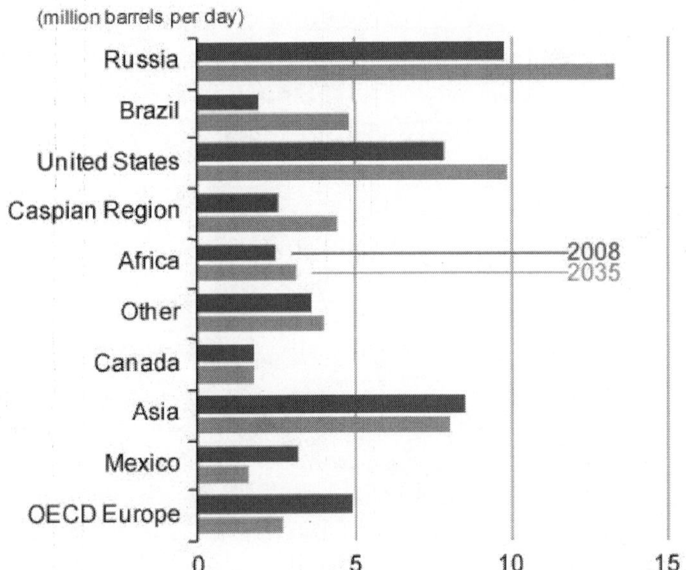

Figure : *Non-OPEC conventional production by region, 2008 and 2035*

In the Reference case, unconventional liquids production from non-OPEC suppliers rises to 6.5 million barrels per day in 2020 and 11.4 million barrels per day in 2035. In both the High Oil Price and Traditional High Oil Price cases, non-OPEC unconventional liquids production rises to about 17.4 million barrels per day in 2035, as significantly higher prices encourage the development of alternative fuel sources to the limits imposed by expected environmental protection measures and industry expansion in general. In contrast, in the Low Oil Price and Traditional Low Oil Price cases, fewer unconventional resources become economically competitive, and non-OPEC production of unconventional liquids rises to only about 7.0 million barrels per day in 2035 in each low price case.

Major Areas of Decline in Non-OPEC Liquids Production

In the *IEO2011* Reference case, Mexico and the North Sea are the only non-OPEC production areas that lose more than 1 million barrels of liquids production per day from 2008 to 2035. The most significant decline in non-OPEC liquids production is projected for OECD Europe, with a decrease from 5.1 million barrels per day in 2008 to 3.0 million barrels per day in 2035. Most of the decline is in North Sea production, which includes offshore operations by Norway, the United Kingdom, the Netherlands, and Germany. Over time, fewer and fewer prospects capable of compensating for declines in existing fields have been discovered. The drop in North Sea liquids production does not vary significantly among the four price cases, both because the projected production is based on depletion of resources and because all the countries currently producing liquids from North Sea operations are expected to continue encouraging investment and providing open access to development.

In Mexico, liquids production sinks to approximately 1.4 million barrels per day in 2025 before rebounding slowly to 1.7 million barrels per day in 2035, still 1.5 million barrels per day below the 2008 production volume of 3.2 million barrels per day. The rebound after 2025 depends entirely on the development of potential resources in the deepwater Gulf of Mexico, which must begin some years in advance of any increase in production levels. The outlook for Mexico's liquids production is markedly different from the IEO projection just 5 years ago, in which production did not fall below 2.9 million barrels per day, and a long-term recovery began in 2013. The difference between the projections is the result of production declines at Cantarell, which have been more severe than expected, as well as diminished expectations for Chicontepec production and more pessimistic assumptions about the level of future investment, both foreign and domestic, in Mexico's deepwater production.

Although the shortage of investment in Mexico is expected to lead to a mid-term decline, Mexico has potential resources to support a long-term recovery in total production, primarily in the Gulf of Mexico. The extent and timing of a recovery will depend in part on the level of economic access granted to foreign investors and operators. Mexico's national oil company, PetrΓ³leos Mexicanos (PEMEX), currently does not have the technical capability or financial means to develop potential deepwater projects in the Gulf of Mexico.

Major Areas of Growth in Non-OPEC Liquids Production

The largest increase in non-OPEC total liquids production is expected for Brazil, where total production in 2035 is 4.1 million barrels per day above the 2008 level of 2.4 million barrels per day. Of that increase, 2.9 million barrels per day is attributed to conventional liquids production. The strong growth in Brazil's conventional production results in part from short- and mid-term increases at producing fields for which expansions currently are either planned or in progress. In addition, recent and expected discoveries in the Campos and Santos basins, including the massive Tupi and related Guara and Iara discoveries, both add to production in the mid- and long term and suggest the presence of other large fields in the same formation. The vast size of the sub-salt potential in Brazil, as well as national economic strategy and industrialization goals, has led Brazil to pursue new petroleum legislation. The legislative change most pertinent to production potential is the requirement that the state oil company, Petrobras, be the sole operator and a minimum 30-percent equity holder for all sub-salt fields.

Although Petrobras has repeatedly proven itself a leader in deepwater development and is known to have the technical capabilities to develop sub-salt prospects, it is not expected to have the resources (financial, labour, etc.) to develop its domestic plays completely on its own. The different *IEO2011* price cases assume different investment terms offered by Brazil to foreign investors and hence different rates of sub-salt development. Although both the High Oil Price case and the Traditional High Oil Price case assume more restrictive terms of access to Brazil's conventional resources, the increase in world liquids demand in the High Oil Price cases supports a production level of 5.3 million barrels per day in 2035, compared with 5.0 million barrels per day in the Traditional High Oil Price case. In contrast, both the Low Oil Price and Traditional Low Oil Price cases assume open terms of access to Brazil's conventional resources, resulting in production increases averaging 3.4 percent per year and conventional production of 5.1 million barrels per day in 2035 in the Low Oil Price case (as a result of lower world liquids demand) and 5.6 million barrels per day in 2035 in the Traditional Low Oil Price case.

In addition to the growth in conventional liquids production, Brazil's biofuel production also increases, from 0.5 million barrels per day in 2008 to 1.7 million barrels per day in 2035 in the Reference case. The growth is a result of steadily increasing yields and expansion of crop production, with most of the increase consisting of ethanol. Brazil's major ethanol production is derived from sugar cane, currently the highest yielding and least expensive feedstock for ethanol. Brazil also has a large amount of land available for sugar cane production, in the form of previously cleared and currently underutilized pasture land. The country's domestic consumption is not expected to rise as fast as its expansion of ethanol production, making Brazil a net ethanol exporter over the course of the projection. Thus, its production depends largely on other countries' policies and demand for ethanol.

In the High Oil Price case, Brazil's ethanol production totals 1.9 million barrels per day in 2035, reflecting higher demand for ethanol both at home and abroad. In the Low Oil Price case, which assumes reduced domestic and international demand for ethanol, Brazil's ethanol production totals 1.1 million barrels per day in 2035. Even in the Low Oil Price case, however, there is only a small drop in Brazil's domestic ethanol consumption, because of the country's mandatory minimum E25 blend and the fact that ethanol makes up nearly 50 percent of the country's domestic gasoline market.

The second-largest contributor to future increases in non-OPEC total liquids production is the United States. U.S. conventional liquids production grows from 7.8 million barrels per day in 2008 to 9.9 million barrels per day in 2035 in the Reference case, as rising world oil prices spur both onshore and offshore drilling. In the short term, the vast majority of the increase in crude oil production comes from deepwater offshore fields. Fields that started producing in 2009, or that are expected to start producing in the next few years, include Great White, Norman, Tahiti, Gomez, Cascade, and Chinook. All are in water depths greater than 2,600 feet, and most are in the U.S. Central Gulf of Mexico. Production from those fields, combined with increased production from fields that started producing in 2007 and 2008, contributes to the near-term growth in U.S. offshore production. The reduction in crude oil production resulting from the current moratorium on deepwater drilling in the Gulf of Mexico is estimated to average about 31,000 barrels per day in the fourth quarter of 2010 and about 82,000 barrels per day in 2011, but production levels are expected to recover in the mid-term. Production from other recently discovered and yet-to-be discovered fields offsets production declines in older fields in the projection, resulting in a net increase in liquids production through 2035.

Is Brazil the World's Next Major Oil Producer?

In 2007, a consortium led by Petrobras, Brazil's national oil company, discovered the Tupi field in the Santos Basin off the coast of Brazil. The field, now known as a "pre-salt deposit," was found 18,000 feet below the ocean surface underneath a 6,000-foot layer of salt. Tupi and other pre-salt finds hold the potential to make Brazil one of the world's most prolific oil exporters. Although Brazil already produces 2.1 million barrels per day of crude oil and lease condensate, it did not become a net exporter until 2009. In the next decade, Brazil aspires to more than double its conventional production and significantly expand its oil exports.

According to Oil & Gas Journal, Brazil's proven oil reserves are estimated currently at 12.9 billion barrels, not including major pre-salt fields. Estimates of Brazil's pre-salt reserves have varied widely. In 2008, Haroldo Lima, Director General of Brazil's National Petroleum Agency, stated that the country's pre-salt deposits could contain between 50 and 70 billion barrels of oil. More recently, in January 2011, Petrobras announced its assessment that the Tupi and Iracema fields (renamed Lula and Cernambi) contain 6.5 billion and 1.8 billion barrels of commercially recoverable oil, respectively. It will be some time before the Brazil's pre-salt reserves are fully quantified, but knowledge of exact reserve levels is not critical to assessing the viability of Brazil's proposal to expand their production in the coming years.

In its 2010-2014 business plan, Petrobras outlined production targets of 3.0 million barrels per day in 2014 and 4.0 million barrels per day in 2020. In the plan, more than one-quarter of the company's Brazilian production in 2020 comes from pre-salt fields. In the *IEO2011* Reference case, Brazil's conventional liquids production increases to 3.3 million barrels per day in 2020 and 4.9 million barrels per day in 2035; and its total liquids supply, including unconventional liquids such as ethanol and biodiesel, increases to 6.6 million barrels per day in 2035. The projections reflect a somewhat more conservative view of the pace of expansion, given the financial, regulatory, and operational challenges that Petrobras will need to overcome in order to realize the full potential of Brazil's pre-salt resources.

Financing the development of pre-salt oil fields will be expensive. One analyst has suggested that Brazil's current undertaking could be "the largest private sector investment program in the history of mankind." The Petrobras business plan includes investments of $224 billion between 2010 and 2014, more than half of which will be spent on exploration and production activities. To facilitate the plan, the company raised $67 billion in the world's largest initial public offering ever in September 2010. However, most of the capital came in the form of a reserves-for-shares swap with the Brazilian government. Petrobras will need to fund the majority of its investments through operating cash flow. The increase in the government's equity points to an expansion of state involvement in the petroleum sector.

The government's capitalization of Petrobras was part of a set of laws passed in 2010 to regulate development of Brazil's pre-salt reserves. The legislation also established a new federal agency (Petrosal) to administer pre-salt production and set up a fund to align the expenditure of pre-salt revenues with Brazil's development goals. Most importantly in terms of Brazil's investment climate, the law changed the country's concession-based system for exploration to a production-sharing agreement (PSA) system. Under the PSA system, Petrobras will hold at least a 30-percent share of each project and be the operator. Some analysts fear that the new system will reduce foreign interest in investing in Brazil and overburden Petrobras. The re-launch of Brazil's latest bid round for oil exploration blocks is scheduled for 2011, pending settlement of a dispute over the distribution of pre-salt royalties among Brazilian states. The results of the bid round will highlight the full impact of the legislative changes on the development of pre-salt resources.

Development of pre-salt deposits represents a daunting task, with considerable technological uncertainty about how the geologic formations will behave once production has begun. In addition, the reserves are located more than 150 miles off Brazil's coast, making them difficult for pipelines and people to reach. Petrobras plans to purchase 45 floating production, storage, and offloading (FPSO) vessels to extract the pre-salt oil; however, only 75 such rigs currently exist in the world.

In addition to massive investments in physical capital, the planned expansion of Brazil's production will require additional human capital. Petrobras plans to train 243,000 technical professionals to work in the petroleum industry in the coming decade and to invest hundreds of millions of dollars in oil-related research and development centers at Brazilian universities. Given the scale of the task, the predominant role played by Petrobras, and local-content requirements, operational challenges introduce a nontrivial amount of uncertainty into projections of Brazil's liquids production.

Brazil's pre-salt discoveries represent some of the most promising oil finds, and its role as an oil producer will grow in the coming decades.

The extent of that expansion is uncertain, however, given the financial, regulatory, and operational challenges involved in such a large-scale undertaking.

U.S. lower 48 onshore production of crude oil continues to grow through 2035, primarily as a result of increased application of EOR techniques. In 2035, EOR accounts for 37 percent of total onshore production in the Reference case. The rate of growth in domestic crude oil production depends largely on assumptions about world oil prices and improvements in technology, because remaining onshore resources typically require more costly secondary or tertiary recovery techniques. On the other hand, if carbon dioxide emissions were captured and sequestered in the future, the availability of relatively plentiful and inexpensive supplies of carbon dioxide could spur additional EOR activities that would make onshore production more economical.

U.S. unconventional liquids production becomes more significant as world oil prices rise, with domestic production of biofuels increasing from 0.7 million barrels per day in 2008 to 2.2 million barrels per day in 2035 in the Reference case. Although advances in coal liquefaction technology have made CTL fuels commercially available in other countries, including South Africa, China, and Germany, the technical and financial risks of building what would be essentially a first-of-a-kind facility in the United States have discouraged significant investment thus far. In addition, the possibility of new legislation aimed at reducing U.S. greenhouse gas emissions creates further uncertainty for future investment in CTL. Similarly, although ongoing improvement in oil shale technology leads to the start of commercial production in 2029 in the Reference case and a rapid increase to 1.1 percent of total U.S. liquids supply in 2035, oil shale development also would have to overcome environmental, technical, and financial uncertainties similar to those for CTL.

Canada's production of conventional liquids declines slowly in the Reference case, by a total of just under 20 thousand barrels per day from 2008 to 2035. However, increased production of unconventional petroleum liquids from oil sands more than offsets the decline in conventional production. As a result, Canada's total liquids production increases from 3.4 million barrels per day in 2008 to 6.6 million barrels per day in 2035.

Russia and Kazakhstan are the other key players in non-OPEC production growth. However, the non-OECD Europe and Eurasia region is prone to territorial disputes, transportation blockages, contractual changes, and political intervention. After declining to 9.0 million barrels per day in 2014, Russia's liquids production begins a slow increase to 11.4 million barrels per day in 2020 in the Reference case, as uncertainty about tax regimes lessens. In addition, annual increases in the world oil price in the IEO2011 Reference case spur liquids development that boosts Russia's production to 13.3 million barrels per day in 2035. Although exploration in eastern Siberia and the Arctic is expected during the projection period, Arctic exploration does not contribute much to production in the Reference case. Across the five IEO2011 scenarios that assume different levels of economic access granted to investors in the long term, Russia's total liquids production in 2035 ranges from 13.3 to 15.3 million barrels per day. In the Low Oil Price case, as access to resources is opened up, production in 2035 totals 14.1 million barrels per more than in the Reference case but less than in the Traditional Low Oil Price case, because worldwide demand for liquids is lower.

In Kazakhstan, mid-term growth in liquids production depends predominantly on the resources of the Kashagan and Tengiz oil fields, as well as the ability of investors to transport production from those projects to the world market. Although known and potential resources are sufficient to support the growth of liquids production in Kazakhstan, they could be undermined by a lack of easy export routes. Currently, exports are limited to six routes: the CPC pipeline, Atyrau-Samara pipeline, and railway shipments can transport a total of 0.8 million barrels per day to Russia; another pipeline can move 0.2 million barrels per day to China; and two barge routes allow shipments of about 0.1 million barrels per day to Azerbaijan and Iran.

Kazakhstan's export potential is affected strongly by its geographical position. Attaining the production levels projected in the Reference case depends not only on resource availability and production but also on the construction of export routes—a task requiring regional cooperation that has not been easy to achieve in the past. A number of possible projects to expand Kazakhstan's capacity for liquids exports have been proposed over the past several years. The most likely expansions in the near term are capacity increases in the pipelines to Russia and China.

In addition to the problem of transportation capacity, Kazakhstan has previously reopened legal contracts with private foreign investors, forcing renegotiation of investment returns and making companies reluctant to increase their investment in the country's energy sector. Across the five *IEO2011* oil price cases (including the Reference case), Kazakhstan's production in 2035 ranges from a low of 3.1 million barrels per day to a high of 3.5 million barrels per day.

OPEC Production

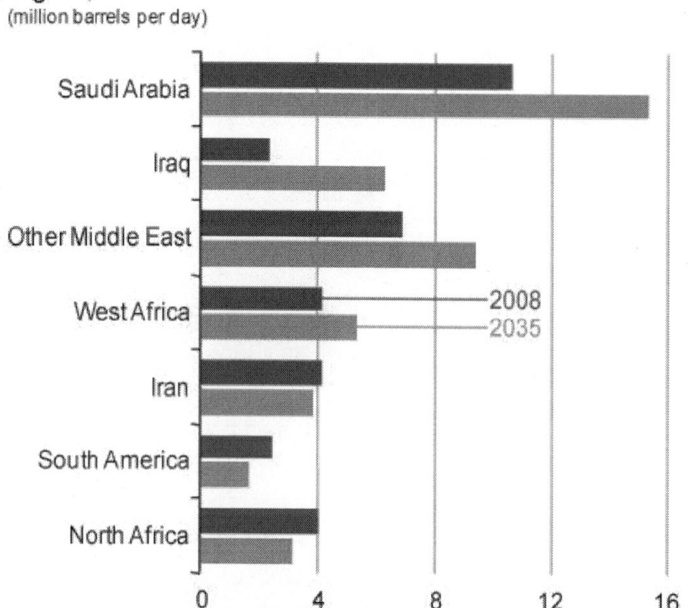

Figure : *OPEC conventional liquids production by country and region 2008 and 2035*

In the *IEO2011* Reference case, total liquids production from OPEC nations increases from the 2008 level of 35.6 million barrels per day at an average annual rate of 1.0 percent, resulting in the production of 46.9 million barrels of liquids per day in 2035. Of the total OPEC increase, 11.0 million barrels per day originates in the Middle East.

Throughout the projection period, Saudi Arabia remains the largest liquids producer in OPEC, with total production increasing from 10.7 million barrels per day in 2008 to 15.4 million barrels per day in 2035, as prices stabilize at historically high levels and world consumption continues to grow. Seventeen percent of the increase (0.8 million barrels per day) is expected to be NGPL production related to expansion of natural gas production. The total production increase equates to an average annual growth rate of 1.4 percent, based on the assumption that Saudi Arabia will continue with its current plan to maintain spare production capacity at levels between 1.5 and 2.0 million barrels per day.

Iraq increases its liquids production by 3.7 percent per year in the *IEO2011* Reference case, the largest annual average growth in total liquids production among all OPEC members. The projection assumes that political, legislative, logistical, investment, and security uncertainties in Iraq will be resolved in the long term, and that OPEC constraints and resource availability will be the factors with the strongest influence on Iraq's willingness and ability to increase production.

In addition to political and legislative uncertainty, import and export infrastructure also are expected to limit production growth in Iraq to 0.6 million barrels per day from 2008 to 2015. If the country is able to achieve long-term political and economic stability and expand the capacity of import and export routes as projected in the Reference case, investment in production capacity could rise by an average of 4.2 percent per year from 2015 and 2030 before slowing to a more modest 3.0 percent per year from 2030 to 2035. The fact that Iraq has the resources necessary to support such growth in the long run, yet produced only 2.4 million barrels per day in 2008, illustrates the significant impacts that the political environment and other above-ground constraints can have on production projections.

Qatar has the second-highest average annual growth rate in total liquids production among OPEC nations from 2008 to 2035 in the Reference case, at 2.7 percent, with total volumes increasing from 1.2 million barrels per day in 2008 to 2.5 million barrels per day in 2035. About 55 percent of the increase consists of crude oil and lease condensate production; NGPL production contributes another 0.3 million barrels per day; and GTL projects add just over 0.2 million barrels per day. Despite the current negative outlook for many previously announced GTL projects around the world, the return and persistence of historically high oil prices in the Reference case supports the operation of Qatar's Pearl facility (0.1 million barrels per day capacity) and expansion of its Oryx facility (adding another 0.1 million barrels per day).

Total liquids production in Iran is restricted by political rather than resource-related factors in the IEO2011 Reference case. The political factors include the effectiveness of the national oil company's operations, the ability of the government and foreign investors to agree on contractual terms, and continuing financial sanctions. In the Reference case, Iran's oil production declines from 2008 through 2035 because of both financial and political constraints on the development of new oil and natural gas prospects. In addition, the amount of natural gas available for improving oil recovery through natural gas reinjection is limited in the projections by natural gas demand for domestic electric power and heat production. Political factors and investment constraints affect Iran's liquids production so severely that production in 2035 varies by 3.5 million barrels per day across the *IEO2011* projections, from 2.7 million barrels per day in the Traditional High Oil Price case to 6.3 million barrels per day in the Traditional Low Oil Price case.

In the OPEC nations of Western Africa, total liquids production increases from 4.2 million barrels per day in 2008 to 5.4 million barrels per day in 2035 in the Reference case. Angola expands production to 2.3 million barrels per day in 2020—almost entirely by increasing crude oil and condensate production from offshore projects—before entering a slow but steady resource-driven decline in the long term. Nigeria's liquids production is likely to be hampered in the short term by conflict and infrastructure difficulties; in the long term, however, a higher level of known resources enables its liquids production to grow by an average of 1.7 percent per year, from 2.2 million barrels per day in 2008 to a total of 3.4 million barrels per day in 2035.

Recent history suggests that Venezuela's national government reacts to high oil prices by tightening the terms for foreign direct investment and limiting access to its reserves. As a result, in the Reference case, with prices rising in real terms through 2035, further mandated changes in contractual terms, along with threats of actions to recapture upside returns from potential investors, are likely to hinder Venezuela's production potential in the short term and discourage investment in and development of additional projects in the long term. The trend is particularly evident in the mature conventional oil basins, with conventional production declining by 0.3 million barrels per day over the projection period from 2008 levels of 2.0 million barrels per day. However, development of several extra-heavy oil projects in the Orinoco belt offsets some of the decline in conventional liquids production. Ecuador rejoined OPEC in October 2007, after having suspended its membership in 1999. Ecuador is a relatively small oil producer in Â comparison with other OPEC members, producing 0.5 million barrels of oil per day in 2008. Liquids production in Ecuador declines through 2015 in the Reference case, as uncertainties associated with the country's Hydrocarbons Law make foreign Â companies reluctant to investment in Ecuador's oil sector. After 2015, although investment in the country's oil sector continues to be hindered by high investment risk, development of its ITT heavy oil field in the Amazon helps to stabilize its production. Consequently, liquids production in Ecuador rebounds to 0.7 million barrels per day in 2025 and remains fairly flat through 2035.

OPEC investment decisions regarding additional new production capacity are the primary difference between the Traditional High and Traditional Low Oil Price cases. In the *IEO2011* High and Low Oil

Price cases, non-OECD demand is also an important market determinant. In the Low Oil Price case, OPEC production increases to 53.7 million barrels per day in 2035, representing a 47-percent share of total world liquids production. The Low Oil Price case assumes that OPEC members will increase investment either through their own national oil companies or by allowing greater economic access to foreign investors, depending on the country. It also assumes that OPEC members will expand production capacity in an attempt to maximize government revenue through increased production. OPEC production in the Traditional Low Oil Price case increases by 32.4 million barrels per day from 2008 to 2035, to 68.0 million barrels per day or approximately 52 percent of total world liquids production in 2035.

In the High Oil Price case, high demand and high prices encourage development of expensive non-OPEC resources. As a result, Â OPEC supports only a 37-percent market share of total world liquids production, with a production level of 45.7 million barrels per day in 2035, less than the Reference case level of 46.9 million barrels per day. Alternatively, in the Traditional High Oil Price case, OPEC member countries maintain record high prices by restricting production targets to a smaller share of world total liquids production each year. As a result, OPEC production accounts for 32 percent of the world total in 2035. Production totals 34.8 million barrels per day in 2025, and after 2026 it begins a slight decline to 34.1 million barrels per day in 2035.

Unconventional Liquids Production

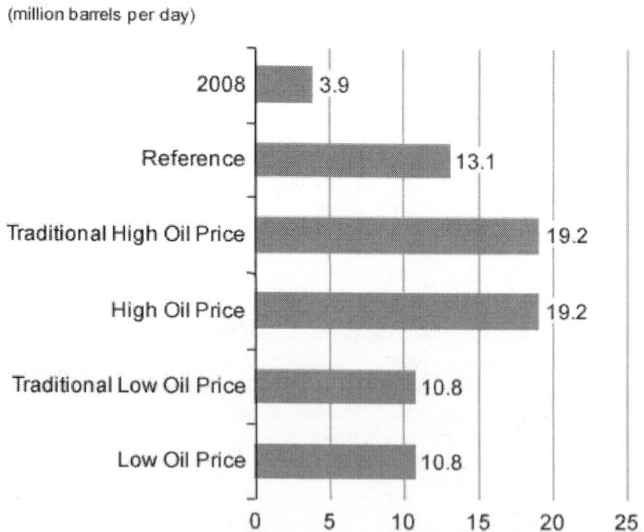

Figure : *Unconventional liquids production in five cases, 2008 and 2035*

Unconventional liquids play an increasingly important role in meeting demand for liquid fuels over the course of the *IEO2011* projections. In the Reference case, 12 percent of world liquids supply in 2035 comes from unconventional sources, including 1.7 million barrels per day from OPEC and 11.4 million from non-OPEC sources. Although the volume and composition of unconventional production vary across the IEO2011 price cases (from 19.2 million barrels per day in the Traditional High Oil Price case to 10.8 million barrels per day in the Low Oil Price case), the geographic origin of each unconventional liquid type is relatively constant across the cases, usually being limited to countries where projects currently are underway or advertised. Because world oil prices largely determine whether relatively expensive unconventional supplies are developed, there is little difference between the volumes of unconventional resources supplied in the Low Oil Price case and in the Traditional Low Oil Price case. The same is true of the two high oil price cases.

OPEC Unconventional Production

OPEC's unconventional production consists predominantly of extra-heavy oil production in Venezuela (from the Orinoco belt) and GTL production in Qatar. In the *IEO2011* Reference case, Venezuela's extra-heavy oil production rises from 0.7 million barrels per day in 2008 to 1.4 million barrels per day in 2035, and Qatar's GTL production increases from a negligible amount in 2008 to 0.2 million barrels per day in 2035. Although the resources to support production at those levels abound in the two countries, large investments will be required to bring them to market, and the timing of such investment is uncertain.

There are four major projects currently operating in Venezuela's Orinoco belt, but they have been suffering from poor maintenance and lack of investment. Venezuela's ability to increase its extra-heavy oil production will depend on the level of foreign investment and expertise it is able to attract for extraction and upgrading projects. In the Reference case, only two Orinoco belt projects are developed over the course of the projection—JunΓ-n 4 (operated by a consortium of Chinese companies) and JunΓ-n 6 (operated by a consortium of Russian companies). The two projects add 0.4 million barrels per day of production capacity each.

In the Low Oil Price case, Venezuela improves contract terms and stabilizes its investment climate to attract more foreign investment in the development of Orinoco resources, including JunΓ-n 2 and the Carabobo area, which contribute 0.2 and 1.2 million barrels per day, respectively. In addition, several other development projects are undertaken in the long term.

Non-OPEC Unconventional Production

Outside OPEC, unconventional liquids production comes from a much more diverse group of countries and resource types. As a whole, non-OPEC unconventional liquids production in the *IEO2011* Reference case increases by 8.2 million barrels per day, from 3.2 million barrels per day in 2008 to 11.4 million barrels per day in 2035. OECD countries account for 71 percent of total non-OPEC unconventional liquids production in 2035. By volume, the countries making the largest contribution to the increase in non-OPEC unconventional liquids are Canada (an increase of 3.3 million barrels per day), the United States (2.3 million barrels per day), Brazil (1.2 million barrels per day), and China (0.9 million barrels per day).

In each of the five oil price cases, Canada's bitumen (oil sands) production makes up more than 40 percent of total non-OPEC unconventional production, ranging from 3.1 million barrels per day in the Low Oil Price and Traditional Low Oil Price cases to 6.5 million barrels per day in the High Oil Price and Traditional High Oil Price cases. Bitumen production in the two high price cases ramps up quickly in the short to mid-term then begins to slow in the long term, closely following the assumed world oil price path in high price cases. In the low oil price cases, production growth stagnates because the price is too low for new projects to be economical. Over time, however, reductions in the cost of the technology lead to an overall increase in production.

Biofuels production in the Reference case increases from 1.5 million barrels per day in 2008 to 4.7 million barrels per day in 2035, at an average annual growth rate of 4.3 percent. The largest increase in biofuels production over the projection period comes from the United States, where production grows by 1.6 million barrels per day, from 0.7 million barrels per day in 2008 to 2.2 million barrels per day in 2035. The growth in U.S. biofuels production is supported by the Energy Independence and Security Act of 2007, which mandates increased use of biofuels. Strong growth in biofuels consumption is also projected for Brazil, where production grows by 1.2 million barrels per day from 2008 to 2035.

Government policies provide the primary incentive for non-OPEC biofuels production. Biofuels are used as a means to reduce greenhouse gas emissions, promote energy security, and support local economic development. To achieve those goals, many countries set mandates for the amount of biofuels to be used and give tax credits to biofuel producers. The United States, for example, mandates 36 billion gallons of biofuels by 2022 under the Energy Independence and Security Act of 2007. The European Union mandates that biofuels must make up 10 percent of the liquid fuels market by 2020, according to the European Union Biofuels Directive. Canadian producers receive payments or operating grants based on output, and the Chinese government has a flexible subsidy scheme with payments based on plant profitability. The Canadian and Chinese tax credits are designed to expire over time as the cost of production falls and oil prices rise.

Despite the wide range of biofuels incentive programs, some recent studies suggest that biofuels may not be as effective in reducing greenhouse gas emissions as previously thought. As a result, many countries have relaxed or postponed renewal of their mandates. For example, Germany reduced its biofuels quota for 2009 from 6.25 percent to 5.25 percent. The global economic recession has also dampened investment in biofuels development. Consequently, world biofuels production in 2030 is 40 percent lower in the *IEO2011* Reference case than was projected in the *IEO2009* Reference case and essentially the same as in the *IEO2010* Reference case.

In the *IEO2011* oil price cases, as in the Reference case, biofuels become more competitive with conventional oil products over time; however, the level of competitiveness depends on the oil price assumption. In the low price cases, only the cheapest and most cost-effective feedstocks and production technologies are competitive with gasoline and diesel fuels. In the high price cases, more feedstocks and production processes are competitive. Total biofuel production in 2035 ranges from 3.5 million barrels per day in the Low Oil Price case to 6.2 million barrels per day in the Traditional High Oil Price case. The growth of biofuel production slows in all cases from 2008 to 2015, as the current generation of crops reach their economic potential, then accelerates after 2016 with the advent of new technologies that use cellulosic feedstocks.

China is the primary CTL producer in all the *IEO2011* cases, with 2035 production levels ranging from 0.2 million barrels per day (or 50 percent of the world total) in the two low oil price cases to 2.1 million barrels per day (51 percent of the world total) in the two high oil price cases. Other major producers are the United States and South Africa, which produce about 0.5 and 0.3 million barrels per day, respectively, in the Reference case; 1.6 and 0.3 million barrels per day in the High Oil Price and Traditional High Oil Price cases; and about 0.1 million barrels per day each in the Low Oil Price and Traditional Low Oil Price cases.

The unconventional liquid product that consistently contributes the least to total unconventional production in each of the IEO2011 cases is GTL. In the Reference case and the two low oil price cases, GTL production is limited primarily to Qatar, although South Africa and Nigeria also produce small volumes. In the two high oil price cases, the United States rapidly becomes the world's third-largest GTL producer, accounting for 96 thousand barrels per day of the world's total of 400 thousand barrels per day in 2035.

World Oil Reserves

As of January 1, 2011, proved world oil reserves, as reported by the *Oil & Gas Journal*, were estimated at 1,471 billion barrels—115 billion barrels (about 9 percent) higher than the estimate for 2010. According to the Oil & Gas Journal, 51 percent of the world's proved oil reserves are located in the Middle East. Just under 79 percent of the world's proved reserves are concentrated in eight countries, of which only Canada (with oil sands included) and Russia are not OPEC members.

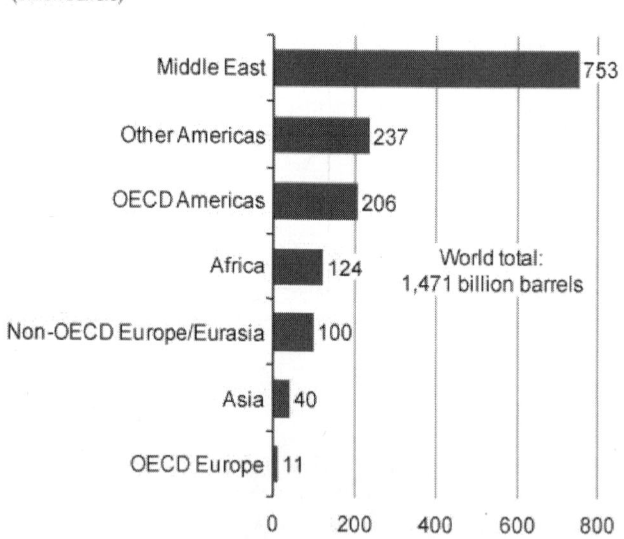

Figure : *World proved oil reserves by geographic region as of Janguary 1, 2011*

In 2011, the largest increase in proved reserves by far was attributed to Venezuela, as the country now reports its Orinoco belt extra-heavy oil in its totals. As a result, Venezuela's reserves alone increased by 113 billion barrels from 2010 to 2011. Smaller but notable increases were reported for Libya, Uganda, and Ghana. Libya's proved reserves increased by almost 2 billion barrels (4 percent). Uganda, which previously did not report any oil reserves, now claims 1.0 billion barrels. Ghana's recent discoveries of the Jubilee, Tweneboa, and Owo fields, among others, raised its reserves from 15 million barrels in 2010 to 660 million barrels in 2011. The largest decreases in regional reserves were attributed to Europe, including notable declines for Norway, Denmark, and the United Kingdom, which in combination saw a 14-percent decline (1,485 billion barrels) in reserves from 2010 to 2011. Although several OPEC member countries in late 2010 reported large additions to reserves, the Oil & Gas Journal chose not to include the new figures, citing the "politics involved in reserves estimates as they relate to output targets" within OPEC.

Country-level estimates of proved reserves from the Oil and Gas Journal are developed from data reported to the U.S. Securities and Exchange Commission (SEC), from foreign government reports, and from international geologic assessments. The estimates are not always updated annually. Proved reserves of crude oil are the estimated quantities that geological and engineering data indicate can be recovered in future years from known reservoirs, assuming existing technology and current economic and operating conditions.

Companies whose stocks are publicly traded on U.S. stock markets are required by the SEC to report their holdings of domestic and international proved reserves, following specific guidelines. In December 2008, the SEC released revisions to its reserves reporting requirements in an attempt to provide investors with a more complete picture of the reserves held by reporting companies, by recognizing the technologies and reserve quantification methods that have evolved over time. Proved reserves include only estimated quantities of crude oil from known reservoirs, and therefore they are only a subset of the entire potential oil resource base. Resource base estimates include estimated quantities of both discovered and undiscovered liquids that have the potential to be classified as reserves at some time in the future. The resource base may include oil that currently is not technically recoverable but could become recoverable in the future as technologies advance.

Readers may notice that, in some cases in the *IEO2011* projections, country-level volumes for cumulative production through 2035 exceed the estimates of proved reserves. This does not imply that resources and the physical limits of production have not been considered in the development of production forecasts, or that the projections assume a rapid decline in production immediately after the end of the projection period as reserves are depleted. EIA considers resource availability in all long-term country-level projections, the aggregation of which gives the total world production projection. However, proved reserves are not an appropriate measure for judging total resource availability in the long run. For example, despite continued production, global reserves historically have not declined as new reserves have been added through exploration, discovery, and reserve replacement.

In order to construct realistic and plausible projections for liquids production, and especially for petroleum liquids production, underlying analysis must both consider production beyond the intended end of the projection period and base production projections on the physical realities and limitations of production. The importance of approaching an assessment of liquids production in this way is illustrated by the recent history of U.S. reserve estimates. Whereas the United States reported 22.5 billion barrels of proved reserves in 1998, proved reserves of 20.7 billion barrels were reported in 2010—a decrease of only 1.8 billion barrels despite the cumulative 26.2 billion barrels of liquids supplied from U.S. reserves between 1998 and 2010.

Proved reserves cannot provide an accurate assessment of the physical limits on future production but rather are intended to provide insight as to company- or country- level development plans in the very near term. In fact, because of the particularly rigid requirements for the classification of resources as proved reserves, even the cumulative production levels from individual development projects may exceed initial estimates of proved reserves.

EIA attempts to address the lack of applicability of proved reserves estimates to long-term production projections by developing a production methodology based on the true physical limits of production, initially-in-place volumes, and technologically limited recovery factors. By basing long-term production assessments on resources rather than reserves, EIA is able to present projections that are physically achievable and can be supported beyond the 2035 projection horizon. The realization of such production levels depends on future growth in world demand, taking into consideration such above-ground limitations on production as profitability and specific national regulations, among others.

According to current estimates, more than 80% of the world's proven oil reserves are located in OPEC Member Countries, with the bulk of OPEC oil reserves in the Middle East, amounting to 65% of the OPEC total. OPEC Member Countries have made significant additions to their oil reserves in recent years, for example, by adopting best practices in the industry, realizing intensive explorations and enhancing recoveries. As a result, OPEC's proven oil reserves currently stand at well above 1,190 billion barrels.

Venezuela Oil Reserves Surpassed Saudi Arabia in 2010-OPEC

In an annual statistical report recently posted on its website, OPEC said Venezuela's proven crude oil reserves had reached 296.5 billion barrels in 2010, up 40.4% year-on-year and higher than Saudi Arabia's 264.5 billion barrels. In the long run, the boost in reserves, which comes along with an upgrade from Iran and Iraq, may empower members of the group who favour a defense of high prices. However, there are doubts over whether all of Venezuela's heavy oil discoveries are actually viable economically.

The data broadly confirms Venezuela's statements, which said it had reached this level of reserves in January this year. OPEC normally relies on its members' assessments for its statistical data.

Iraq's and Iran's proven reserves were also respectively upgraded by 24.4% to 143.1 billion barrels, and by 10.3% to 151.2 billion barrels, roughly in line with the countries' earlier disclosures.

Venezuela, Iran and Iraq were part of a group that refused to endorse a Saudi-led push to hike output at an acrimonious June 8 OPEC meeting.

The amount of oil each member can produce—particularly if it is combined with spare capacity—is a key metric of clout within OPEC. But it's unclear how much Venezuela's reserves can be turned into production.

Analysts have questioned how economic Venezuelan reserves additions could be, as most come from the heavy and extra-heavy oil in the Orinoco Belt, which is difficult and expensive to extract.

Venezuela's statistics have long been a controversial topic in oil circles, though disagreements on the matter have recently eased. The International Energy Agency last month said it revised the method used to calculate the country's oil-production figures, bringing the agency's estimates closer to those of Caracas.

How much Oil do we Really Have?

As oil prices remain volatile the markets do their best to forecast future prices. Unfortunately this is not an easy task. While it may appear extraordinary to outsiders one of the main problems in the oil market is the reliability of basic statistics.

The oil industry calls the problem 'data transparency'.

As an example this week is a 'revision' to oil demand growth in the United States in 2004.

Previously the growth in oil demand was thought to be 2.4%, about 484,000 barrels per day. In fact it was 697,000 barrels per day or 3.5%.

That is in fact 46% more than was previously stated - a huge revision.

"Oil market data is generally a black art like using a set of chicken bones," says Paul Horsnell of Barclays Capital. "If Columbus had thought he'd hit India when in fact he was in the Caribbean, that's about the level of oil market data."

"The revisions to US demand growth are small in percentage terms, they are generally 99% accurate. But the change is huge in barrel terms, and this is from the USA who have the best oil data in the world."

The barrel difference was in fact 213,000 per day. Added up that is 77.75 million extra barrels per year, about one day of global production.

"Oil data is like paint thrown across a canvas, you get the broad outline of the situation. But even then it's not just a Jackson Pollock painting, the paint actually moves of its own accord after it has been applied," says Mr Horsnell.

Phantom Reserves

One of the major problems surrounding oil data is in reserves.

These are the basins of crude oil that lie underground.

They are either held by governments or the 'oil majors' like BP, ExxonMobil or Shell, or a combination of both.

Many countries simply do not allow outsiders to audit the size of these fields.

This is especially true of the major Middle East oil producers of OPEC and the countries of the former Soviet Union.

Some believe that reserves stated by OPEC countries such as Kuwait and Saudi Arabia are not accurate.

"There are a lot of questions to answer over OPEC reserves," says Bruce Evers of Investec Bank. "The quality of overall oil market data is poor, but with OPEC there remains considerable debate over the reliability of their reserve estimates."

Sudden revisions

One of the main reasons is that in the 1980s OPEC decided to switch to a quota production system based on the size of reserves.

The larger the reserves a country said it had the more it could pump.

The more it could pump the more money it could make.

As a result in 1985 Kuwait revised its reserve estimates by 50% overnight.

It was soon followed by United Arab Emirates, Iran, and Iraq. In 1988 Saudi Arabia became the last to join the revised reserve estimates party, adding a whopping 88bn barrels.

Unexplained Changes

"Something needs to be done," says Mr Evers. "OPEC have never fully explained the reasons behind these changes, they have never issued any guidelines. The market needs to know."

Although previous estimates may have been conservative, what troubles some analysts is that twenty years later, these reserve estimates are unchanged, in fact some have increased.

Whilst it is obviously possible to add reserves by new field discoveries it can seem a perplexing situation to market makers.

Kuwait for example still claim exactly the same reserve level as they had in 1985 despite pumping millions of barrels every day since then.

Nor are company estimates any better, with Shell forced to make four revisions downwards of its official reserves since 2002, losing around 4.8bn barrels and damaging its share price.

Unclear Figures

Even current figures for OPEC production are unclear.

OPEC say they are producing exactly 28 million barrels a day (mbpd).

This includes their latest 500,000 barrels per day increase announced at their last quarterly meeting by Kuwaiti oil minister Al-Sabbah.

But OPEC have also admitted that their members break their own quotas to take advantage of high prices.

So is it really 28mbpd?

The International Energy Agency says OPEC pumped 29.3 mbpd in May 2005.

The IEA say this is actually a fall from April 2005 of 55,000bpd.

Who is correct? "There is no official OPEC output data," says Mr Horsnell. "They just kind of pass on the data they are given by their member countries. It is really not that easy for OPEC, you can't blame them, it is down to their members."

Forecasting Demand

"I don't rate IEA data either," says Mr Evers. "They have horrendously underestimated demand in the past, it is one of the reasons we are where we are now. They are little more than a data collection agency, and the data they are given is already tarnished."

It is no easier to forecast the future demand for oil, and analysts are growing increasingly sceptical of oil company attempts to do so.

Energy Files director Dr Michael Smith said "it is no longer appropriate to accept glib demand forecasts from oil companies, financial institutions and government suggestions that oil consumption will grow to up to 120 million barrels per day by 2020 and that automobile and airline traffic will increase at extraordinary rates are futile and damaging."

But Paul Horsnell says that gaps between data-sets can in fact show up areas of the oil market that need careful study.

"Take Russian production as an example," he says. "There are all kinds of rosy forecasts and then there are people like me who think it's all rather bad news. But there are many reasons about why it is impossible to measure oil, it's a liquid for a start.

"There are huge margins of error with oil data and it has to be treated as such. It's the nature of the product. Thinking you can measure it to the eighth decimal point, well, it's just a waste of time."

As oil prices continue to soar, the lack of accurate data could make it harder for the oil market to predict its future direction.

Lennard's Carrying Co Ltd v Asiatic Petroleum Co Ltd

Lennard's Carrying Co Ltd v Asiatic Petroleum Co Ltd [1915] AC 705 is a famous decision by the House of Lords on the ability to impose liability upon a corporation. The decision expands upon the earlier decision in *Salomon v Salomon & Co.* [1897] AC 22 and first introduced the "alter ego" theory of corporate liability.

Facts

A ship owned by Lennard's Carrying Co was transporting some goods to the Asiatic Petroleum Company, a joint venture of the Shell and Royal Dutch oil companies. The ship sank and the cargo was lost due to the negligent acts of Mr Lennard in violation of the Merchant Shipping Act 1894. Asiatic sued the company for negligence under the Act. At issue was whether the guilty acts of a director would be imposed upon the corporation.

Judgment

The House of Lords held that liability could be imposed on a corporation for the acts of the directors by virtue that the directors are the controlling minds of the company.

Viscount Haldane explained the "directing mind" principle of corporate liability:

> *"...a corporation is an abstraction. -It has no mind of its own any more than it has a body of its own; its active and directing will must consequently be sought in the person of somebody who for some purposes may be called an agent, but who is really the directing mind and will of the corporation, the very ego and centre of the personality of the corporation. ... It must be upon the true construction of that section in such a case as the present one that the fault or privity is the fault or privity of somebody who is not merely a servant or agent for whom the company is liable upon the footing respondeat superior, but somebody for whom the company is liable because his action is the very action of the company itself. It is not enough that the fault should be the fault of a servant in order to exonerate the owner, the fault must also be one which is not the fault of the owner, or a fault to which the owner is privy; and I take the view that when anybody sets up that section to excuse himself from the normal consequences of the maxim respondeat superior the burden lies upon him to do so."*

In considering the case of Mr Lennard himself he stated:

> *"...whatever is not known about Mr. Lennard's position, this is known for certain, Mr. Lennard took the active part in the management of this ship on behalf of the owners, and Mr. Lennard, as I have said, was registered as the person designated for this purpose in the ship's register. Mr. Lennard therefore was the natural person to come on behalf of the owners and give full evidence not only about the events of which I have spoken, and which related to the seaworthiness of the ship, but about his own position and as to whether or not he was the life and soul of the company. For if Mr. Lennard was the directing mind of the company, then his action must, unless a corporation is not to be liable at all, have been an action which was the action of the company itself..."*

Significance

Prior to this case the primary means of imposing liability on a corporation was through vicarious liability, however, that only applied to employees of the company, which excluded the act of the directors. After the Lennard case, the alter ego theory has become the most powerful method of imposing liability on a corporation. It has proved to be particularly effective for imposing criminal liability.

Buncefield Fire

Figure: *The fire just ten minutes after the explosion as seen from Hunters Oak*

The Buncefield fire was a major conflagration caused by a series of explosions on 11 December 2005 at the Hertfordshire Oil Storage Terminal, an oil storage facility located near the M1 motorway by Hemel Hempstead in Hertfordshire, England. The terminal was the fifth largest oil-products storage depot in the United Kingdom, with a capacity of about 60,000,000 imperial gallons (272,765,400 l) of fuel. The terminal is owned by TOTAL UK Limited (60%) and Texaco (40%).

The first and largest explosion occurred at 06:01 UTC near tank 912, which led to further explosions which eventually overwhelmed 20 large storage tanks. The emergency services announced a major emergency at 06:08 and a fire fighting effort began. The cause of the explosion seems to have been a fuel-air explosion of unusually high strength. The British Geological Survey monitored the event, which measured 2.4 on the Richter scale. News reports described the incident as the biggest of its kind in peacetime Europe and certainly the biggest such explosion in the United Kingdom since the 1974 Flixborough Disaster. The flames had been extinguished by the afternoon of 13 December 2005. However, one storage tank re-ignited that evening, which the fire-fighters left to burn rather than attempt to extinguish it again. The Health Protection Agency and the Major Incident Investigation Board provided advice to prevent incidents such as these in the future. The primary need is for safety measures to be in place to prevent fuel from exiting the tanks in which it is stored. Added safety measures are needed for when fuel does escape, mainly to prevent it forming a flammable vapour and stop pollutants from poisoning the environment.

Incident

Explosion and Fire: The first and largest explosion occurred at 06:01 UTC on Sunday, 11 December 2005 near container 912. Further explosions followed which eventually overwhelmed 20 large storage tanks. From all accounts, it seems to have been an unconfined vapour cloud explosion of unusually high strength—also known as a fuel-air explosion. Because of an inversion layer, the explosions were heard up to 125 miles (201 km) away; there were reports that they were audible in Belgium, France, and the Netherlands.

The British Geological Survey monitored the event, which measured 2.4 on the Richter scale. It was reported that people were woken in south London, and as far west as Wokingham (about 28 miles (45 km)), where in its southern suburb, Finchampstead, numerous people felt the shockwave after the initial explosion. Subsequent explosions occurred at 06:27 and 06:28.

Figure: *The fire seen from a vantage point between the Northgate and 3Com Corporation buildings*

Witnesses many miles from the terminal observed flames hundreds of feet high; the smoke cloud was visible from space, and from as far north as Lincolnshire (about 70 miles (113 km)) away. Damage from the blasts included broken windows at various buildings including the Holy Trinity church and Leverstock Green School, blown-in or warped front doors, and an entire wall being removed from a warehouse more than half a mile (800 m) from the site. Buildings in neighbouring St Albans also suffered; Townsend School had serious blast damage, and a window was blown out of St Albans Abbey (about 5 miles (8 km)).

Several nearby office blocks were hit so badly that almost every window, front and back, was blown in as the explosion ripped through them. During the working day, these offices would have been full of people, and many deaths may have resulted. Reports also indicated that cars in nearby streets caught fire. The roof of at least one house was blown off. Buildings in the vicinity were evacuated by police, not only because of the smoke and possibility of more explosions, but because of the danger of structural damage making the buildings unstable. There were 43 reported injuries; two people were deemed to be seriously injured enough to be kept in hospital, one in Watford General Hospital, with breathing difficulties, and another in Hemel Hempstead Hospital, although they were not in a life-threatening condition. Some early media reports spoke of eight fatalities, but these may have been persons missing.

All members of staff from the terminal were accounted for. Hertfordshire police and fire services and the Member of Parliament for the area, Mike Penning, said that there were seven fuel tanks on the site which, as of 14:00 on 12 December, had not been affected. These tanks were at risk of exploding if the fire were to spread.

Tackling the Blaze

The emergency services announced a major emergency at 06:08 and a huge fire fighting effort began. At peak times this effort consisted of 25 fire engines, 20 support vehicles and 180 fire fighters. Around 150 firefighters were called immediately to the incident, and began tackling the blaze at 08:20 on the morning of 12 December, putting in containment measures before applying a large quantity of foam. The incident occurred close to junction 8 of the M1 motorway, which led to its closure and the setting up of a public exclusion area. It was estimated that this incident would be the largest "single-seat" fire in the world ever to be fought by a fire brigade, and foam supplies from sites all over the UK were drawn upon.

Figure: *This satellite photo shows black smoke from the explosion spreading in two main streams from the explosion site at the apex of the inverted 'v'. By the time the fire had been extinguished the smoke had reached the English channel. The orange dot is a marker, not the actual fire.*

Plans had been in place to start using foam at midnight on 11 December, but were delayed by last-minute concerns over possible pollution of local rivers and underlying water sources. Six high volume pumps were used to extract 25,000 litres (5,499 imp gal) of water per minute—417 litres (92 imp gal) per second—from a reservoir 1.5 miles (2 km) from the fire, with six more high volume pumps deployed at various locations to serve as boosters. Thirty-two thousand litres (7,039 imp gal) of fire fighting foam per minute were directed against the fire for just over four hours, after which the pumping rate was reduced. Half of the 20 individual fires were reported extinguished by midday.

By 16:30 on Monday 12 December, it was reported that a further two tank fires had been extinguished, but that one of the tanks extinguished earlier had ruptured and re-ignited, and was now threatening to cause the explosion of an adjacent tank. This led to the M1 motorway being closed again; the public exclusion area was widened, and firefighters were temporarily withdrawn until the risk posed by the threatened tank could be assessed.

Firefighting operations were resumed at about 20:00, and it was anticipated that all fires could be extinguished during the night. Further damage occurred to one of the storage tanks in the early hours of Tuesday morning, causing firefighters to be withdrawn once again, but operations resumed at 08:30. By midday on the 13 December, all but three fires had been extinguished, although the largest tank was still burning. Bronze command—operations on the ground—was visited by the Bishop of St Albans, the local vicar, and the industrial chaplain supporting the fire crews, to see how they were coping.

Firefighters were confident that the remaining fires could be extinguished during the day—Tuesday 13 December. The smoke plume had been considerably reduced and was more grey, indicating the amount of vapourised water now combining with the smoke. It was reported at 16:45 that all tank fires had been extinguished, although some smaller fires persisted. 75% of firefighters for Hertfordshire were involved in fighting the fire, supported by 16 other brigades. The entire gold command operation, involving many agencies as well as all the emergency services, was run from Hertfordshire Constabulary's headquarters in Welwyn Garden City, some distance from the fire.

A further fire broke out during the early morning of 14 December. Firefighters were of the view that extinguishing it would leave the risk of petroleum vapour re-igniting or exploding, so it would be better to allow the fire, which was well contained, to burn itself out. Hertfordshire Fire Service's deputy chief Mark Yates stated that escaping petroleum vapour was the most likely cause of the original explosion and fire.

Smoke Cloud

Figure: *The smoke plume seen from Dunsmore, Buckinghamshire, about 20 miles (32 km) away*

The black smoke cloud, which was clearly visible from satellite photographs, drifted at a high altitude, around 9,000 feet (2,700 m), towards Reading and Swindon, and could be seen across much of South East England.

The small particles in the smoke contained hydrocarbons, which can be an irritant but have a low toxicity and were not expected to cause any long-term harm. The Met Office issued warnings that the smoke in the atmosphere could come down in rainfall during the night of 11 December.

The fire resulted in 244 people requiring medical aid—mainly on the first day of the fire. From those 117 had symptoms attributable to the incident, of which 38 were members of the public. The majority of those visiting hospitals were from the rescue services and attended for precautionary check ups. Most of them had no symptoms, except for 63 emergency workers who suffered respiratory complaints, of which half were sore throats.

For the first two days of the fire, the high thermal energy made the plume highly buoyant; this, together with settled weather conditions, allowed the plume to rise to a great height with little cross-mixing. When the fire was reduced in intensity it was reported to be possible that the plume would be less buoyant and that ground-level smoke concentrations could then rise significantly. By 12 December, it was reported that the smoke cloud had reached northern France; it was expected to arrive in northern Spain by the weekend.

To investigate the smoke cloud the Facility for Airborne Atmospheric Measurements, a research aircraft operated jointly by NERC and the Met Office, made two flights on 12 and 13 December. In the first flight the edge of the plume was followed along the south coast of England. Carbon monoxide, nitrogen oxides and ozone concentrations were found to be low with soot particles being the major component in the cloud. The second flight went into the centre of the plume to obtain data to help forecasting and emergency teams.

Reactions and Response

Evacuations and Closures: Hundreds of homes in the Hemel Hempstead area were evacuated, and about 2,000 people had to find alternative accommodation; emergency services asked residents of the smoke-affected areas to close their windows and doors and to stay inside. Hertfordshire Constabulary advised people who had houses with smashed windows to seek refuge with friends or family nearby if possible. Some people whose homes were damaged by the blast were placed in hotels, while others stayed in a nearby shopping centre. Total, the operator of the Buncefield depot, set up a helpline for people whose properties had been damaged by the explosion, and called in local authorities and the Salvation Army to provide accommodation or other help.

Concerns for public safety resulted in about 227 schools, libraries, and other public buildings across Hertfordshire and Buckinghamshire closing on 12 and 13 December. Police and local authorities advised residents to consult the *Hertfordshire Direct* website for up-to-date information. Seventy-eight schools in Luton borough were closed on 13 December, along with a limited number of schools in Bedfordshire, on the advice of Hertfordshire's Health Protection Agency that all schools within a 10-mile (16 km) radius of the incident site should be closed because of concerns surrounding the effect of the smoke plume on children's health. Schools reopened as normal on 14 December.

Figure: *Smoke from the blast, visible from Hemel Hempstead, above the closed M1 motorway.*

Transport Disruption

The incident occurred close to junction 8 of the M1 motorway. The motorway was shut between junctions 12 and 6a—about 18 miles (29 km) shortly after the incident. Other roads in the vicinity, including the short M10 motorway (now part of the A414 road), were also closed.

Some local petrol stations reported long queues as people started panic buying. A spokesman for the Department of Trade and Industry gave assurances that no petrol shortage was likely to result from the incident.

The oil terminal supplied 30% of Heathrow Airport's fuel, and because of the fire, the airport had to start rationing fuel. Some long-haul flights to Australia, the Far-East, and South Africa had to pit-stop at Stansted Airport or other European airports to refuel, while short-haul operators were asked to fuel their planes for the round trip before flying to Heathrow. Some aircraft were only allowed 40% of the fuel they would normally take on board. Fuel shortages continued for months after the explosion.

Business Disruption

In the Maylands industrial area the worst affected buildings were the Northgate Information Solutions headquarters and the Fujifilm building. These buildings were so badly damaged they were rendered completely unusable. Demolition of the Fujifilm building began soon afterwards, and by June 2006 it had been completely removed from the site. Although the Northgate and Fujifilm buildings were closest to the blast, the surrounding Catherine House (to the north), Keystone Distribution building (to the west), 3Com Corporation and RO buildings (to the south), were also extensively damaged. In all, six buildings were designated for demolition and 30 more required major repairs before they could be reoccupied.

As a result of the destruction of the equipment in the Northgate building several websites hosted there were inaccessible—including that of the Labour Party. Addenbrooke's Hospital in Cambridge was also affected; its IT system dealing with admissions and discharges had to be replaced for several days by a manual system.

A number of companies were affected by inability to reach their premises even where the premises themselves were largely unaffected by the blast. Criticism was expressed by local citizens and the local MP that originally the depot had been constructed away from other buildings, but that developmental pressures had led to both houses and commercial premises being built near the depot.

Groundwater Pollution

In May 2006 Three Valleys Water announced that it had detected the persistent, bioaccumulative, and toxic fluorosurfactant perfluorooctane sulfonate (PFOS)—which is used in fire fighting foam—in a ground water bore hole close to the Buncefield site. It stated that no water from this well entered the public water supply and that a nearby well and pumping station had been closed since the fire as a precaution. The chemical is a known health risk and the UK government had been about to ban its use.

However just before the announcement, the Drinking Water Inspectorate announced that it was increasing the safe level of the chemical in drinking water. Hemel Hempstead MP, Mike Penning accused the government of changing the rules to suit the situation in which PFOS levels in drinking water in the area may rise in the future. Most of the fuel burned out—rather than spilling into the soil, so the impact on surrounding land and the water table was limited.

Inquiry

A government inquiry held jointly by the Health and Safety Executive (HSE) and the Environment Agency was started, but calls for a full public enquiry were declined. The Board included Lord Newton of Braintree, Prof Dougal Drysdale—an authority on fire safety and Dr Peter Baxter, a medical expert. Environment Agency and HSE staff were also on the board. Its aim was to identify the immediate causes of the explosion, rather than consider who was to blame for any deficiencies, so as not to prejudice further legal proceedings.

Figure: *Smoke from the fire over Hampstead Heath, London*

An initial progress report by the Major Incident Investigation Board on 21 February 2006 did not go into the causes of the explosion, but summed up the event and the immediate reaction from the emergency services. A second progress report, published on 11 April 2006, looked at the environmental impact.

A further announcement was made on 9 May 2006 about the sequence of events which caused the explosion. Starting at 19:00 on the evening of 10 December, 2005, Tank 912, towards the north west of the main depot, was filled with unleaded petrol—from the Coryton Refinery located in Essex, England. At midnight the terminal closed, and a check was made of the contents of tanks, which found everything normal. Normally the gauges monitor the level of the fuel in the tank as it fills from the particular pipeline. From about 03:00 the level gauge for Tank 912 began to indicate an unchanging level reading, despite it being filled at 550 cubic metres (19,423 cu ft) per hour.

Calculations show that the tank would have begun to overflow at about 05:20. There is evidence suggesting that a high-level switch, which should have detected that the tank was full and shut off the supply, failed to operate. The switch failure should have triggered an alarm, but it too appears to have failed. Forty-one minutes later, an estimated 300 tonnes of petrol would have spilled down the side of the tank through the roof vents onto the ground inside a bund wall—a semi-enclosed compound surrounding several tanks.

An overflow such as this results in the rapid formation of a rich fuel and air vapour. CCTV footage showed such a vapour flowing out the bund wall from around 05:38. By 05:50 the vapour started flowing off the site, near the junction of Cherry Tree and Buncefield Lane. Around 05:50 the rate at which fuel was being pumped into the tank increased dramatically. Initially the fuel was pumped in at 550 cubic metres (19,423 cu ft) per hour, but it increased to about 890 cubic metres (31,430 cu ft) per hour. By 06:01, when the first explosion occurred, the cloud which was initially about 1 metre (3 ft) deep, thickened to 2 metres (7 ft) and had spread beyond the boundaries of the site.

The extent of the damage meant it was not possible to determine the exact source of ignition, but possibilities include an emergency generator and the depot's fire pump system. The investigators did not believe that it was caused either by the driver of a fuel tanker, as had been speculated, or by anyone using a mobile phone. It was felt unlikely that the explosion had a widespread effect on air quality at ground level.

Legal Action

Civil Liability: A total of 2,700 claims were filed by residents, businesses and insurers. A group of 146 claimants were hoping to bring a class action against Hertfordshire Oil Storage Ltd. On 17 March 2006 a High Court official, Senior Master Turner, adjourned a hearing on whether to permit the class action until October 2006. Claimants including insurance companies, small businesses and about 280 families whose properties were damaged or destroyed were claiming up to £1 billion in damages. Several court cases resulted from the explosion, although the main trial to determine who was liable for the damage commenced at the High Court in October 2008. An example of loss is Cheetah Couriers—who suffered a 20% drop in turnover because of the explosions, resulting in losses of around £300,000 to £400,000. The company was located in offices on an industrial estate 400 metres (1,312 ft) from the depot.

Figure: *The Buncefield depot is behind the Northgate building (at the right of this photo). The building lost the glass from all of its windows.*

An initial trial concluded on 23 May 2008 when Mr Justice David Steel issued a summary judgment after hearing that both Total and Hertfordshire Oil Storage Ltd (HOSL) had agreed that negligence was the cause. In the main trial, Total UK claimed that the duty supervisor at the time was responsible for the explosion, but refused to admit either civil or criminal liability for the incident. Total UK argued that it should not be liable for damages because it could not reasonably have foreseen that it would cause the destruction it did. On 20 March 2009 the High Court found Total liable for the blast, saying that it was satisfied that Total had control of tank filling operations at the Buncefield depot. The judgement left the company facing damage claims of around £700 million.

Total are appealing this judgement in a case due to be heard in 2010.

Criminal Liability

The site is covered by the COMAH regulations. The Control of Major Accidents and Hazards Regulations are jointly enforced by the "competent authority" which is formed of the Environment Agency and the Health and Safety Executive. They carried out an investigation during and following the fire.

In April 2010 the five companies accused of causing the explosion faced a criminal prosecution brought by the Health and Safety Executive and the Environment Agency. Two defendants, Total UK and British Pipeline Agency Limited, had already pleaded guilty to offences under the Health and Safety at Work Act. The remaining three, Hertfordshire Oil Storage Ltd, TAV Engineering Ltd, and Motherwell Control Systems were found guilty in June 2010. TAV Engineering Ltd and Motherwell Control Systems were found guilty of failing to protect their employees. Hertfordshire Oil Storage Ltd was found guilty of failing to prevent major accidents and limit their effects and then pleaded guilty to causing pollution to enter controlled waters underlying the vicinity around the site, contrary to the Water Resources Act.

Sentencing took place in July 2010. Total UK was fined £3.6m, plus £2.6m in costs. Hertfordshire Oil Storage Limited was fined £1.45m and £1m in costs. The British Pipeline Agency was fined £300,000 plus £480,000 costs. Motherwell Control Systems and TAV Engineering were fined £1,000 each. Local MP Mike Penning called the modest fines "insulting".

The Terminal

The Hertfordshire Oil Storage Terminal (HOSL – Hertfordshire Oil Storage Ltd), generally known as the Buncefield complex, was the fifth largest oil-products storage depot in the UK, with a capacity of about 60,000,000 imperial gallons (272,765,400 l) of fuel, although it was not always full. This was about 8% of UK oil storage capacity.

The HOSL is a major hub on the UK's oil pipeline network (UKOP) with pipelines to Humberside and Merseyside and is an important fuel source to the British aviation industry, providing aircraft fuel for local airports including London Gatwick, London Heathrow and Luton airports. About half of the complex is dedicated to the storage of aviation fuel. The remainder of the complex stores oil, kerosene, petrol and diesel fuel for petrol stations across much of the South-East of England. The terminal is owned by TOTAL UK Limited (60%) and Texaco 40%.

The seat of the fire, and the worst damaged section, was "HOSL West", used by Total and Texaco to store a variety of fuels, and the neighbouring British Pipeline Agency area.

Initial Speculation on Causes

The police issued a statement saying that they were treating the incident as an accident as opposed to a terrorist attack. Italian television stations early on the morning of the fire described the event as a possible terrorist attack and went to the extent of showing features on the July 2005 terrorist bombings. Speculation about the possible terrorist nature of the blasts was prompted by the fact that a videotape allegedly released by al-Qaeda four days previously had called for attacks on fuel depots and refineries containing oil "stolen" from Muslim countries. However, the cause of the blasts will likely not be known until a full investigation is completed.

Figure: *Clear view skies on Monday, 12 December 2005, except for the fire in Hemel Hempstead*

An oil industry specialist speculated on BBC News that a vapour leak could have built up to explosive concentrations because of the ground frost in the area keeping vapour concentration at ground level. This would have resulted in a fuel-air explosion. It is industry practice for detection systems to be in place to reveal leakages. In order for this scenario to be fulfilled, there must have been a leakage that was not picked up by the leak detection system.

A BBC News 24 interview with a petrol tanker driver, who was about to load his tanker at 06:00, reported a cloud of mist rolling in from the tank farm area behind the loading bay. All electric lights were turned off and they were ordered to leave the site on foot. As he was doing so, the blast blew him off his feet. In another interview, a security guard in a nearby office building reported an unusual smell of petrol inside his building before the explosion. Hertfordshire police reported speaking to a tanker driver concerned that switching the engine cut-off on his tanker might have triggered the explosion.

Other safety experts spoke of a known "weekend effect" in industry, in which weekend maintenance creates an unsafe condition. A retired military explosives safety officer submitted a published paper on the explosion to the HSE inquiry. The paper was intended to help those who lived close to petrol storage depots and who were worried about the risks they faced. It contained different views from those of other experts whose opinions had been voiced publicly, and was critical of the HSE's general safety culture.

Aftermath

Lessons Learned: The Health Protection Agency and the Major Incident Investigation Board (MIIB) provided the needed advice for risk assessments to create guidelines to prevent incidents such as these from happening again. The most important lesson learned from the incident was the need for an increased environmental measurement capability.

Buncefield was clearly a major emergency, but luckily the public health impact was rather small. The situation could have been very different if the initial explosion had happened at a different time, or if the weather conditions had been less favourable for dispersing the plume. So we need to analyse our response carefully and make sure any lessons are learnt.

— *Professor Pat Troop, Chief Executive of the Agency.*

The MIIB focused on three main work streams subsuming the lessons to be learned from the incident:

1. Design and operation of storage sites
2. Emergency response to incidents
3. Advice to planning authorities

The primary need identified was for additional safety measures to prevent fuel escaping from its storage tanks, and to deal adequately with fuel when it does escape, preventing it from forming a flammable vapour and pollutants from poisoning the environment. This report demand that the fuel industry should extensively strengthen safety measures at storage sites handling large quantities of fuel.

Soon after the incident the Health Protection Agency was stripped of its remit to provide air quality data and it was passed on to the Environment Agency who form part of the Major Accident Investigation Board.

Remembrance

An anniversary service was held in Holy Trinity Church Leverstock Green on Sunday, 10 December 2006, at which the Bishop of St Albans spoke, calling again for a full public inquiry, for assurances that the local hospital would maintain its accident and emergency department, and for the community to continue to build on good relationships formed because of the blast.

Reconstruction

To rebuild the damaged parts of the site, the relevant approval from Dacorum Borough Council would be needed. The BP section of the site—a good way from the explosion, survived with very little damage, but is inoperative as of 2009. BP is exploring plans for the future use of this part of the site, and has indicated a number of priorities, including the reopening the fuel pipelines to Heathrow. They consider using their section to store aviation fuel and as a distribution centre for motor fuel, but at a much-reduced level. In late 2009, Total UK submitted plans for the reconstruction of the oil depot.

2009 Jaipur Fire

The Jaipur oil depot fire broke out on 29 October 2009 at 7:30 PM (IST) at the Indian Oil Corporation (IOC) oil depot's giant tank holding 8,000 kilolitres (280,000 cu ft) of oil, in Sitapura Industrial Area on the outskirts of Jaipur, Rajasthan, killing 12 people and injuring over 200. The blaze continued to rage out of control for over a week after it started and during the period half a million people were evacuated from the area. The oil depot is about 16 kilometers (9.9 mi) south of the city of Jaipur

The incident occurred when petrol was being transferred from the Indian Oil Corporation's oil depot to a pipeline. There were at least 40 IOC employees at the terminal, situated close to the Jaipur International Airport) when it caught fire with an explosion. The Met department recorded a tremor measuring 2.3 on the Richter scale around the time the first explosion at 7:36 pm which resulted in shattering of glass window nearly 3 kilometres (1.9 mi) from the accident site.

The Fire

The fire was a major disaster in terms of deaths, injury, loss of business, property and man-days, displacement of people, environmental impact in Jaipur, the capital city of the Indian state of Rajasthan and a popular tourist destination. As per eyewitnesses having factories and hotels around Indian Oil's Sitapura (Jaipur) Oil Terminal they felt presence of petrol vapour in the atmosphere around 4:00 p.m. on 29 October 2009. Within the next few hours the concentration of petrol vapour intensified making it difficult to breathe. The Ayush Hotel in the vicinity of the terminal asked all its guests to vacate the Hotel to avert any tragedy. The police, civil administration and fire emergency services were oblivious of the situation developing in Indian Oil Terminal.

Around half past six the staff in the terminal had contained the leak and flow of petrol panicked and reported the matter to nearby Sanganer Sadar Police Station. Within the next 30 minutes the local police chief and District Collector were on the spot along with Indian Oil General Manager, but with no plan to deal with the situation. The nearby industries, which were running second shifts, were cautioned to vacate the area. At 7:35 p.m. a huge ball of fire with loud explosion broke out engulfing the leaking petrol tank and other nearby petrol tanks with continuous fire with flames rising 30–35 m (98–115 ft) and visible from a 30 km (19 mi) radius. The traffic on adjacent National Highway No. 12 was stopped leading to a 20 km (12 mi) long traffic jam. The Jaipur International Airport is just 5 km (3.1 mi) away from the accident site. Both the Army and experts from Mumbai were employed on 30 October 2009 to contain the fire, which started when an oil tanker caught fire at the depot in the Sitapura Industrial Area. The district administration disconnected electricity and evacuated nearby areas to limit the damage.

The fire still raged on 31 October 2009, in the Indian Oil Corporation Depot, at Jaipur, after a defective pipe line leak that set fire to 50,000 kilolitres (1,800,000 cu ft) of diesel and petrol out of the storage tanks at the IOC Depot. By then, the accident had already claimed 11 lives and seriously injured more than 150. The District Administration and Indian Oil Corporation had no disaster management plan to deal with this kind of calamity. The local fire officers were ill equipped to deal with fire accidents of this magnitude. They remained onlookers and no efforts were made to breach the terminal wall to get closer to kerosene and diesel tanks to cool them with water jets.

Inventory

The following products were stored in eleven tanks inside the terminal:

- Petrol (18,810 kl (664,000 cu ft))
- Kerosene (2,099 kl (74,100 cu ft))

- High Speed Diesel (39,966 kl (1,411,400 cu ft))
- Interface (2,809 kl (99,200 cu ft)).

Aftermath

About 11 people lost their lives due to burns and asphyxia and more than 300 suffered injuries. Many of the dead were the employees of Indian Oil Corporation.

Disaster Management Plan

THE DISASTER MANAGEMENT ACT, 2005 envisages that each revenue District must have a Disaster Management Plan. While 31 revenue Districts of Rajasthan had placed the Disaster Management Plan on Rajasthan Government website Jaipur District did not have any Disaster Management Plan. A Disaster Management Plan for Jaipur District has been put on Internet on 17 November 2009 i.e. 20 days after the accident took place on 29 October 2009. In the meanwhile Jaipur suffered two more disasters when Swine Flu infected a number of school children prompting Government to order closure of schools, and derailment of a Train Mandore Express killing six persons and injuring more than 50 persons.

Central Pollution Control Board (CPCB) report

Air pollution across Jaipur was way above maximum permitted limits when the Indian Oil Corporation (IOC) depot on the edge of the city was caught fire. It significant effect on the air in Delhi or Agra, the Central Pollution Control Board (CPCB) reported. Almost 60,000 kilolitres (2,100,000 cu ft) of oil in 11 storage tanks went up in flames on the evening of Oct 29 and the blaze raged till Nov 6.

Investigations

The Petroleum Minister of India Murli Deora had appointed a 5-member committee to investigate the causes of Fire and submit its report within 60 days. The Industries & Education Institutions in Sitapura Industrial Area have filed about 150 complaints with Sanganer Sadar police station about deaths, injury and loss of property due to negligence of Indian Oil Corporation Limited.

Central Bureau of Investigation Case

Variation in stock of liquid petroleum products due to temperature variation, evaporation, handling (and also due to pilferage) result into what is known as *stock loss*. Percentage stock loss for every product for every depot is fixed based on historical operating data. Monitoring of stock loss is done on shift basis daily.

Abnormal variation in stock loss beyond permitted limit invites explanation and even disciplinary actions for the officers at the Depots and Terminals. The Competent Authorities for such chargesheeting for Depot level Officers for such lapses are Executive Director (Supplies) and Director (Marketing) who prefer to selectively issue chargesheets to defaulting officers to protect their favourites.

First Information Report

The Chief Judicial Magistrate, Jaipur City, Jaipur Mr. Mahaveer Swami ordered registering of a number of First Information Report (FIR) against Indian Oil Corporation Limited officers and Civil Administration for non-performance of statutory duty and negligence.

Civil Administration

The Director General of Police, Rajasthan to investigate against Mr. B. L. Soni, Inspector General of Police Jaipur Range I, Mr. Kuldeep Ranka, District Collector, Jaipur and Mr. Biju George Joseph, Superintendent of Police Jaipur (East) for commission of offences u/ss 120B, 166, 167, 201, 202, 203, 204, 217, 218, 221 IPC. The order was passed on 10 December 2009, a month after the fire got extinguished.

Indian Oil Corporation Limited

As per the orders passed on 4 December 2009 by the Chief Judicial Magistrate, Jaipur Mr. Mahaveer Swami, the Police Station Adarsh Nagar, Jaipur has registered FIR 337/09 under sections 166, 304A, 511, 120B against 20 accused;

1. Indian Oil Corporation Limited (IOC), Through Company Secretary Mr. Raju Rangnathan,
2. Sarthak Behuria, Chairman IOC
3. B M Bansal, Director (Planning & Business Development) IOC
4. S V Narasimhan, Director (Finance) IOC
5. V C Agrawal, Director (Human Resources) IOC
6. G C Daga, Director (Marketing) IOC
7. B N Bankapur, Director (Refineries) IOC
8. Anand Kumar, Director (Research & Development) IOC
9. K. K. Jha, Director (Pipelines) IOC
10. S Sundareshan, Additional Secretary, Ministry Of Petroleum & Natural Gas, & Director IOC
11. P K Sinha, Additional Secretary & Financial Advisor, Ministry Of Petroleum & Natural Gas, & Director IOC

12. Prof.(Mrs.) Indira J. Parikh, Former Prof. IIM, Ahmedabad and President, FLAME, Pune, & Director IOC
13. Anees Noorani, Managing Director, Zodiac Clothing Company Ltd., & Director IOC
14. Michael Bastian, Former Chairman & Managing Director, Syndicate Bank, & Director IOC
15. Dr.(Mrs.) Indu Shahani, Principal, HR College of Commerce & Economics, Mumbai and Sheriff of Mumbai, & Director IOC
16. Prof. Gautam Barua, Director, Indian Institute of Technology Guwahati, & Director IOC
17. N.K. Poddar, Senior Advocate, Kolkata, & Director IOC
18. K. S. Kanoujiya Senior Terminal Manager IOC
19. Gautam Bose, General Manager IOC, and
20. other unknown accused.

Section 120B: Punishment of Criminal Conspiracy

(1) Whoever is a party to a criminal conspiracy to commit an offence punishable with death, 2[imprisonment for life] or rigorous imprisonment for a term of two years or upwards shall, where no express provision is made in this Code fro the punishment of such a conspiracy, be punished in the same abetted such offence.

(2) Whoever is a party to a criminal conspiracy other than a criminal conspiracy to commit an offence punishable as aforesaid shall be punished with imprisonment of either description for a term not exceeding six months, or with fine or with both.]

Section 166: Public servant disobeying law, with intent to cause injury to any person Whoever, being a public servant, knowingly disobeys any direction of the law as to the way in which he is to conduct himself as such public servant, intending to cause, or knowing it to be likely that he will, by such disobedience, cause injury to any person, shall be punished with simple imprisonment for a term which may extend to one year, or with fine, or with both.

Section 304A: Causing death by negligence Whoever causes the death of any person by doing any rash or negligent act not amounting to culpable homicide, shall be punished with imprisonment of either description for a term which may extend to two years, or with fine, or with both.]

Section 511: Punishment for attempting to commit offences punishable with imprisonment for life or other imprisonment Whoever attempts to commit an offence punishable by this Code with 1[imprisonment for life] or imprisonment, or to cause such an offence to be committed, and in such attempts does any act towards the commission of the offence, shall, where no express provision is made by this Code for the punishment of such attempt, be punished with 2[imprisonment of any description provided for the offence, for a term which may extend to one-half of the imprisonment for life or, as the case may be, one-half of the longest term of imprisonment provided for that offence], or with such fine as is provided for the offence, or with both.

Sanganer Sadar Police Station

In addition to the above two more FIR 241/09 dated 2 November 2009 by Mr. Prit Pal Singh of Genus Overseas an Industrial unit in Sitapura and FIR 242/09 dated 3 November 2009 by Mr. B. L. Meharada of BLM Institute have been registered against Indian Oil by Police Station Sanganer Sadar.

Sanganer Court

A city court in Sanganer has ordered registering of FIR on the complaint of Ayush Hotel Sitapura.

Arrests

On 2 July 2010, eight months after the devastating fire at an Indian Oil Corp (IOC) fuel depot that killed 11 people, police arrested 9 senior company officials including its General Manager on charges of criminal negligence. IOC General Manager for Rajasthan Mr. Gautam Bose and 8 other officers were arrested under various sections of the Indian Penal Code (IPC) including section 304-II (culpable homicide not amounting to murder).

Section 304-II of IPC carries a maximum prison term of 10 years. Those arrested in connection with the 29 October fire caused by leakage of petrol during transfer from storage tank, included chief of operations at IOC's Jaipur Office, Mr. Rajesh Sayal.

The others arrested are Mr. Shashank Shekhar, Manager Operation, Mr. K S Kanojia, Senior Terminal Manager, Mr. Arun Poddar, Manager Terminal, Mr. Kapil Goyal, Deputy Manager Terminal, Mr. Ashok Gupta, Operation Officer, Mr. Kailash Nath Agarwal, Chargeman, and Mr. S S Gupta, DGM Pipeline who is presently posted in Ghaziabad. While 8 accused have been enlarged on bail, Mr. Ashok Kumar Gupta is still in judicial custody after 4 months. The next hearing in the matter is fixed on 11 November 2010.

Widows Request Compensation

Ms. Savita Saroha and Ms. Alka Kumar whose husbands Mr. S. K. Saroha and Mr. Ravindra Kumar died in the Fire on 29 October 2010 have moved to Rajasthan High Court for equitable and fair compensation. The duo allege that they were not given the compensation of Rs. 10,00,000.00 (One Million Rupees) promised by Mr. Murli Deora the Minister for Petroleum and Natural Gas, Government of India. The widows are also upset that the company Indian Oil and the arrested officers have tried to pass on blame on their husbands. They are now opposing the accused officers in High Court against quashing of First Information Report and grant of bail to them.

Compensation

The State Government promptly announced a cash compensation of Rs. 2,000,000.00 to the dead and in addition Indian Oil Corporation paid Rs. 10,000,000.00 to the next of the kin of dead and varied amount of compensation between Rs.1,000,000.00 and 2,000,000.00 to the injured. It has been decided to review the location of all Oil Terminals throughout India and shift these terminals beyond city limits within a period of next 12–18 months.

Sitapura Industries Association

The SITAPURA INDUSTRIES ASSOCIATION has 1383 units, consisting of 325 garment, 115 jewellers, 110 handicraft, and other units like chemical, cable, manufacturing, IT, BPO, Auto parts, Educational Institutes and Hospitals having an investment of over 75,000 crore. The SITAPURA INDUSTRIES ASSOCIATION have played an important part in shaping the economy of the State of Rajasthan and generation of employment (approximately 1,000,000 direct/indirect workers).

The SITAPURA INDUSTRIES ASSOCIATION has played an important role in exports and generation of foreign exchange. That on 29 October 2009 at about 4:00 p.m. some leakage of Petrol started in IOC Terminal and by 6:00 p.m. the fumes had spread far and wide in and around the Indian Oil Corporation terminal. That a huge explosion and fire erupted at 7:35 p.m. and the noise and shock waves were so intense that it gave an impression of an earthquake to the Industries of the area.

The neighbouring industries adjacent to the Indian Oil Corporation terminal suffered major structural damages, loss of inventory, equipment, and finished goods. As a consequence of the Fire and associated hazards the District Collector, Jaipur declared a 5 km. zone as dangerous area and prohibited entry of the persons and vehicles in the area. The SITAPURA INDUSTRIES ASSOCIATION claims to have lost Rs.400.00 crore worth of property, equipment and inventory instantaneously on 29 October 2009.

Thereafter the loss of production, dispatch and consequent loss of goodwill is valued at Rs. 200.00 Crore per day. The industries were allowed free access to their units since 5 November 2009. The total estimated loss is valued at 1800.00 crore. As an EPZ is part of the SITAPURA INDUSTRIAL AREA it houses a number of export-oriented units. The peak season for the export oriented units was at handshake. Due to fire and subsequent pollution and dispersion of carbon soot particles in atmosphere almost 100% finished garments would fail in stringent quality test and would have to be dumped in the domestic market at throwaway prices. As the industries are most likely to falter on their export commitment, the loss of Goodwill will takes years to rebuild.

Government Report

On 10 December 2009, the Indian Minister of State of Petroleum and Natural Gas Jitin Prasada said the government today ruled out a C.B.I. / probe into the November fires and informed the Lok Sabha and the Indian press that a Committee had- 'ruled out sabotage or terrorisum', blamed both 'corporate neglect' and 'servere radiant heat' from the October fires, and denied any connection with a similar, but smaller blast that month in Kashmir./

Oil Tanker

An oil tanker, also known as a petroleum tanker, is a merchant ship designed for the bulk transport of oil. There are two basic types of oil tankers: the crude tanker and the product tanker. Crude tankers move large quantities of unrefined crude oil from its point of extraction to refineries. Product tankers, generally much smaller, are designed to move petrochemicals from refineries to points near consuming markets.

Oil tankers are often classified by their size as well as their occupation. The size classes range from inland or coastal tankers of a few thousand metric tons of deadweight (DWT) to the mammoth ultra large crude carriers (ULCCs) of 550,000 DWT. Tankers move approximately 2,000,000,000 metric tons (2.2×10^9 short tons) of oil every year. Second only to pipelines in terms of efficiency, the average cost of oil transport by tanker amounts to only two or three United States cents per 1 US gallon (3.8 L).

Some specialized types of oil tankers have evolved. One of these is the naval replenishment oiler, a tanker which can fuel a moving vessel. Combination ore-bulk-oil carriers and permanently moored floating storage units are two other variations on the standard oil tanker design. Oil tankers have been involved in a number of damaging and high-profile oil spills. As a result, they are subject to stringent design and operational regulations.

Figure : *The commercial oil tanker AbQaiq, in ballast*

History

The technology of oil transportation has evolved alongside the oil industry. Although anthropogenic use of oil reaches to prehistory, the first modern commercial exploitation dates back to James Young's manufacture of parafin in 1850. In these early days, oil from Upper Burma was moved in earthenware vessels to the river bank where it was then poured into boat holds.

Figure: *The Falls of Clyde is the oldest surviving American tanker and the world's only surviving sail-driven oil tanker.*

In the 1850s, the Pennsylvania oil fields became a major supplier of oil, and a center of innovation after Edwin Drake had struck oil near Titusville, Pennsylvania. The first oil well in the United States was dug here in 1859, initially yielding around ten barrels per day. Within two years, the Titusville field was providing 3,000 barrels (480 m^3) per day. By this time, petroleum oil had already begun to supplant fish, whale, and vegetable oils for applications such as indoor and outdoor lighting, and transatlantic export had already begun. Break-bulk boats and barges were originally used to transport Pennsylvania oil in 40-US-gallon (150 l) wooden barrels. But transport by barrel had several problems. The first problem was weight: the standard empty barrel weighed 64 pounds (29 kg), representing 20% of the total weight of a full barrel. Other problems with barrels were their expense, their tendency to leak, and the fact that they were generally used only once. The expense was significant, for example, in the early years of the Russian oil industry, barrels accounted for half the cost of petroleum production.

The movement of oil in bulk was attempted in many places and in many ways. Modern oil pipelines have existed since 1860. In 1863, two sail-driven tankers were built on England's River Tyne. These were followed in 1873 by the first oil-tank steamer, the *Vaderland,* which was built by Palmers Shipbuilding and Iron Company for Belgian owners. The vessel's use was curtailed by U.S. and Belgian authorities citing safety concerns. By 1871, the Pennsylvania oil fields were making limited use of oil tank barges and cylindrical railroad tank-cars similar to those in use today.

The Nobel Brothers

In 1876, Ludvig and Robert Nobel, brothers of Alfred Nobel, founded Branobel (short for Brothers Nobel) in the Russian Empire, active mostly in the oil-rich region around Baku (now Azerbaijan). During the late 19th century Branobel was one of the largest oil companies in the world.

Ludvig was a pioneer in the development of early oil tankers. He first experimented with carrying oil in bulk on single-hulled barges. Turning his attention to self-propelled tankships, he faced a number of challenges. A primary concern was to keep the cargo and fumes well away from the engine room to avoid fires. Other challenges included allowing for the cargo to expand and contract due to temperature changes, and providing a method to ventilate the tanks.

The world's first successful oil tanker was Nobel's *Zoroaster*. He designed this ship in Gothenburg, Sweden, with Sven Almqvist. The contract to build it was signed in January 1878, and it made its first run later that year from Baku to Astrakhan. The *Zoroaster* design was widely studied and copied, with Nobel refusing to patent any part of it. In October 1878, he ordered two more tankers of the same design: the *Buddha* and the *Nordenskjold. Zoroaster* carried its 242 long tons of kerosene cargo in two iron tanks joined by pipes. One tank was forward of the midships engine room and the other was aft. The ship also featured a set of 21 vertical watertight compartments for extra buoyancy. The ship had a length overall of 184 feet (56 m), a beam of 27 feet (8.2 m), and a draft of 9 feet (2.7 m).

Unlike later Nobel tankers, the *Zoroaster* design was built small enough to sail from Sweden to the Caspian by way of the Baltic Sea, Lake Ladoga, Lake Onega, the Rybinsk and Mariinsk Canals and the Volga River. Nobel then began to adopt a single-hull design, where the ship's hull forms part of its tank structure.

In November 1880, he ordered his first single-hulled tanker, the *Moses*. Within a year, he ordered seven more single-hulled tankers: the *Mohammed, Tatarin, Bramah, Spinoza, Socrates, Darwin, Koran, Talmud*, and *Calmuck*.

Branobel experienced one of the first oil tanker disasters. In 1881, the *Zoroaster*'s sister-ship, the *Nordenskjold* exploded in Baku while taking on kerosene. The pipe carrying the cargo was jerked away from the hold when the ship was hit by a gust of wind. Kerosene then spilled onto the deck and down into the engine room, where mechanics were working in the light of kerosene lanterns. The ship then exploded, killing half the crew. Nobel responded to the disaster by creating a flexible, leak proof loading pipe which was much more resistant to spills.

In 1883, oil tanker design took a large step forward. Working for the Nobel company, Colonel Henry F. Swan designed a set of three Nobel tankers. Instead of one or two large holds, Swan's design used several holds which spanned the width, or beam, of the ship. These holds were further subdivided into port and starboard sections by a longitudinal bulkhead. Earlier designs suffered from stability problems caused by the free surface effect, where oil sloshing from side to side could cause a ship to capsize. But this approach of dividing the ship's storage space into smaller tanks virtually eliminated free-surface problems. This approach, almost universal today, was first used by Swan in the Nobel tankers *Blesk, Lumen*, and *Lux*.

In 1903, the Nobel brothers built two oil tankers which ran on internal combustion engines, as opposed to the older steam engines. The *Vandal*, the first diesel-electric ship, was capable of carrying

750 long tons of refined oil was powered by three 120 horsepower (89 kW) diesel motors. The larger *Sarmat* employed four 180 h.p. engines. The first seagoing diesel-powered tanker, 4,500 ton *Mysl*, was built by Nobel's competitors in Kolomna. Nobel responded with *Emanuel Nobel* and *Karl Hagelin*, 4,600 long ton kerosene tankers with 1,200 horsepower (890 kW) engines.

The *Glückauf* represented a large step forward in tanker design. Another design of Colonel Swan, the ship has been called the "true progenitor of all subsequent tanker tonnage." Its features included cargo valves operable from the deck, cargo main piping, a vapor line, cofferdams for added safety, and the ability to fill a ballast tank with seawater when empty of cargo. Wilhelm Anton Riedemann, an agent for the Standard Oil Company purchased *Glückauf* and several of her sister ships. After the *Glückauf* was lost in 1893, Standard Oil purchased the sister ships.

Chapter 3

Petro Giants

Eni

Eni S.p.A. is an Italian multinational oil and gas company, present in 70 countries, and currently Italy's largest industrial company with a market capitalization of 87.7 billion euros (US$138 billion), as of July 24, 2008. The Italian government owns a 30% golden share in the company, 20% held through the state Treasury and 10% held through the Cassa depositi e prestiti.

History—1950s–1960s

Despite initial postwar plans to break up Agip, administrator Enrico Mattei converted it to a state monopoly, renamed Eni. The name derives from the initials of the company's original full title Ente Nazionale Idrocarburi, but is no longer used as an acronym. The Italian Government authorized its establishment on February 10, 1953 in order to implement a national energy strategy based on the concentration of all the activities in the energy sector into one group. Eni was to supply energy to Italy and contribute to the country's industrial development. The head of Eni, Mattei, a centre left politician, had developed cooperation with communist countries, and the import of oil from the Soviet Union became an important part of Eni's operations. At the same time, Eni was involved in a series of high profile political corruption scandals.

Current Operations

Exploration and Production

Its crude oil production comes primarily from Libya, Egypt, Nigeria, the Congo, the North Sea, and Angola, with smaller amounts of crude oil production in Tunisia and in the United States. Eni's China production began in 1992, although it currently amounts to only 1 percent of Eni's total crude oil production.

In 2007, oil and natural gas production for the full year averaged 1.74 millions boe per day, making Eni Europe's third largest refiner, after Royal Dutch Shell and Total S.A..

Eni carried out several hydrocarbon discoveries in recent years; the main discoveries were made in: Angola, Brazil, Congo, Egypt, Indonesia, Nigeria, Norway, Pakistan, Scotland, the Gulf of Mexico and Alaska. In 2007, a total of 81 new exploratory wells were drilled (43.5 of which represented Eni's share). Moreover, the company acquired oil and gas assets in the Gulf of Mexico from Dominion Resources and in onshore Congo from Maurel & Prom with total expenditures amounting to €4.52 billion. In January 2010 a consortium led by Eni was awarded a license to develop the Zubair field, one of the largest oil fields in Iraq.

Natural Gas

Eni operates in the supply, transport, distribution and sale of natural gas. Gas sales reached 99 billion cubic meters in 2007. In June 2008 the company bought a 57% stake in Distrigas, a Belgian company that supplies natural gas to industries, resellers and electricity producers. In March 2009 it bought the remaining 43%.

In December 2010, Eni entered into the shale gas exploration market by acquiring Minsk Energy Resources owning three licences in the Polish Baltic basin.

Power

Eni's electricity generation sites in Italy, as of January 2010, are the following:

Natural Gas Power Plants

- Brindisi - 1321 MW
- Ferrara - 61 MW
- Ferrera Erbognone - 1030 MW
- Livorno - 199 MW
- Mantova - 836 MW
- Ravenna - 972 MW
- Taranto - 300 MW.

Photovoltaic Power Plants:

- Nettuno - 30 MW.

Engineering and Construction

Eni operates in engineering, oilfield services and construction both offshore and onshore through Saipem, a subsidiary listed on the Italian Stock Exchange (Eni's interest is 43%).

Split Proposal

Activist asset manager Knight Vinke, which owns 1% of the outstanding shares of the company, in October 2009 has begun pressing Eni's management to operate a spin off of Eni's gas activities. In its opinion this would solve the undervaluation of the company and release up to 50 billion euros ($70bn) of hidden value.

Controversies

The Central Energy Italian Gas Holding scandal in 2005 involved Eni and Gazprom

In 2009, the European Commission filed formal antitrust charges against Eni. The commission believes that Eni has conspired to keep competitors from using its gas pipelines.

In 2009 again, according to the WikiLeaks cables, US ambassador Lanier told Washington that bribery allegations were made in Uganda by Eni which at the time was in competition for oil assets in the country against Tullow Oil. The bribes were taken by the newly appointed Ugandan prime minister, Amama Mbabazi.

Subsidiaries

- AGIP - (Azienda Generale Italiana Petroli - General Italian Oil Company) is an Italian automotive gasoline and diesel retailer.
- AGI (100% owned) - Agenzia Giornalistica Italia (Italian Journalist Agency) is one of the main Italian news agencies.
- Distrigas (100% owned) - a natural gas company based in Belgium
- Polimeri Europa (100% owned) - Polimeri Europa is a petrochemical company that manages the production and marketing of petrochemical products such as olefines, aromatics and intermediates (base chemicals), styrenes, elastomers and polyethylene, being also able to count on a range of proprietary technologies, advanced plant facilities and a broad-based distribution network.
- Saipem (43% owned) - Saipem is an oil and gas industry contractor. Saipem has contracted for designing and constructing several pipelines, including Blue Stream, Greenstream, Nord Stream and South Stream.

- Snam Rete Gas (50% owned) - Snam Rete Gas (BIT: SRG) owns Italy's largest natural gas pipeline system and is one of the twoLNG operators in Italy.
- Eni UK - carries out operations in the British section of the North Sea, in the Irish Sea and off the coast of the Shetland Islands. Has been present in UK since 1964. In 2006 Eni UK's average net production of hydrocarbons was more than 141,000 boe/d.
- Eni India is expected to start drilling at a deepwater block 2, near Andaman and Nicobar Islands in Q2 of 2011 as it has received 2 year extension for the completion of drilling program. The program was delayed due to various environmental issues and scarcity of oil rigs. ENI India had won this block in 2005 and partners with ONGC and GAIL India.

BG Group

BG Group plc (LSE: BG.) is a global oil and gas company headquartered in Reading, United Kingdom. It has operations in 25 countries across Africa, Asia, Australasia, Europe, North America and South America and produces around 680,000 barrels of oil equivalent per day. It has a major Liquefied Natural Gas (LNG) business and is the largest supplier of LNG to the United States. As at 31 December 2009 it had total proven commercial reserves of 2.6 billion barrels (410,000,000 m^3) of oil equivalent.

BG Group is listed on the London Stock Exchange and is a constituent of the FTSE 100 Index.

History

British Gas

The company was created in 1997 when British Gas plc divested Centrica and became BG plc, which was reorganised in 1999 as BG Group plc.

Lattice Group de-merger

On 23 October 2000, a further demerger separated the company into Lattice Group and BG Group. Lattice took ownership of *Transco* (the gas transporter for the UK), Advantica (gas engineering and consultancy specialist) along with the property and transport companies and BG Group took ownership of gas fields and other assets. In 2002, Lattice merged with National Grid Company to become National Grid Transco which was renamed National Grid in 2005.

NYSE Delisting

In September 2007, BG Group delisted its ADRs from the New York Stock Exchange after expressing concerns over the tougher rules and high costs associated with the Sarbanes-Oxley Act. Instead its shares began trading on the US over-the-counter market known as the Pink Sheets "International Premier QX".

Acquisitions

In June 2008 BG Group launched a US$13.1 billion hostile and ultimately unsuccessful bid to acquire Origin Energy, Australia's largest coal-seam gas producer: BG Group were out-manoeuvred by ConocoPhillips who offered to invest US$9.1 billion in a joint venture with Origin.

In October 2008 BG Group agreed to buy *Queensland Gas* for US$3.4bn so enabling it to operate in Asia's liquified natural gas market.

Coal Gas Liquefaction Project

On 1 November 2010, BG Group Announced plans to invest £9.3bn on the world's first project to liquefy and ship gas produced from coal deposits. This will be the first in a series of "coal seam methane" projects in the region of eastern Australia and will be operational by 2014. BG Group will construct a 540 km underground pipeline in Queensland which will transport gas producing coal deposits to a terminal in Gladstone on the east coast.

Operations

BG Group's main business is exploration for and the extraction of natural gas, liquefied natural gas and to a lesser extent oil. It sells these products to wholesale customers such as retail gas suppliers and electricity generating companies.

It also owns some gas pipelines and is involved in some power generation projects. It is active around the world, with only a minority of its business being in the UK. BG Group is a multinational company with operations in 27 countries.

Key areas for the company include:

- Australia
  - QGC
- Brazil
  - Interests in the Tupi, Iara, Guara and Iracema fields in the Santos Basin

- Egypt
  - Operates the Rosetta and West Delta Deep Marine gas fields, LNG export
- India
  - Interest in the Panna, Mukta and Tapti fields, Gujarat Gas Company and the Mhanagar Gas Company (gas distribution)
- Kazakhstan
  - Interest in the Karachaganak gas field
- Norway
  - Exploration licences with several discoveries
- Thailand
  - Interest in the Bongkot gas field
- Trinidad & Tobago
  - NCMA gas fields, Dplphin gas field, LNG export
- Tunisia
  - Operates the Miskar gasfield
- UK
  - Interests in several oil and gas fields in the UKCS, including operating the Armada, Everest and Lomond gas fields and the Blake oil field, Interest in the Dragon LNG import terminal
- USA
  - Interest in LNG Terminals, shale gas joint venture operation in the Haynesville and Marcellus plays

As of 31 December 2009 BG had proven reserves of $11,181\times10^9$ cu ft (3.166×10^{11} m^3) of natural gas and 736 million barrels of oil and condensate. Annual production in 2009 was 234.9 million barrels of oil equivalent (mmboe)

Senior Management

Frank Chapman was appointed Chief Executive of the BG Group in October 2000. His remuneration for this role in 2008 consisted of £1,081,588 base salary and a £1,944,000 bonus.

Lukoil

Lukoil/LUKoil is Russia's second largest oil company and its second largest producer of oil. In 2009, the company produced 97.615 million tons of oil; 1.972 million barrels per day (313,500 m^3/d).

Headquartered in Moscow, Lukoil is the second largest public company (next to ExxonMobil) in terms of proven oil and gas reserves. In 2008, the company had 19.3 billion barrels of oil equivalent per SPE standards. This accounts to some 1.3% of global oil reserves. The company has operations in more than 40 countries around the world.

History

Lukoil was formed in 1991, when three state-run, western Siberian companies, Langepasneftegaz, Urayneftegaz, and Kogalymneftegaz, merged. The initials of the three companies are preserved in the name Lukoil. The central figure in the company's founding was the Soviet deputy minister of oil production Vagit Alekperov. He came to believe the only way Russians could compete against Western companies was to copy their business model. That meant vertically integrating the three branches of the industry – exploration, refining, and distribution – that were strictly separate under the old Soviet system.

In 1994, Lukoil became the first company to begin offering shares of stock on the new Russian Trading System.

Exploration and Production

Lukoil carries out exploration and/or production of oil and gas in Russia and (as of 2008) thirty other countries: Kazakhstan, Azerbaijan, Uzbekistan, Egypt, Iran, Iraq, Colombia, Venezuela, Belgium, Saudi Arabia, Bulgaria and more.

In September 2004, ConocoPhillips purchased a 7.6 percent stake in Lukoil and signed an agreement that could increase this figure in the future to up to 20 percent. The two oil companies have agreed to develop jointly an oil and gas field in the northern Timan-Pechora area of Russia (Komi Republic) and intend to secure the rights to develop the West Qurna Field in Iraq, one of the country's largest.

Development of the Aral Sea

Ergash Shaismatov, the Deputy Prime Minister of Uzbekistan, announced on 30 August 2006 that the Uzbek government and an international consortium consisting of state-run Uzbekneftegaz, Lukoil Overseas, Petronas, Korea National Oil Corporation, and China National Petroleum Corporation signed a production sharing agreement to explore and develop oil and gas fields in the Aral Sea, saying, "The Aral Sea is largely unknown, but it holds a lot of promise in terms of finding oil and gas. There is risk of course but we believe in the success of this unique project." The consortium was created in September 2005.

Lukoil oil production by region, million tonnes

Region	2004	2005	2006	2007	2009
Russia	82.720	86.277	89.561	91.100	91.868
Western Siberia	56.351	58.469	59.764	59.917	52.962
Urals	10.082	10.307	10.923	11.257	12.042
Volga	3.175	3.210	3.214	3.240	3.072
Timan-Pechora	11.732	12.476	13.601	14.576	21.662
Other	1.380	1.815	2.059	2.110	2.130
International	3.480	3.881	5.674	5.545	5.747
Total	86.200	90.158	95.235	96.645	97.615

Oil Refining and Petrochemical Facilities

Lukoil owns seven oil-processing companies in Eastern Europe with total capacity of 54,1 mln tpa and holds 49% share of ISAB refinery complex in Sicily:

Name	Location	Launched	Acquired	Capacity, mln tpa
Lukoil-Nizhegorodnefteorgsintez	Kstovo	1958	2000	15,0
Lukoil-Permnefteorgsintez	Perm	1958	1991	12,0
Lukoil-Volgogradneftepererabotka	Volgograd	1957	1991	9,9
Lukoil-Ukhtaneftepererabotka	Ukhta	1934	2000	3,7
Lukoil-Odessky Neftepererabatyvayuschiy zavod	Odessa	1937	1999	3,6
Lukoil Neftochim Burgas License to operate revoked, see footnote	Burgas	1964	1999	7,5
Petrotel-Lukoil	Ploieşti	1904	1998	2,4
ISAB	Priolo Gargallo	1975	2008*	16,0*
TRN	Vlissingen	1973	2009*	7,9*

* – 49% and 45% shares respectively

— The Bulgarian Facility has had it's license to operate revoked as of July 2011 for failure to install Excise Metering Devices that connect directly to the Nation Revenue Agency, the plant is currently in the process of stopping production as of 29 July 2011.

However on 1 August 2011 the Bulgarian court returned the license and the refinery is expected to begin work.

The company also owns several petrochemical plants in Budennovsk, Saratov and Kalush, all managed by "Lukoil-Neftechim".

Proven Reserves

As of January 2009, the company had proven reserves of 14.5 billion barrels (2.31×10^9 m^3) of oil and 29.3 trillion cubic feet (830 km^3) of gas, per PRMS (previously called SPE) requirements.

Gasoline Retail Sales

Lukoil sells gasoline in 59 regions of Russia and in 22 other countries (Azerbaijan, Belarus, Belgium (through its subsidiary "Jet" until late 2008, and progressively directly under the Lukoil brand), Bulgaria, Croatia (operated by Lukoil Croatia, but under the brand name "Europa-Mil"), Cyprus, Czech Republic, Slovakia (Rebranded from "Jet" to "Lukoil"), Estonia, Finland (Teboil), Georgia, Hungary, Latvia, Lithuania, Republic of Macedonia, Moldova, Montenegro, Poland (Rebranded from "Jet" to "Lukoil" in August 2008), Romania, Serbia, Turkey, USA and Ukraine). As of the end of 2006, it has 197 tank farms and 6,090 gas stations.

In 2000, Lukoil purchased Getty Oil, and converted a small number of Getty stations in the United States to Lukoil in 2003.

In 2004, Lukoil acquired Schlotzmeyer Bros., who formerly owned the Mobil stations in New Jersey and Pennsylvania. Many of these stations had Circle K stores, which Lukoil converted to its own Kwik Farms brand. However, many Mobil franchisees in the area did not want to convert their stations to Lukoil because it sold its fuel at the same prices as more established brands.

In 2008, Lukoil purchased petroleum distribution company Akpet in Turkey. As a result of this acquisition, Lukoil market share in Turkish retail market increased to 5% with 8 storage facilities and over 600 petroleum stations across the country.

Controversy

Environmental Record

According to Lukoil, their numbers in 2007 recorded a drop of 7.8% in the volume of pollutant effects and a drop of 3.8% in the area of contaminated lands compared to 2006. These numbers came after an appeal from EMERCON of Russia (the Ministry of the Russian Federation for Civil Defence, Emergencies and Natural Disaster Recovery), which proposed that Lukoil participate in the development of monitoring, prevention, and emergency recovery systems.

In an effort to increase their productivity, Lukoil organized a contract to begin an oil pumping block in the Azerbaijan sector of the

Caspian Sea. They arranged an Environmental Impact Assessment of the drill site in order to organize a second exploration drill. This block, D-222, is the largest prospective structure in the north-east section of the Caspian Sea.

The key issue of the assessment was the amount of damage the block would be doing to the fish stock in the area. Taking into account the depth of the operation of about 700 meters, the amount of harm would be minimal with most of the fish harmed being plankton and benthos. A rescue and salvage ship will be placed into operation to mitigate the impact on the area. They have also developed contingency plans for oil spills, and implemented an environmental monitoring system.

Management and Major Shareholders

Company's top managers control over half of Lukoil shares while about 20% is owned by ConocoPhillips. The rest of shares is a free-float. On 24 March 2010, ConocoPhillips announced it would begin selling half of its 20% stake in the company.

Board of Directors elected at the Annual General Shareholders Meeting on 28 June 2005 consists of:

- Valery Grayfer (Chairman, General Director of the JSC RITEK)
- Vagit Alekperov (President of the OAO Lukoil).

Motorsports

Lukoil Racing team is the leading Russian motorsport organization; its operations including management, driver training and support, engineering expertise and a quality technical environment, which enables continuous development, building, testing and race preparation.

Lukoil has been involved in motorsport for over 10 years. The Lukoil Racing Team has achieved notable successes both in Russia and in Europe, winning more than 60 championships over the years. No other auto racing team has gained such success in the history of the USSR and Russia.

Nippon Oil

The Nippon Oil Corporation is a Japanese petroleum company. Its businesses include the exploration, importation, and refining of crude oil; the manufacture and sale of petroleum products, including fuels and lubricants; and other energy-related activities. Its products are sold under the brand name ENEOS, which is also the name used for its service stations. It is the largest oil company in Japan, and in recent years it has been expanding its operations in other countries.

History

The company was established 1888 as the "Nippon Oil", "Nisseki" for short. In 1999, the company merged with and absorbed the former "Mitsubishi Oil" (,*Mitsubishi Sekiyu*?). The merged company was called "Nippon Mitsubishi Oil" (,*Nisseki Mitsubishi*?) until 2002, when it adopted its present name.

In late 2009, Nippon Oil announced its most recent merger activity. An excerpt from the press release is attached...

> *"Nippon Oil Corporation and Nippon Mining Holdings, Inc. have been working towards their business integration based on the business integration agreement entered into on October 30, 2009 and the share transfer plan for the establishment of the holding company, assuming the approval of the general meetings of shareholders of Nippon Oil and Nippon Mining and of the regulatory authorities.*
>
> *As the Companies have agreed upon the operational structure of oil refineries, manufacturing facilities and branch offices of JX Nippon Oil & Energy Corporation to be established on July 1, 2010 ("JX Nippon Oil & Energy," a wholly owned petroleum refining and marketing business company of JX Holdings, Inc. to be established on April 1, 2010) and the branding to be used by JX Nippon Oil & Energy..."*

Worldwide Operations

The company has world wide locations including JX Nippon Oil & Energy USA Inc in Itasca, Illinois, Torrance, California, and Nippon Oil Lubricants (America), LLC, in Childersburg, Alabama. ENEOS is JX Group's corporate brand. They have brought their premium brand motor oil ENEOS and SUSTINA into the United States recently. The product line includes the extremely difficult to formulate 0W-50 viscosity oil. New line of premium full synthetic motor oil SUSTINA is now available in the United States. NOC employs over 4,222 people with additional employees from oversea divisions, and operates the following refineries throughout Japan:

- Muroran Refinery (Nippon Petroleum Refining Co., Ltd.)
- Sendai Refinery (NPRC)
- Yokohama Refinery (NPRC)
- Negishi Refinery (NPRC)

- Mizushima Refinery (NPRC)
- Osaka Refinery (NPRC)
- Marifu Refinery (NPRC).

Nippon Oil Exploration also owns a 5% share of Syncrude, a Canadian oil sands mining company, through its fully owned subsidiary Mocal Energy.

The company also has technical collaboration with Tide Water Oil Co., an Indian petroleum products manufacturer. Superior quality lubricants under the brand name ENEOS are manufactured and marketed in India by Tide Water Oil Co. in India.

2011 Earthquake and Tsunami

On 11 March 2011, a 145,000-barrel-per-day refinery in Sendai was set ablaze by a magnitude 9 earthquake. Workers were evacuated, but tsunami warnings hindered efforts to extinguish the fire until 14 March, when officials planned to do so.

Environmental Record

While developing the Rang Don Oil Field and Helang Gas Field NOEX, part of the Nippon Oil Corporation, conducted environmental impact assessments. These assessments helped them implement management plans based on the results of the assessments, specifically, how to reduce the impact of the fields on surrounding sea areas.

In 2005 Nippon Oil and Ebara-Ballard announced they were going to start field testing a 1 kW household proton-exchange membrane fuel cell system that uses coal oil as fuel. It was the world's first household test with the system. The system achieves a greater power-generation efficiency than normal heating. The system can operate in temperatures as low as -10 deg C.

In 2007 Nippon Oil was the recipient of the Nippon Keidanren Chairman's Prize in recognition of its achievements in a number of areas. They were the first in the Japanese petroleum industry to achieve a zero emission status at their refineries. They are also developing fuel cell systems as well as producing and selling sulfur-free fuel. The Rang Dong Oil Field in also one of the biggest CO2 reduction projects in the world. The project utilizes associated gas produced along with crude oil for additional energy production.

Connection to Human Rights Abuses

The construction of the Yetagun pipeline in Myanmar has been linked to 'severe human rights abuses' by Burmese troops. The company stated it 'was not aware of such abuses.' However critics claim that such foreign investment by Nippon Oil and other multinationals: 'provides a crucial source of support to the junta, allowing it to ignore demands that it return Burma to civilian rule and end human rights abuses.'

Sponsorship

Nippon Oil was formerly a sponsor of the Honda Racing F1 Team and is a current sponsor of the F.C. Tokyo football club. It also sponsors other motor sports teams, such as Team Lexus LeMans ENEOS SC430 in the Japanese Super GT series in the GT500 class. In the late 1980s and early 1990s JSPC, it sponsored the Trust Racing Team Porsche.

Occidental Petroleum

Occidental Petroleum Corporation (Oxy) is a California-based oil and gas exploration and production company with operations in the United States, the Middle East, North Africa, and South America. "Oxy" is the largest oil producer in Texas and the largest natural gas producer and second-largest producer of oil and gas combined in California, with additional operations in Kansas, North Dakota, Utah, Oklahoma, Colorado and New Mexico. The company nickname began in 1964 in reference to Occidental's NYSE stock ticker (OXY). Headquartered in Los Angeles, California, Oxy is the fourth-largest U.S. oil and gas company, based on equity market capitalization. As of 2010, the company has more than 30,000 employees and contractors worldwide.

Oxy's role in oil and natural gas exploration and production, to which they have pledged a commitment to responsibility, has also been a source of criticism. The company states that it is "committed to respecting the environment, protecting safety and upholding high standards of social responsibility throughout its worldwide operations." Critics have raised concerns about Occidental's historical operations in these areas.

Oxy's subsidiaries include wholly owned chemical manufacturers Occidental Chemical Corporation (OxyChem), OxyVinyls, and INDSPEC Chemical Corporation. Oxy indirectly owns Armand Products Company with Church & Dwight Co., Inc.. Carbocloro S.A. Indústrias Químicas, is a joint venture between OxyChem and UNIPAR in Brazil.

History

Occidental was founded in 1920. In 1957, Dr. Armand Hammer was elected president and CEO. In 1961, the company discovered the second largest natural gas field in California in the Arbuckle area of the Sacramento basin at Lathrop. Over the next 10 years, Occidental expanded internationally with operations in Libya, Peru, Venezuela, Bolivia, Trinidad, and the United Kingdom.

Occidental won exploration rights in Libya in 1965 and operated there until all activities were suspended in 1986 after the United States imposed economic sanctions on Libya. On July 6, 1988, an explosion and subsequent inferno on the Piper Alpha platform, operated by Occidental Petroleum (Caledonia) Ltd in the UK North Sea, resulted in 167 fatalities in what remains the world's most deadly offshore disaster.

Occidental entered the chemical business with the acquisition of Hooker Chemicals in 1968, 26 years after the contamination at Love Canal. Today, Dallas-based Occidental Chemical is a leading chemical manufacturer with interests in basic chemicals, vinyls and performance chemical products.

In 1990, Dr. Ray R. Irani became Occidental Petroleum Corporation's Chairman and CEO. He held the additional title of President from 2005 to 2007. Irani and Occidental President, Stephen Chazen, ordered a reduction in company expenditures that resulted in hundreds of company job terminations, the majority of whom were veteran employees, in 2007-2008, at the height of the recession, even as Irani collected a massive $460 million dollar total compensation package for 2006 and the company enjoyed record profits. According to the Associated Press, within the last decade, he has received $857 million. "We're not in the business to employ people. We're in the business to make a profit," Irani has said. Chazen collected $38,080,344 and Irani $76,107,010 in fiscal year 2010, nearly doubling his 2009 compensation despite shareholder outrage over the Occidental board of directors executive pay policies.

A survey of Fortune 500 corporate general counsel compensation revealed that Occidental general counsel Donald de Brier was second highest on the list at approximately $6 million with total compensation reaching $34, 528,779. Irani retired as CEO on May 10, 2011 after the California State Teachers' Retirement System and Relational Investors, two major institutional Occidental Investors, objected to the company's compensation policies and announced plans to replace long-term board members who were described as "ossified" in a letter written in protest of Irani's salary. They also termed Irani's salary a "corporate giveaway program." Irani's salary was considered excessive and not truly performance based for decades by a number of corporate governance authorities who noted that Irani's compensation had exceeded that of the head of energy giant ExxonMobil, Rex Tillerson, who leads a company with a market cap that is five times larger than Occidental Petroleum. Former CFO and current President Stephen Chazen was named CEO of Occidental to replace the 76 year-old Irani who plans to stay on as executive Chairman until 2014.

Despite retiring as CEO, Irani continues to exclusively utilize the company's Boeing Business Jet, enjoys lavish perqs, and is often jointly interviewed with Stephen Chazen in business publications, causing some to question whether he has truly relinquished leadership of the company. Since 1990, Occidental has gone from a collection of unrelated businesses to one that focuses on oil and gas. During Irani's tenure as CEO, Occidental's market capitalization increased to more than $80 billion from $5.4 billion.

In 2005, Occidental was among 53 entities which contributed the maximum of $250,000 to the second inauguration of President George W. Bush. In 2008, Oxy contributed $301,579 to Democratic candidates and $204,587 to Republican candidates.

Financial Performance

At year-end 2010, Occidental was the fourth-largest U.S. oil and gas company measured by market capitalization, with a market capitalization of $79.7 billion at that date. This represented a fifteenfold increase in the company's market capitalization since the end of 1990, when it was approximately $5.4 billion.

At year-end 2010, Occidental was ranked No. 33 on the Standard & Poor's 500 Index. Shares of Occidental rose by nearly 21 percent in 2010, compared with a 12 percent increase in the Chicago Board Options Exchange index of oil companies.

Table: *Occidental Petroleum Financial Performance*

Fiscal year	*Market capitalization (billions)*	*Revenue (billions)*	*Income before income taxes (loss) (billions)*
2005	$32.112	$16.259	$7.133
2006	$41.070	$18.160	$7.830
2007	$63.794	$20.013	$8.572
2008	$48.585	$24.480	$11.371
2009	$66.050	$15.531	$4.669
2010	$79.735	$19.157	$7.359

Operations

Oil and Gas

Occidental's growth strategy in oil and gas relies on three components: enhanced oil recovery (EOR), exploration and acquisitions. Occidental's oil and gas operations are focused in three core areas, the United States, the Middle East/North Africa, and South America. Occidental had approximately 3.36 billion barrels (534,000,000 m^3) of oil equivalent net proved reserves at December 31, 2010. In 2010, the company had its highest annual daily sales volume in history – 748,000 barrels (118,900 m^3) of oil equivalent.

The United States accounted for 66 percent of Occidental's oil and gas reserves and 51 percent of the current production in 2010. Occidental is the largest producer of natural gas and second-largest producer of oil and gas on a barrels of oil equivalent basis in California, where in 2009 it made what is believed to be the largest oil and natural gas discovery in the state in 35 years. It also operates the THUMS Islands in the San Pedro Bay. Occidental's total share of oil and gas 2010 production in California was approximately 139,000-barrel (22,100 m^3) of oil equivalent per day and its properties held approximately 768-million-barrel (122,100,000 m^3) of oil equivalent in proved reserves.

Occidental also has significant oil and natural gas holdings in the Permian Basin of West Texas and Southeast New Mexico. Occidental is the largest oil producer in the Permian Basin, where it produced roughly 197,000 barrels (31,300 m^3) of oil equivalent per day in 2010 and held 1.2 billion barrels (190,000,000 m^3) of proved reserves as of December 31, 2010. In the Permian Basin, Oxy is the largest operator of EOR oil projects that inject carbon dioxide into underground formations to extract the oil and gas that remains after primary recovery operations. In 2010, the company's 31 CO_2 projects produced nearly 85,000 barrels (13,500 m^3) of oil per day as a result of EOR, according to Oil & Gas Journal's biennial EOR survey. Occidental's Mid-Continent Gas operations are concentrated in the Permian Basin, Kansas, Colorado, Utah and Oklahoma. These operations produced approximately 62,000 barrels (9,900 m^3) of oil equivalent per day in 2010 and had proved reserves of 266 million barrels (42,300,000 m^3) of oil equivalent, as of December 31, 2010. In 2010, Oxy announced the acquisition of new shale oil properties in Williston Basin in North Dakota as well as natural gas and oil properties in South Texas.

Occidental's Middle East and North Africa operations accounted for 38 percent of its worldwide production in 2010, producing approximately 287,500 barrels (45,710 m^3) of oil equivalent. The region also holds 26 percent of the company's proved reserves. In the Middle East, Occidental has operations in Libya, Oman, Qatar, Bahrain, Iraq and Yemen. Oxy is the second-largest oil producer in Oman. In Qatar, it is a partner in the giant Dolphin natural gas project, which delivers gas to Oman and the United Arab Emirates.

The company has its only operation in North Africa in Libya. In 2005, Occidental and partner Liwa won eight out of 15 exploration spots on the EPSA-4 auction, making both companies among the first to enter the Libyan market since the United States lifted its embargo on that country. In early 2011, Occidental won a contract to join Abu Dhabi's state oil company in developing the Shah natural-gas project, one of the largest natural gas fields in the Middle East. In South America, Occidental operates in Bolivia and Colombia. Occidental's share of production from its Colombia assets was approximately 32,000 barrels (5,100 m^3) of oil per day in 2010.

In Colombia, Occidental and Ecopetrol, the state-owned oil company, discovered the giant Caño Limón oilfield in 1983. It proved to be the largest discovery in Colombia's oil history and helped return the country to the oil-exporter status. In 2010, Occidental announced the sale of its oil and gas operations in Argentina to Sinopec, a subsidiary of China Petrochemical Corporation; the transaction was completed in early 2011. Occidental formerly operated in Ecuador, but the government ended the company's interests in block 15 in the Ecuadorian Amazon in 2006.

Chemical

Oxy's subsidiaries include wholly owned chemical manufacturers Occidental Chemical Corporation (OxyChem), OxyVinyls, and INDSPEC Chemical Corporation. OxyChem is a Dallas, Texas-based manufacturer of polyvinyl chloride (PVC) resins, chlorine and caustic soda used in plastics, pharmaceuticals and water treatment chemicals. Other products manufactured by the company include caustic potash, chlorinated organics, sodium silicates, chlorinated isocyanurates and calcium chloride. OxyChem has manufacturing facilities in the United States, Canada, Chile and Brazil.

Through joint ventures, Oxy indirectly owns Armand Products Company, with OxyChem and Church & Dwight Co., Inc., which sells potassium carbonate and potassium bicarbonate. Carbocloro S.A. Indústrias Químicas, a joint venture between OxyChem and UNIPAR, manufactures and sells chlor-alkali products in Brazil.

On October 11, 2008, an accidental spill of oleum, a chemical similar to sulfuric acid, occurred at INDSPEC's facility in Petrolia, Pennsylvania. The accident caused contamination of the ventilation system and a cloud of toxic gas in the Petrolia sky. 2,500 residents of the area were asked to evacuate.

Oil Shale

Starting in 1972, Occidental Oil Shale, Inc., a subsidiary of Occidental Petroleum, began research on a shale oil extraction process, ending research in 1991. The company conducted the first modified *in situ* oil shale experiment in 1972 at Logan Wash, Colorado. The process used explosives to create underground chambers (retorts) of fractured oil shale. About 20% was mined out after which blasting was used to fracture oil shale. The commercial-sized retort covered 333 by 166 feet (101 by 51 m) area and had height of 400 feet (120 m). Oil shale was then ignited on the top by external fuel and air or steam was injected to control the process. As a result, combustion moved from the top to the bottom of retort.

During the process four major zones could be identified. In the pre-heat zone air contacted processed hot shale (spent shale) which pre-heated air. In the combustion zone, oxygen in air was used to burn carbon residue in the spent shale. Below this zone, heated gas caused retorting process converting kerogen in oil shale to oil shale gas and shale oil vapours. In the final zone oil and gas were cooled and collected through separation sump and collecting well. All together, six retorts have been burned at the site.

Phibro

CFO Stephen Chazen led Occidental's October 12, 2009 acquisition of Citigroup's controversial Phibro energy-trading business, paying $250 million for the unit and the services of Phibro chief Andrew J. Hall. Hall's compensation of $100 million in 2009 was seen as a problem for troubled Citibank which struggled with continuing losses before selling the unit. So far the Occidental-owned Phibro has had mixed results. Occidental suffered significant trading losses in 2010, causing the company to fall short of analyst expectations, and landed in the red again in the second quarter of 2011 despite Chazen's public support of Hall.

Corporate Social Responsibility

Occidental's role in oil and natural gas exploration and production has also been a source of criticism. The company states that it is "committed to respecting the environment, maintaining safety and upholding high standards of social responsibility throughout the company's worldwide operations." Critics have raised concerns about Occidental's historical operations in these areas. Occidental Petroleum is a signatory participant of the Voluntary Principles on Security and Human Rights.

Libya

Occidental has been criticized for lobbying for a special exemption, on behalf of Libyan dictator Muammar Qaddafi, to a federal law designed by Senator Frank Lautenberg (D-NJ) to assist American terror victims seize assets of countries found culpable in terror attacks such as the Libyan bombing of the Pan Am flight in Lockerbie in 1988 which resulted in the deaths of 270 passengers and crew, including 189 Americans. In 2008 the company hired Hogan & Hartson, a Washington D.C. law firm to successfully secure the exemption for Libya, a country where Occidental had major oil drilling operations prior to the anti-Qaddafi uprising in February 2011. Occidental's Chairman, Ray Irani, told investors during a conference call in 2007 that "Libya is a very attractive place" in describing that country's oil reserves. Irani led Occidental back into Libya in 2005, personally negotiating with Qaddafi, the terms of a new contract after the sanctions imposed by President Reagan as a result of Libya's terror attacks were finally lifted by the U.S. government. The company has since withdrawn from Libya pending resolution of the current crisis.

Libyan Investment Authority

The United States Securities and Exchange Commission was in June 2011 investigating Occidental's possible role in illegal actions relating to the Libyan Investment Authority or LIA, an investment firm controlled by Libyan dictator Muammar Qaddafi. United Kingdom prosecutors, in cooperation with the SEC, have undertaken similar investigations of Occidental's actions during this same period to determine if Occidental, as well as other oil companies, violated international bribery laws. The Libyan government has invested $80 million dollars in Occidental. These funds were subsequently seized by the U.S. government in reaction to Qaddafi's attacks on Libyan civilians.

Environmental Record

Oxy has been noted within the oil and gas industry as being among the first to employ carbon dioxide (CO2) injection for enhanced oil recovery; this technique is a means of long-term geologic storage of CO2, which could reduce future greenhouse gas emissions to the atmosphere. Occidental was recognized by the EPA in 2008 as Production Partner of the Year and in 2009 for Continuing Excellence (5 Years). Occidental is a member of the Wildlife Habitat Council (WHC). The WHC has certified the habitat conservation and education programs at eight of the company's sites.

Researchers at the University of Massachusetts Amherst identified Occidental Petroleum as the 47th-largest corporate producer of air pollution in the United States, with about 1.2 million pounds of toxic chemicals released annually into the air. Pollutants emitted by the company included chlorine, antimony compounds, benzotrichloride, and hydrochloric acid.

Love Canal

In 1942, Hooker Chemical and Plastics began disposing chemical waste in the Love Canal region. Other companies as well as the military had used it as a chemical disposal site since the 1920s. In 1947, Hooker Chemicals became the owner and the sole user of the land. In 1952, the site was filled to capacity and closed off. Later in the 1950s, the local school board requested Hooker, after threatening to resort to eminent domain, to sell the land. The school board intended to build a school on an unused area of the dump. Hooker Chemical sold the land to the school board at $1, with the warning that the site contained waste products from the manufacturing of chemicals, and disclaimed all subsequent liability. A school was built on the site, and later a middle-class residential district was built upon the land adjacent to the site. The construction broke through the 4-foot (1.2 m) clay seal containing the waste. In 1968, Hooker Chemical was purchased by Occidental Petroleum. In 1978, residents became concerned about unusual health issues in the Love Canal region, including high rates of cancer and birth defects. This subsequently became a national news story, and in 1980, president Jimmy Carter declared a federal emergency in the area. Residents were eventually relocated, and Occidental paid $129 million in restitution.

Colombia

Occidental met with substantial resistance from 1992 to 2001 when it tried to drill for oil in the territory of the U'wa people in northeast Colombia. The locals were concerned about environmental damage and feared that development would bring strangers and invite violence to the region. There also were tribal beliefs that oil is the "blood of the earth" and should not be removed. They believed that oil infrastructure would be a target for violent leftist guerillas in the country. After years of shareholder resolutions, legal battles, protests, and a failed test well, the company abandoned the project. Repsol YPF took over the project and continues to work on it.

Caño Limón

On December 13, 1998, seventeen civilians, including 7 children, were killed when the Colombian Air Force dropped a cluster bomb in the hamlet of Santo Domingo, Colombia, after AirScan, Occidental's security contractor, from a private aircraft, incorrectly identified it as a hostile guerrilla target. Groups such as FARC and the National Liberation Army were active in the area. Three employees of AirScan were flying the Skymaster plane from which they provided the Colombian military with the coordinates to drop the bombs. The operation had been planned by the CAF and AirScan at the Occidental's complex in Caño Limón. A lawsuit was attempted in April 2003 against Occidental by Luis Alberto Galvis Mujica, a witness and survivor of the accident. Plaintiffs claims were dismissed by the trial court. The dismissal was appealed to 9th U.S. Circuit Court of Appeals, which sent the back case to the trial court to resolve a single issue. The trial court declined to reconsider the case, thereby reinstating the dismissal. The case is once again on appeal.

Maynas Carijano v. Occidental Petroleum

On May 10, 2007, a group of 25 indigenous Achuar Peruvians filed suit against Occidental, demanding clean-up and reparations for environmental damages allegedly caused by Occidental over 30 years. The plaintiffs claimed that the company violated the industry standards and the environmental regulations by dumping a total of 9 billion barrels (1.4×10^9 m^3) of toxic oil by-products in watersheds used by the Achuar people to fish, drink, and bathe. The Achuar were represented by Los Angeles-based EarthRights International and the law firm Schonbrun DeSimone Seplow Harris & Hoffman LLP.

On March 3, 2010, EarthRights International (ERI) argued to the Ninth Circuit Court of Appeals that the landmark environmental and public health case brought by indigenous Peruvian Achuar and the U.S. NGO Amazon Watch against Los Angeles-based oil giant Occidental Petroleum (Oxy), Maynas Carijano v. Occidental Petroleum, should be litigated in Los Angeles, where Oxy is headquartered. The appeals court will be deciding whether the oil giant will face suit in its own hometown or whether the case will move to Peru.

Political Record

Greenmail

In 1984, David Murdock owned about 5% of the company's shares. When Murdock called on the management to take measures to increase the share price, it chose to pay greenmail to buy back shares from him at $40.10, while the market price was $28.75.

Gore Family

Occidental's coal interests were represented for many years by attorney and former U.S. Senator Albert Gore, Sr., among others. Gore, who had a long-time close friendship with Hammer, became the head of the subsidiary Island Creek Coal Company, upon his election loss in the Senate. Much of Occidental's coal and phosphate production was in Tennessee, the state Gore represented in the Senate, and Gore owned shares in the company. Former Vice President Albert Gore, Jr. received much criticism from environmentalists, when the shares passed to the estate after the death of Albert Gore Sr., and Albert Gore Jr. was a son and the executor of the estate. Albert Gore Jr. did not exercise control over the shares, which were eventually sold when the estate closed.

In 1998, the US government sold the Elk Hills naval petroleum reserve to Occidental for $3.65 billion. According to the government, the reserve was no longer strategically necessary, and the reserve was sold to reduce the national debt and the size of the government. To ensure competition, the field was sold in segments and offered to multiple bidders. Critics cited Vice President Al Gore's involvement with the company as evidence of graft.

Safety Record

OxyChem has achieved Star Status under OSHA's Voluntary Protection Programs as being among the safest work sites in the U.S.

Piper Alpha

On July 6, 1988 Occidental's Piper Alpha offshore production platform in the UK North Sea was destroyed when an out of service gas condensate pump was started with its pressure safety valve removed. The subsequent gas leak, explosion and fire resulted in the deaths of 167 workers in what remains the world's most deadly offshore disaster.

OMV

OMV (originally ΦMV for "Osterreichische Mineralölverwaltung", meaning Austrian mineral oil authority) is Austria's largest oil-producing, refining and gas station operating company with important activities in other Central European countries. It is Austria's largest listed industrial company (concerning turnover) and one of the largest integrated oil and gas groups in Central Europe.

History

OMV was founded in 1956 as a joint stock company. In 1960, the company commissioned the Schwechat Refinery near Vienna. International activities of OMV started in 1985 with exploration and production activities in Libya. In 1990, OMV enlarged its activities into retail sale inaugurating its first filling station followed by the first filling station on abroad (Hungary) in 1991. In 1995, the company changed its name from ΦMV to OMV.

In 2000s OMV had several important acquisitions. In 2002, it bought 25.1% of shares in Rompetrol Group In 2003, it took over the international portfolio of Preussag Energie and 45% of Bayernoil-Raffinerieverbund. One year later, it acquired 51% of the Romanian oil and gas group Petrom SA, which was the largest acquisition in the company's history. In 2005, OMV sold its stake in the Rompetrol Group and together with IPIC of Abu Dhabi acquired petrochemical company Borealis. In June 2006, OMV established the OMV Future Energy Fund for identifying projects in the field of renewable energy, providing assistance with their implementation and financing. In 2007, OMV tried to take over Hungarian oil company MOL, but was forced to withdraw its merger proposal in 2008. In 2008, OMV and Gazprom to develop the Central European Gas Hub, based on the Baumgarten underground gas storage, into a leading hub platform in continental Europe and to establish a gas exchange there for trading on spot and futures markets for gas products.

Operations

In 2006, OMV has consolidated sales of €18.97 billion, a workforce of 40,993 employees, and a market capitalization of approximately €14 billion. It has refining and marketing activities in 13 countries and explorations and production activities in 18 countries on five continents. OMV operates refineries in Germany, Austria and Romania and it runs over 2500 gas stations in Central Europe, with brands OMV, Avanti, Stroh and PETROM.

Subsidiaries

OMV holds stakes in several oil and petrochemical companies. Most important shareholdings are:

- Petrom S.A. (51%)
- Borealis A/S (36%)
- Agrolinz Melamine International (AMI) GmbH (51%)
- Bayernoil Raffineriegesellschaft GmbH (45%)
- EconGas GmbH (50%)
- Petrol Ofisi A.[a]. (55.40%)
- Nabucco Gas Pipeline International GmbH (16.67%).

OMV Aktiengesellschaft

According to OMV:

- OMV Aktiengesellschaft
  - — OMV Refining & Marketing GmbH (100%)
  - — OMV Exploration & Production GmbH (100%)
  - — OMV Gas & Power GmbH (100%)
  - — OMV Solutions GmbH (100%)
  - — Petrom SA (51%)
  - — Petrol Ofisi (41.58%)
  - — OMV Deutschland (10%)
  - — Borealis (36 %).

Refining and Marketing

According to OMV:

- Refining & Marketing GmbH (100%)
  - — OMV Deutschland (90%)
    - * Bayernoil Raffinerie GmbH (45%)
  - — Adria Wien Pipeline (76 %)
  - — Borealis (36%)
  - — OMV Supply & Trading (100%)
  - — OMV Trading Services (100%)
  - — OMV Wärme VertriebsGmbH (100%)
  - — OMV Èeská republika (100%)
  - — OMV Slovensko (100%)
  - — OMV Hungaria (100%)
  - — OMV Slovenija (92.25%)
  - — OMV Hrvatska (100%)

— OMV Bosnia-Hercegovina (100%)

— OMV Italia (100%).

Exploration and Production

According to OMV:

- OMV (ALBANIEN) Adriatic Sea Exploration GmbH
- OMV Petroleum Exploration GmbH
- OMV Austria Exploration & Production GmbH
- OMV (BULGARIA) offshore Exploration GmbH
- OMV (EGYPT) Exploration GmbH
- OMV Exploration & Production Limited
- OMV (FAROE ISLANDS) Exploration GmbH
- OMV Global Oil & Gas GmbH
- OMV (RUSSLAND) Exploration & Production GmbH
- OMV (Tunesien) Exploration GmbH
- OMV (Tunesien) Production GmbH
- OMV (TUNESIEN) Sidi Mansour GmbH
- OMV (U.K.) Limited
- OMV (IRELAND) Exploration GmbH
- OMV (Yemen Block S 2) Exploration GmbH
- OMV (IRAN) onshore Exploration GmbH
- OMV (IRELAND) Killala Exploration GmbH
- OMV New Zealand Ltd.
- OMV (NORGE) AS
- OMV of Libya Limited Exploration GmbH
- OMV (YEMEN) Al Mabar Exploration GmbH
- OMV (YEMEN) South Sanau Exploration GmbH
- OMV Oil Exploration GmbH
- OMV Oil & Gas Exploration GmbH
- OMV Oil Production GmbH
- OMV (PAKISTAN) Exploration GmbH
- PEI Venezuela GmbH
- Preussag Energie International GmbH.

Gas and Power

According to OMV:

- OMV Gas & Power GmbH (100%)
  - — OMV Gas GmbH (100%)
    - * AGGM Austrian Gas Grid Management AG (100%)
    - * AGCS Gas Clearing and Settlement AG (23.1%)
    - * TAG Trans Austria Gasleitung GmbH (11%)
  - — OMV Power International GmbH (100%)
  - — OMV Gaz ve Enerji Ltd. Sti. (100%)
  - — Nabucco Gas Pipeline International GmbH (16.67%)
  - — EconGas GmbH (59.26%)
  - — Central European Gas Hub AG (100%)
  - — Adria LNG d.o.o. (25.58%)
  - — Gate terminal b.v. (5%).

Shareholders

OMV is a publicly traded company. The main shareholders are ΦIAG (Austrian state holding - 31.5%) and IPIC (20%) with 48.3% of shares freely floating in the market (without treasury shares).

Controversies—Petrom

The acquisition of 51% stake in Petrom S.A. was considered controversial as the privatization contract was not been made public and it consists of several disputed clauses. The privatization allegedly produced a market monopoly. Critics say that OMV can use the resources Petrom owns until their exhaustion. Also fixing of tax for gas and oil exploration at 3 to 13.5 percent from the final delivery price for 10 years was criticized. Some critics claimed, that the price €1.5 billion was too low.

MOL

In June 2007, OMV made an unsolicited bid to take over MOL, which was rejected by the Hungarian company. MOL criticized OMV's advertisement in which OMV had suggested the two had already worked together on the European market. MOL thought that to be misleading and unethical and asked OMV to remove the name MOL from those advertisements. OMV dismissed its bid after negative results of the investigation by the European competition authorities.

OMV sold its entire stake to Surgutneftegas in March 2009.

The End of Cheap Oil

In 1973 and 1979 a pair of sudden price increases rudely awakened the industrial world to its dependence on cheap crude oil. Prices first tripled in response to an Arab embargo and then nearly doubled again when Iran dethroned its Shah, sending the major economies sputtering into recession. Many analysts warned that these crises proved that the world would soon run out of oil. Yet they were wrong.

Their dire predictions were emotional and political reactions; even at the time, oil experts knew that they had no scientific basis. Just a few years earlier oil explorers had discovered enormous new oil provinces on the north slope of Alaska and below the North Sea off the coast of Europe. By 1973 the world had consumed, according to many experts' best estimates, only about one eighth of its endowment of readily accessible crude oil (so-called conventional oil). The five Middle Eastern members of the Organization of Petroleum Exporting Countries (OPEC) were able to hike prices not because oil was growing scarce but because they had managed to corner 36 percent of the market. Later, when demand sagged, and the flow of fresh Alaskan and North Sea oil weakened OPEC's economic stranglehold, prices collapsed.

The next oil crunch will not be so temporary. Our analysis of the discovery and production of oil fields around the world suggests that within the next decade, the supply of conventional oil will be unable to keep up with demand. This conclusion contradicts the picture one gets from oil industry reports, which boasted of 1,020 billion barrels of oil (Gbo) in "Proved" reserves at the start of 1998. Dividing that figure by the current production rate of about 23.6 Gbo a year might suggest that crude oil could remain plentiful and cheap for 43 more years—probably longer, because official charts show reserves growing.

Unfortunately, this appraisal makes three critical errors. First, it relies on distorted estimates of reserves. A second mistake is to pretend that production will remain constant. Third and most important, conventional wisdom erroneously assumes that the last bucket of oil can be pumped from the ground just as quickly as the barrels of oil gushing from wells today. In fact, the rate at which any well—or any country—can produce oil always rises to a maximum and then, when about half the oil is gone, begins falling gradually back to zero. From an economic perspective, when the world runs completely out of oil is thus not directly relevant: what matters is when production begins to taper off. Beyond that point, prices will rise unless demand declines commensurately.

Using several different techniques to estimate the current reserves of conventional oil and the amount still left to be discovered, we conclude that the decline will begin before 2010. We have spent most of our careers exploring for oil, studying reserve figures and estimating the amount of oil left to discover, first while employed at major oil companies and later as independent consultants. Over the years, we have come to appreciate that the relevant statistics are far more complicated than they first appear.

Consider, for example, three vital numbers needed to project future oil production. The first is the tally of how much oil has been extracted to date. The second is an estimate of reserves, the amount that companies can pump out of known oil fields before having to abandon them. Finally, one must have an educated guess at the quantity of conventional oil that remains to be discovered and exploited. Together they add up to ultimate recovery, the total number of barrels that will have been extracted when production ceases many decades from now. The obvious way to gather these numbers is to look them up in any of several publications. That approach works well enough for cumulative production statistics because companies meter the oil as it flows from their wells. The record of production is not perfect , but errors are relatively easy to spot and rectify. Most experts agree that the industry had removed just over 800 Gbo from the earth at the end of 1997.

Getting good estimates of reserves is much harder, however. Almost all the publicly available statistics are taken from surveys conducted by the *Oil and Gas Journal* and *World Oil*. Each year these two trade journals query oil firms and governments around the world. They then publish whatever production and reserve numbers they receive but are not able to verify them. The results, which are often accepted uncritically, contain systematic errors. For one, many of the reported figures are unrealistic. Estimating reserves is an inexact science to begin with, so petroleum engineers assign a probability to their assessments. For example, if, as geologists estimate, there is a 90 percent chance that the Oseberg field in Norway contains 700 million barrels of recoverable oil but only a 10 percent chance that it will yield 2,500 million more barrels, then the lower figure should be cited as the so-called P90 estimate (P90 for "probability 90 percent") and the higher as the P10 reserves.

In practice, companies and countries are often deliberately vague about the likelihood of the reserves they report, preferring instead to publicize whichever figure, within a P10 to P90 range, best suits them. Exaggerated estimates can, for instance, raise the price of an oil company's stock. The members of OPEC have faced an even greater temptation to inflate their reports because the higher their reserves, the more oil they are allowed to export. National companies, which have exclusive oil rights in the main OPEC countries, need not (and do not) release detailed statistics on each field that could be used to verify the country's total reserves. There is thus good reason to suspect that when, during the late 1980s, six of the 11 OPEC nations increased their reserve figures by colossal amounts, ranging from 42 to 197 percent, they did so only to boost their export quotas.

Another source of systematic error in the commonly accepted statistics is that the definition of reserves varies widely from region to region. In the U.S., the Securities and Exchange Commission allows companies to call reserves "proved" only if the oil lies near a producing well and there is "reasonable certainty" that it can be recovered profitably at current oil prices, using existing technology. So a proved reserve estimate in the U.S. is roughly equal to a P90 estimate. Regulators in most other countries do not enforce particular oil-reserve definitions. For many years, the former Soviet countries have routinely released wildly optimistic figures—essentially P10 reserves. Yet analysts have often misinterpreted these as estimates of "proved" reserves. *World Oil* reckoned reserves in the former Soviet Union amounted to 190 Gbo in 1996, whereas the *Oil and Gas Journal* put the number at 57 Gbo. This large discrepancy shows just how elastic these numbers can be.

Using only P90 estimates is not the answer, because adding what is 90 percent likely for each field, as is done in the U.S., does not in fact yield what is 90 percent likely for a country or the entire planet. On the contrary, summing many P90 reserve estimates always understates the amount of proved oil in a region. The only correct way to total up reserve numbers is to add the mean, or average, estimates of oil in each field. In practice, the median estimate, often called "proved and probable," or P50 reserves, is more widely used and is good enough. The P50 value is the number of barrels of oil that are as likely as not to come out of a well during its lifetime, assuming prices remain within a limited range. Errors in P50 estimates tend to cancel one another out. We were able to work around many of the problems plaguing estimates of conventional reserves by using a large body of statistics maintained by Petroconsultants in Geneva. This information, assembled over 40 years from myriad sources, covers some 18,000 oil fields worldwide. It, too, contains some dubious reports, but we did our best to correct these sporadic errors.

According to our calculations, the world had at the end of 1996 approximately 850 Gbo of conventional oil in P50 reserves—substantially less than the 1,019 Gbo reported in the *Oil and Gas Journal* and the 1,160 Gbo estimated by *World Oil*. The difference is actually greater than it appears because our value represents the amount most likely to come out of known oil fields, whereas the larger number is supposedly a cautious estimate of proved reserves. For the purposes of calculating when oil production will crest, even more critical than the size of the world's reserves is the size of ultimate recovery—all the cheap oil there is to be had. In order to estimate that, we need to know whether, and how fast, reserves are moving up or down. It is here that the official statistics become dangerously misleading. According to most accounts, world oil reserves have marched steadily upward over the past 20 years. Extending that apparent trend into the future, one could easily conclude, as the U.S. Energy Information Administration has, that oil production will continue to rise unhindered for decades to come, increasing almost two thirds by 2020.

Such growth is an illusion. About 80 percent of the oil produced today flows from fields that were found before 1973, and the great majority of them are declining. In the 1990s oil companies have discovered an average of seven Gbo a year; last year they drained more than three times as much. Yet official figures indicated that proved reserves did not fall by 16 Gbo, as one would expect rather they expanded by 11 Gbo. One reason is that several dozen governments opted not to report declines in their reserves, perhaps to enhance their political cachet and their ability to obtain loans. A more important cause of the expansion lies in revisions: oil companies replaced earlier estimates of the reserves left in many fields with higher numbers. For most purposes, such amendments are harmless, but they seriously distort forecasts extrapolated from published reports.

To judge accurately how much oil explorers will uncover in the future, one has to backdate every revision to the year in which the field was first discovered—not to the year in which a company or country corrected an earlier estimate. Doing so reveals that global discovery peaked in the early 1960s and has been falling steadily ever since. By extending the trend to zero, we can make a good guess at how much oil the industry will ultimately find. We have used other methods to estimate the ultimate recovery of conventional oil for each country and we calculate that the oil industry will be able to recover only about another 1,000 billion barrels of conventional oil. This number, though great, is little more than the 800 billion barrels that have already been extracted.

It is important to realize that spending more money on oil exploration will not change this situation. After the price of crude hit all-time highs in the early 1980s, explorers developed new technology for finding and recovering oil, and they scoured the world for new fields. They found few: the discovery rate continued its decline uninterrupted. There is only so much crude oil in the world, and the industry has found about 90 percent of it. Predicting when oil production will stop rising is relatively straightforward once one has a good estimate of how much oil there is left to produce. We simply apply a refinement of a technique first published in 1956 by M. King Hubbert. Hubbert observed that in any large region, unrestrained extraction of a finite resource rises along a bellshaped curve that peaks when about half the resource is gone. To demonstrate his theory, Hubbert fitted a bell curve to production statistics and projected that crude oil production in the lower 48 U.S. states would rise for 13 more years, then crest in 1969, give or take a year. He was right: production peaked in 1970 and has continued to follow Hubbert curves with only minor deviations. The flow of oil from several other regions, such as the former Soviet Union and the collection of all oil producers outside the Middle East, also follows Hubbert curves quite faithfully.

The global picture is more complicated, because the Middle East members of OPEC deliberately reined back their oil exports in the 1970s, while other nations continued producing at full capacity. Our analysis reveals that a number of the largest producers, including Norway and the U.K., will reach their peaks around the turn of the millennium unless they sharply curtail production. By 2002 or so the world will rely on Middle East nations, particularly five near the Persian Gulf (Iran, Iraq, Kuwait, Saudi Arabia and the United Arab Emirates), to fill in the gap between dwindling supply and growing demand. But once approximately 900 Gbo have been consumed, production must soon begin to fall. Barring a global recession, it seems most likely that world production of conventional oil will peak during the first decade of the 21st century.

Perhaps surprisingly, that prediction does not shift much even if our estimates are a few hundred billion barrels high or low. Craig Bond Hatfield of the University of Toledo, for example, has conducted his own analysis based on a 1991 estimate by the U.S. Geological Survey of 1,550 Gbo remaining—55 percent higher than our figure. Yet he similarly concludes that the world will hit maximum oil production within the next 15 years. John D. Edwards of the University of Colorado published last August one of the most optimistic recent estimates of oil remaining: 2,036 Gbo. (Edwards concedes that the industry has only a 5 percent chance of attaining that very high goal.) Even so, his calculations suggest that conventional oil will top out in 2020. Factors other than major economic changes could speed or delay the point at which oil production begins to decline. Three in particular have often led economists and academic geologists to dismiss concerns about future oil production with naive optimism.

First, some argue, huge deposits of oil may lie undetected in far-off corners of the globe. In fact, that is very unlikely. Exploration has pushed the frontiers back so far that only extremely deep water and polar regions remain to be fully tested, and even their prospects are now reasonably well understood. Theoretical advances in geochemistry and geophysics have made it possible to map productive and prospective fields with impressive accuracy.

As a result, large tracts can be condemned as barren. Much of the deepwater realm, for example, has been shown to be absolutely nonprospective for geologic reasons. What about the much touted Caspian Sea deposits? Our models project that oil production from that region will grow until around 2010. We agree with analysts at the USGS World Oil Assessment program and elsewhere who rank the total resources there as roughly equivalent to those of the North Sea that is, perhaps 50 Gbo but certainly not several hundreds of billions as sometimes reported in the media.

A second common rejoinder is that new technologies have steadily increased the fraction of oil that can be recovered from fields in a basin—the so-called recovery factor. In the 1960s oil companies assumed as a rule of thumb that only 30 percent of the oil in a field was typically recoverable; now they bank on an average of 40 or 50 percent. That progress will continue and will extend global reserves for many years to come, the argument runs.

Of course, advanced technologies will buy a bit more time before production starts to fall. But most of the apparent improvement in recovery factors is an artifact of reporting. As oil fields grow old, their owners often deploy newer technology to slow their decline. The falloff also allows engineers to gauge the size of the field more accurately and to correct previous underestimation—in particular P90 estimates that by definition were 90 percent likely to be exceeded. Another reason not to pin too much hope on better recovery is that oil companies routinely count on technological progress when they compute their reserve estimates. In truth, advanced technologies can offer little help in draining the largest basins of oil, those onshore in the Middle East where the oil needs no assistance to gush from the ground. Last, economists like to point out that the world contains enormous caches of unconventional oil that can substitute for crude oil as soon as the price rises high enough to make them profitable. There is no question that the resources are ample: the Orinoco oil belt in Venezuela has been assessed to contain a staggering 1.2 trillion barrels of the sludge known as heavy oil.

Tar sands and shale deposits in Canada and the former Soviet Union may contain the equivalent of more than 300 billion barrels of oil. Theoretically, these unconventional oil reserves could quench the world's thirst for liquid fuels as conventional oil passes its prime. But the industry will be hard-pressed for the time and money needed to ramp up production of unconventional oil quickly enough Such substitutes for crude oil might also exact a high environmental price. Tar sands typically emerge from strip mines. Extracting oil from these sands and shales creates air pollution. The Orinoco sludge contains heavy metals and sulfur that must be removed. So governments may restrict these industries from growing as fast as they could. In view of these potential obstacles, our skeptical estimate is that only 700 Gbo will be produced from unconventional reserves over the next 60 years.

Meanwhile global demand for oil is currently rising at more than 2 percent a year. Since 1985, energy use is up about 30 percent in Latin America, 40 percent in Africa and 50 percent in Asia. The Energy Information Administration forecasts that worldwide demand for oil will increase 60 percent (to about 40 Gbo a year) by 2020.

The switch from growth to decline in oil production will thus almost certainly create economic and political tension. Unless alternatives to crude oil quickly prove themselves, the market share of the OPEC states in the Middle East will rise rapidly. Within two years, these nations' share of the global oil business will pass 30 percent, nearing the level reached during the oil-price shocks of the 1970s. By 2010 their share will quite probably hit 50 percent.

Reliance Petroleum

Reliance Petroleum Limited (BSE: 532743) was set up by Reliance Industries Limited (RIL), one of India's largest private sector companies based in Mumbai. Currently, RPL is subsidiary of RIL, and has interests in the downstream oil business. RPL also benefits from a strategic alliance with Chevron India Holdings Pte Limited, Singapore, a wholly owned subsidiary of Chevron Corporation USA (Chevron), which currently holds a 5% equity stake in the Company.

Jamnagar Refinery

Refining activities of Reliance Industries Limited are carried out at the Jamnagar refinery complex with refining capacity of 27 million tonnes per annum (540,000 barrels per day). The refinery is able to process a wide variety of crudes- from very light to very heavy (from 18 to 45 degree API) and from sweet to very sour (with sulphur content from 0 to 4.5%). RPL commenced its crude processing on 25 December 2008. The secondary processing units are now under synchronization and commissioning. The entire refinery complex is expected to attain full capacity shortly.

With an annual crude processing capacity of 580,000 barrels (92,000 m^3) per stream day (BPSD), RPL will be the sixth largest refinery in the world. It will have a complexity of 14.0, using the Nelson Complexity Index, ranking it amongst the highest in the sector. The polypropylene plant will have a capacity to produce 0.9 million metric tonnes per annum. The refinery project is being implemented at a capital cost of Rs 270,000 million being funded through a mix of equity and debt. This represents a capital cost of less than US $10,000 per barrel per day and compares very favourably with the average capital cost of new refineries announced in recent years. The International Energy Agency (IEA) estimates the average capital cost of new refinery in the OECD nations to be in the region of US $15,000 to 20,000 per barrel per day. The low capital cost of RPL becomes even more attractive when adjusted for high complexity of the refinery.

Expansion

Reliance petroleum is in the process of purchasing the downstream business of Mobil in Australia. This will give them two more refineries and 800 service stations in Australia.

Chapter 4

Management and Evaluation of Oil Shale Reserves

Price of Petroleum

The price of petroleum as quoted in news generally refers to the spot price per barrel (159 liters) of either WTI/light crude as traded on the New York Mercantile Exchange (NYMEX) for delivery at Cushing, Oklahoma, or of Brent as traded on the Intercontinental Exchange (ICE, into which the International Petroleum Exchange has been incorporated) for delivery at Sullom Voe.

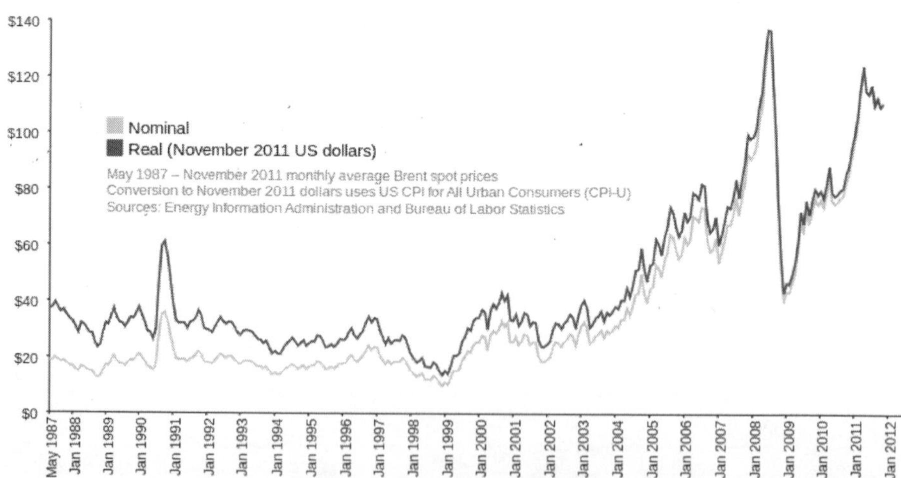

Figure: *Brent barrel petroleum spot prices since May 1987. Due to exchange rate fluctuations, the real price line is only relevant to the United States and countries with a currency tied to the U.S. dollar at a constant rate throughout the period.*

The price of a barrel of oil is highly dependent on both its grade, determined by factors such as its specific gravity or API and its sulphur content, and its location. Other important benchmarks include Dubai, Tapis, and the OPEC basket. The Energy Information Administration (EIA) uses the imported refiner acquisition cost, the weighted average cost of all oil imported into the US, as its "world oil price".

The demand for oil is highly dependent on global macroeconomic conditions. According to the International Energy Agency, high oil prices generally have a large negative impact on the global economic growth. The Organization of the Petroleum Exporting Countries (OPEC) was formed in 1960 to try and counter the oil companies cartel, which had been controlling posted prices since the so-called 1927 Red Line Agreement and 1928 Achnacarry Agreement, and had achieved a high level of price stability until 1972.

Figure: *Weekly reports on crude oil inventories or total stockpiles in storage facilities like these tanks have a strong bearing on oil prices*

The price of oil underwent a significant decrease after the record peak of US$145 it reached in July 2008. On December 23, 2008, WTI crude oil spot price fell to US$30.28 a barrel, the lowest since the financial crisis of 2007–2010 began, and traded at between US$35 a barrel and US$82 a barrel in 2009. On 31 January 2011, the Brent price hit $100 a barrel for the first time since October 2008, on concerns about the political unrest in Egypt.

Recent Price History

A recent low point was reached in January 1999 of $17 (all prices are in US$ per barrel), after increased oil production from Iraq coincided with the Asian Financial Crisis, which reduced demand. Prices then increased rapidly, more than doubling by September 2000 to $35, then fell until the end of 2001 before steadily increasing, reaching $40–50 by September 2004. In October 2004, light crude futures contracts on the NYMEX for November delivery exceeded $53 and for December delivery exceeded $55. Crude oil prices surged to a record high above $60 in June 2005, sustaining a rally built on strong demand for gasoline and diesel and on concerns about refiners' ability to keep up. This trend continued into early August 2005, as NYMEX crude oil futures contracts surged past $65 as consumers kept up the demand for gasoline despite its high price.

Crude oil futures peaked at a close of over $77 in July 2006, and in December 2006 at about $63. That is just about where they began the year 2006. In September 2007, US crude (WTI) crossed $80. Multiple factors caused this high price. OPEC announced an output increase lower than expected. US stocks fell lower than experts predicted, changes in federal oil policies, and six pipelines were attacked by a leftist group in Mexico. In October 2007 US light crude rose above $90 for the first time, due to a combination of tensions in eastern Turkey and the reducing strength of the US dollar.

On January 2, 2008, a single trade was made at $100, but the price did not stay above $100 until late February.

Oil broke through $110 on March 12, 2008, $125 on May 9, 2008, $130 on May 21, 2008, $135 on May 22, 2008, $140 on June 26, 2008 and $145 on July 3, 2008. On July 11, 2008, oil prices rose to a new record of $147.27 following concern over recent Iranian missile tests.

On July 14, 2008, President George W. Bush lifted the executive order removing the ban on offshore drilling that had been enacted by President George H. W. Bush in 1990 and renewed by President William J. Clinton. This action was viewed initially as only symbolic or political since the 1982 Congressional moratorium on offshore drilling was unaffected by President Bush's action. Oil prices declined by more than $20 over the next two weeks, settling around $125 a barrel on July 24, 2008. A strong contributor to this price decline was the drop in demand for oil in the US. Miles driven there in a month were down in March–May 2008 compared to 2007, with the 4% decline in May being the largest drop in history. Oil further dropped down to its lowest price in

3 months, at around $112 a barrel, on August 11, 2008, and on September 15, oil price fell below $100 for the first time in seven months. On September 24, 2008, Speaker of the House, Nancy Pelosi allowed the 26-year moratorium to expire. On October 11, oil fell as much as $8.97, or 10.17% to $77.70 per barrel as global equities slid.

Oil traded below $70 on October 16, 2008. On December 21, 2008, oil was trading at $33.87 a barrel, less than one fourth of the peak price reached four months earlier. Prices initially continued falling in 2009, descending by mid-February to below $34, but prices then steadily rose over the next two years, hitting $113.93/barrel in April 2011.

Benchmark Pricing

After the collapse of the OPEC-administered pricing system in 1985, and a short lived experiment with netback pricing, oil-exporting countries adopted a market-linked pricing mechanism. First adopted by PEMEX in 1986, market-linked pricing received wide acceptance and by 1988 became and still is the main method for pricing crude oil in international trade. The current reference, or pricing markers, are Brent, WTI, and Dubai/Oman.

Market Listings

Oil is marketed among other products in commodities markets. See above for details. Widely traded oil futures, and related natural gas futures, include:

- Petroleum
  - Nymex Crude Future
  - Dated Brent Spot
  - WTI Cushing Spot
  - Nymex Heating Oil Future
  - Nymex RBOB Gasoline Future
- Natural gas
  - Nymex Henry Hub Future
  - Henry Hub Spot
  - New York City Gate Spot.

Most of the above oil futures have delivery dates in all 12 months of the year.

Speculation

The surge in oil prices in the past several years has led some experts to argue that at least some of the rise is due to speculation in the futures markets. This has led to an investigation, which reached an interim conclusion that speculation was largely not responsible for the rise. Economist James K. Galbraith believes that much of the rise is due to the "Enron loophole" drafted in a rider by former Texas senator Phil Gramm, which allowed energy futures to avoid Commodity Futures Trading Commission oversight.

Galbraith cites Masters, a hedge fund manager, who observed that index speculation tied to commodities by pension funds and other investment vehicles rose from $13 billion in 2003 to $250 billion in 2008. Galbraith observed that with Goldman Sachs predicting a rise in the price to $200 and Gazprom $250, suppliers may react to the rise by restricting supply until they can sell their product at a higher price. In 2009, Seismic Micro-Technology conducted a survey of geophysicists and geologists about the future of crude oil. Of the survey participants 80 percent predicted the price for a barrel of oil will rise to be somewhere between $50 and $100 per barrel by June 2010. Another 50 percent saying it will rise even further to $100 to $150 a barrel in the next five years.

Oil prices could go to $200- $300 a barrel if the world's top crude exporter Saudi Arabia is hit by serious political unrest, according to former Saudi oil minister Sheikh Yamani. Yamani has said that underlying discontent remained unresolved in Saudi Arabia. "If something happens in Saudi Arabia it will go to $200 to $300. I don't expect this for the time being, but who would have expected Tunisia?" Yamani told Reuters on the sidelines of a conference of the Centre for Global Energy Studies (CGES) which he chaired on April 5th 2011.

Futures Investigation

The U.S. Commodity Futures Trading Commission (CFTC) announced "Multiple Energy Market Initiatives" on May 29, 2008. Part 1 is "Expanded International Surveillance Information for Crude Oil Trading." The CFTC announcement stated it has joined with the United Kingdom Financial Services Authority and ICE Futures Europe in order to expand surveillance and information sharing of various futures contracts. This announcement has received wide coverage in the financial press, with speculation about oil futures price manipulation. The interim report by the Interagency Task Force, released in July, found that speculation had not caused significant changes in oil prices and that fundamental supply and demand factors provide the best explanation for the crude oil price increases. The report found that the primary reason for the price increases was that the world economy had expanded at its fastest pace in decades, resulting in substantial increases in the demand for oil, while the oil production grew sluggishly, compounded by production shortfalls in oil-exporting countries.

The report stated that as a result of the imbalance and low price elasticity, very large price increases occurred as the market attempted to balance scarce supply against growing demand, particularly in the last three years. The report forecast that this imbalance would persist in the future, leading to continued upward pressure on oil prices, and that large or rapid movements in oil prices are likely to occur even in the absence of activity by speculators. The task force continues to analyze commodity markets and intends to issue further findings later in the year.

Definition of Reserves

Estimating shale oil reserves is complicated by several factors. Firstly, the amount of kerogen contained in oil shale deposits varies considerably. Secondly, some nations report as reserves the total amount of kerogen in place, including all kerogen regardless of technical or economic constraints; these estimates do not consider the amount of kerogen that may be extracted from identified and assayed oil shale rock using available technology and under given economic conditions. By most definitions, "reserves" refers only to the amount of resource which is technically exploitable and economically feasible under current economic conditions. The term "resources", on the other hand, may refer to all deposits containing kerogen. Thirdly, shale oil extraction technologies are still developing, so the amount of recoverable kerogen can only be estimated.

There are a wide variety of extraction methods, which yield significantly different quantities of useful oil. As a result, the estimated amounts of resources and reserves display wide variance. The kerogen content of oil shale formations differs widely, and the economic feasibility of its extraction is highly dependent on international and local costs of oil. Several methods are used to determine the quantity and quality of the products extracted from shale oil. At their best, these methods give an approximate value to its energy potential. One standard method is the Fischer Assay, which yields a heating value, that is, a measure of caloric output. This is generally considered a good overall measure of usefulness. The Fischer Assay has been modified, standardized, and adapted by the American Petroleum Institute. It does not, however, indicate how much oil could be extracted from the sample. Some processing methods yield considerably more useful product than the Fischer Assay would indicate. The Tosco II method yields over 100% more oil, and the Hytort process yields between 300% to 400% more oil.

***Table** : Largest oil shale deposits (over 1 billion metric tons*

Deposit	*Country*	*Period*	*In-place shale oil resources (million barrels)*	*In-place oil shale resources (million metric tons)*
Green River Formation	USA	Tertiary	1,466,000	213,000
Phosphoria Formation	USA	Permian	250,000	35,775
Eastern Devonian	USA	Devonian	189,000	27,000
Heath Formation	USA	Early Carboniferous	180,000	25,578
Olenyok Basin	Russia	Cambrian	167,715	24,000
Congo	Democratic Republic of Congo	?	100,000	14,310
Irati Formation	Brazil	Permian	80,000	11,448
Sicily	Italy	?	63,000	9,015
Tarfaya	Morocco	Cretaceous	42,145	6,448
Volga Basin	Russia	?	31,447	4,500
St. Petersburg, Baltic Oil Shale Basin	Russia	Ordovician	25,157	3,600
Vychegodsk Basin	Russia	Jurassic	19,580	2,800
Wadi Maghar	Jordan	Cretaceous	14,009	2,149
Dictyonema shale	Estonia	Ordovician	12,386	1,900
Timahdit	Morocco	Cretaceous	11,236	1,719
Collingwood Shale	Canada	Ordovician	12,300	1,717
Italy	Italy	Triassic	10,000	1,431

Geographical Allocation

There is no comprehensive overview of oil shales geographical allocation around the world. Around 600 known oil shale deposits are diversely spread throughout the earth, and are found on every continent with the possible exception of Antarctica, which has not yet been explored for oil shale. Oil shale resources can be concentrated in a large confined deposit such as the Green River formations, which were formed by a large inland lake. These can be many meters thick but limited by the size of the original lake. They may also resemble the deposits found along the eastern American seaboard, which were the product of a shallow sea, in that they may be quite thin but laterally expansive, covering thousands of square kilometers.

The table below reports reserves by estimated amount of shale oil. Shale oil refers to synthetic oil obtained by heating organic material (kerogen) contained in oil shale to a temperature which will separate it into oil, combustible gas, and the residual carbon that remains in the spent shale. All figures are presented in barrels and metric tons.

Shale oil: resources and production at end-2005 by regions and countries with resources over 10 billion barrels (1.6 km^3) of in-place shale oil.

Region	***In-place shale oil resources (million barrels)***	***In-place oil shale oil resources (million barrels)***	***Production in 2002 (thousand metric tons (oil))***
Africa	159,243	23,317	-
Democratic Republic of the Congo	100,000	14,310	-
Morocco	53,381	8,187	-
Asia	45,894	6,562	180
China	16,000	2,290	180
Europe	368,156	52,845	345
Russia	247,883	35,470	-
Italy	73,000	10,446	-
Estonia	16,286	2,494	345
Middle East	38,172	5,792	-
Jordan	34,172	5,242	-
North America	2,100,469	303,758	-
United States	2,085,228	301,566	-
Canada	15,241	2,192	-
Oceania	31,748	4,534	-
Australia	31,729	4,531	-
South America	82,421	11,794	157
Brazil	82,000	11,734	159
World total	2,826,103	408,602	684

Africa

Major oil shale deposits are located in the Democratic Republic of Congo (equal to 14.31 billion metric tons of shale oil) and Morocco (12.3 billion metric tons or 8.16 billion metric tons of shale oil). Deposits in Congo are not properly explored yet. In Morocco, oil shale deposits have been identified at ten localities with the largest deposits in Tarfaya and Timahdite.

Although reserves in Tarfaya and Timahdit are well explored, the commercial exploitation has not started yet and only a limited program of laboratory and pilot-plant research has been undertaken. There are also oil shale reserves in Egypt, South Africa, Madagascar, and Nigeria. The main deposits of Egypt are located in Safaga-Al-Qusair and Abu Tartour areas.

Asia

Major oil shale deposits are located in China, which has an estimated total of 32 billion metric tons, of which 4.4 billion metric tons are technically exploitable and economically feasible; Thailand (18.7 billion metric tons), Kazakhstan (several deposits; major deposit at Kenderlyk Field with 4 billion metric tons), and Turkey (2.2 billion metric tons). Smaller oil shale reserves have also been found in Assam (India), Pakistan, Uzbekistan, Turkmenistan, Myanmar, Armenia, and Mongolia. The principal Chinese oil shale deposits and production lie in Fushun and Liaoning; others are located in Maoming in Guangdong, Huadian in Jilin, Heilongjiang, and Shandong. In 2002, China produced more than 90,000 metric tons of shale oil. Thailand's oil shale deposits are near Mae Sot, Tak Province, and at Li, Lamphun Province. Deposits in Turkey are found mainly in middle and western Anatolia.

Professor Alan R. Carroll of University of Wisconsin–Madison estimates that Upper Permian lacustrine oil shale deposits of northwest China, absent from previous global oil shale assessments, are comparable to the Green River Formation.

Europe

The biggest oil shale reserves in Europe are located in Russia (equal to 35.47 billion metric tons of shale oil). Major deposits are located in the Volga-Petchyorsk province and in the Baltic Oil Shale Basin. Other major oil shale deposits in Europe are located in Italy (10.45 billion metric tons of shale oil), Estonia (2.49 billion metric tons of shale oil), France (1 billion metric tons of shale oil), Belarus (1 billion metric tons of shale oil), Sweden (875 million metric tons of shale oil), Ukraine (600 million metric tons of shale oil) and the United Kingdom (500 million metric tons of shale oil). There are oil shale reserves also in Germany, Luxembourg, Spain, Bulgaria, Hungary, Poland, Serbia, Austria, Albania, and Romania.

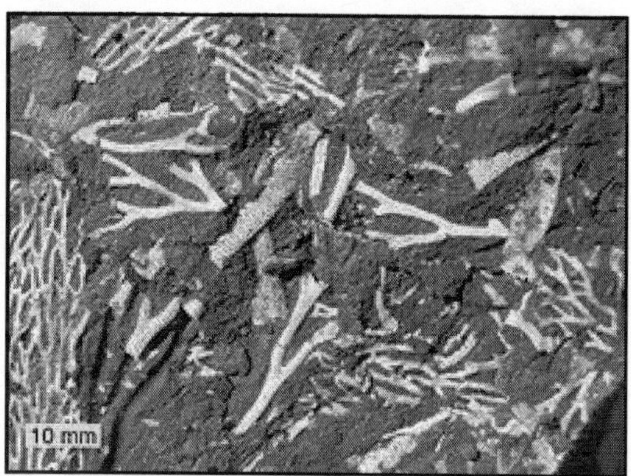

***Figure** : Outcrop of Ordovician kukersite oil shale, northern Estonia*

Middle East

Significant oil shale deposits are located in Jordan (5.242 billion metric tons of shale oil or 65 billion metric tons of oil shale) and Israel (550 million metric tons of shale oil or 6.5 billion metric tons of oil shale). Jordanian oil shales are high quality, comparable to western US oil shale, although their sulfur content is high. The best-explored deposits are El Lajjun, Sultani, and the Juref ed Darawishare located in west-central Jordan, while the Yarmouk deposit, close to its northern border, extends into Syria. Most of Israel's deposits are located in the Rotem Basin region of the northern Negev desert near the Dead Sea. Israeli oil shale is relatively low in heating value and oil yield.

North America

At 301 billion metric tons, the oil shale deposits in the United States are easily the largest in the world. There are two major deposits: the eastern US deposits, in Devonian-Mississippian shales, cover 250,000 square miles (650,000 km^2); the western US deposits of the Green River Formation in Colorado, Wyoming, and Utah, are among the richest oil shale deposits in the world. In Canada 19 deposits have been identified. The best-examined deposits are in Nova Scotia and New Brunswick.

Oceania

Australia's oil shale resource is estimated at about 58 billion metric tons or 4.531 billion metric tons of shale oil, of which about 24 billion barrels (3.8 billion cubic metres) is recoverable. The deposits are located in the eastern and southern states with the biggest potential in the eastern Queensland deposits. Oil shale has also been found in New Zealand.

South America

Brazil has the world's second-largest known oil shale resources (the Irati shale and lacustrine deposits) and is currently the world's second largest shale oil producer, after Estonia. Oil shale resources occur in São Mateus do Sul, Paraná, and in Vale do Paraiba. Brazil has developed the world's largest surface oil shale pyrolysis retort at Petrosix, with a 11-meter (36 ft)-diameter vertical shaft. Brazilian production in 1999 was about 200,000 metric tons. Small resources are also found in Argentina, Chile, Paraguay, Peru, Uruguay, and Venezuela.

OPEC

OPEC (Organization of Petroleum Exporting Countries) is an intergovernmental organization of twelve developing countries made up of Algeria, Angola, Ecuador, Iran, Iraq, Kuwait, Libya, Nigeria, Qatar, Saudi Arabia, the United Arab Emirates, and Venezuela. OPEC has maintained its headquarters in Vienna since 1965, and hosts regular meetings among the oil ministers of its Member Countries. Indonesia withdrew in 2008 after it became a net importer of oil, but stated it would likely return if it became a net exporter again.

According to its statutes, one of the principal goals is the determination of the best means for safeguarding the organization's interests, individually and collectively. It also pursues ways and means of ensuring the stabilization of prices in international oil markets with a view to eliminating harmful and unnecessary fluctuations; giving due regard at all times to the interests of the producing nations and to the necessity of securing a steady income to the producing countries; an efficient and regular supply of petroleum to consuming nations, and a fair return on their capital to those investing in the petroleum industry.

OPEC's influence on the market has been widely criticized, since it became effective in determining production and prices. Arab members of OPEC alarmed the developed world when they used the "oil weapon" during the Yom Kippur War by implementing oil embargoes and initiating the 1973 oil crisis. Although largely political explanations for the timing and extent of the OPEC price increases are also valid, from OPEC's point of view, these changes were triggered largely by previous unilateral changes in the world financial system and the ensuing period of high inflation in both the developed and developing world. This explanation encompasses OPEC actions both before and after the outbreak of hostilities in October 1973, and concludes that "OPEC countries were only 'staying even' by dramatically raising the dollar price of oil."

OPEC's ability to control the price of oil has diminished somewhat since then, due to the subsequent discovery and development of large oil reserves in Alaska, the North Sea, Canada, the Gulf of Mexico, the opening up of Russia, and market modernization. As of November 2010, OPEC members collectively hold 79% of world crude oil reserves and 44% of the world's crude oil production, affording them considerable control over the global market. The next largest group of producers, members of the OECD and the Post-Soviet states produced only 23.8% and 14.8%, respectively, of the world's total oil production. As early as 2003, concerns that OPEC members had little excess pumping capacity sparked speculation that their influence on crude oil prices would begin to slip.

History

Venezuela and Iran were the first countries to move towards the establishment of OPEC in the 1960s by approaching Iraq, Kuwait and Saudi Arabia in 1949, suggesting that they exchange views and explore avenues for regular and closer communication among petroleum-producing nations. The founding members are Iran, Iraq, Kuwait, Saudi Arabia, and Venezuela. Later members include Algeria, Ecuador, Gabon, Indonesia, Libya, Qatar, Nigeria, and the United Arab Emirates.

In 10–14 September 1960, at the initiative of the Venezuelan Energy and Mines minister Juan Pablo Pérez Alfonzo and the Saudi Arabian Energy and Mines minister Abdullah al-Tariki, the governments of Iraq, Iran, Kuwait, Saudi Arabia and Venezuela met in Baghdad to discuss ways to increase the price of the crude oil produced by their respective countries.

OPEC was founded to unify and coordinate members' petroleum policies. Original OPEC members include Iran, Iraq, Kuwait, Saudi Arabia, and Venezuela. Between 1960 and 1975, the organization expanded to include Qatar (1961), Indonesia (1962), Libya (1962), the United Arab Emirates (1967), Algeria (1969), and Nigeria (1971). Ecuador and Gabon were early members of OPEC, but Ecuador withdrew on December 31, 1992 because it was unwilling or unable to pay a $2 million membership fee and felt that it needed to produce more oil than it was allowed to under the OPEC quota, although it rejoined in October 2007.

Similar concerns prompted Gabon to suspend membership in January 1995. Angola joined on the first day of 2007. Norway and Russia have attended OPEC meetings as observers. Indicating that OPEC is not averse to further expansion, Mohammed Barkindo, OPEC's Secretary General, recently asked Sudan to join. Iraq remains a member of OPEC, but Iraqi production has not been a part of any OPEC quota agreements since March 1998.

In May 2008, Indonesia announced that it would leave OPEC when its membership expired at the end of that year, having become a net importer of oil and being unable to meet its production quota. A statement released by OPEC on 10 September 2008 confirmed Indonesia's withdrawal, noting that it "regretfully accepted the wish of Indonesia to suspend its full Membership in the Organization and recorded its hope that the Country would be in a position to rejoin the Organization in the not too distant future." Indonesia is still exporting light, sweet crude oil and importing heavier, more sour crude oil to take advantage of price differentials (import is greater than export) due to Air pollution in Indonesia still being low as compared to China or The United States.

1973 Oil Embargo

The persistence of the Arab-Israeli conflict finally triggered a response that transformed OPEC into a formidable political force. After the Six Day War of 1967, the Arab members of OPEC formed a separate, overlapping group, the Organization of Arab Petroleum Exporting Countries, for the purpose of centering policy and exerting pressure on the West over its support of Israel. Egypt and Syria, though not major oil-exporting countries, joined the latter grouping to help articulate its objectives. Later, the Yom Kippur War of 1973 galvanized Arab opinion. Furious at the emergency re-supply effort that had enabled Israel to withstand Egyptian and Syrian forces, the Arab world imposed the 1973 oil embargo against the United States and Western Europe, while non-Arab OPEC members did not..

1975 Hostage Incident

On 21 December 1975 Ahmed Zaki Yamani and the other oil ministers of the members of OPEC were taken hostage by a six-person team led by terrorist Carlos the Jackal (which included Gabriele Krocher-Tiedemann and Hans-Joachim Klein), in Vienna, Austria, where the ministers were attending a meeting at the OPEC headquarters. Carlos planned to take over the conference by force and kidnap all eleven oil ministers in attendance and hold them for ransom, with the exception of Ahmed Zaki Yamani and Iran's Jamshid Amuzegar, who were to be executed.

Carlos led his six-person team past two police officers in the building's lobby and up to the first floor, where a police officer, an Iraqi plain clothes security guard and a young Libyan economist were shot dead.

As Carlos entered the conference room and fired shots in the ceiling, the delegates ducked under the table. The terrorists searched for Ahmed Zaki Yamani and then divided the sixty-three hostages into groups. Delegates of friendly countries were moved toward the door, 'neutrals' were placed in the centre of the room and the 'enemies' were placed along the back wall, next to a stack of explosives. This last group included those from Saudi Arabia, Iran, Qatar and the UAE. Carlos demanded a bus to be provided to take his group and the hostages to the airport, where a DC-9 airplane and crew would be waiting. In the meantime, Carlos briefed Ahmed Zaki Yamani on his plan to eventually fly to Aden, where Yamani and the Iranian minister would be killed.

The bus was provided the following morning at 6.40 as requested and 42 hostages were boarded and taken to the airport. The group was airborne just after 9.00 and explosives placed under Yamani's seat. The plane first stopped in Algiers, where Carlos left the plane to meet with the Algierian Foreign minister. All 30 non-Arab hostages were released, excluding Amuzegar.

The refueled plane left for Tripoli where there was trouble in acquiring another plane as had been planned. Carlos decided to instead return to Algiers and change to a Boeing 707, a plane large enough to fly to Baghdad nonstop. Ten more hostages were released before leaving.

With only 10 hostages remaining, the Boeing 707 left for Algiers and arrived at 3.40 a.m. After leaving the plane to meet with the Algerians, Carlos talked with his colleagues in the front cabin of the plane and then told Yamani and Amouzegar that they would be released at mid-day. Carlos was then called from the plane a second time and returned after two hours.

At this second meeting it is believed that Carlos held a phone conversation with Algerian President Houari Boumédienne who informed Carlos that the oil ministers' deaths would result in an attack on the plane. Yamani's biography suggests that the Algerians had used a covert listening device on the front of the aircraft to overhear the earlier conversation between the terrorists, and found that Carlos had in fact still planned to murder the two oil ministers. Boumédienne must also have offered Carlos asylum at this time and possibly financial compensation for failing to complete his assignment.

On returning to the plane Carlos stood before Yamani and Amuzegar and expressed his regret at not being able to murder them. He then told the hostages that he and his comrades would leave the plane after which they would all be free. After waiting for the terrorists to leave, Yamani and the other nine hostages followed and were taken to the airport by Algerian Foreign Minister Abdelaziz Bouteflika. The terrorists were present in the next lounge and Khalid, the Palestinian, asked to speak to Yamani. As his hand reached for his coat, Khalid was surrounded by guards and a gun was found concealed in a holster.

Some time after the attack it was revealed by Carlos' accomplices that the operation was commanded by Wadi Haddad, a Palestinian terrorist and founder of the Popular Front for the Liberation of Palestine. It was also claimed that the idea and funding came from an Arab president, widely thought to be Muammar al-Gaddafi.

In the years following the OPEC raid, Bassam Abu Sharif and Klein claimed that Carlos had received a large sum of money in exchange for the safe release of the Arab hostages and had kept it for his personal use. There is still some uncertainty regarding the amount that changed hands but it is believed to be between US$20 million and US$50 million. The source of the money is also uncertain, but, according to Klein, it was from "an Arab president." Carlos later told his lawyers that the money was paid by the Saudis on behalf of the Iranians and was, "diverted en route and lost by the Revolution".

The 1980s Oil Gluts

After 1980, oil prices began a six-year decline that culminated with a 46 percent price drop in 1986. This was due to reduced demand and over-production that produced a glut on the world market. Around this period, Iraq also increased its oil production to help pay for the Iran-Iraq War. Overall OPEC lost its unity and thus its net oil export revenues fell in the 1980s.

Responding to War and Low Prices

Leading up to the 1990-91 Gulf War, Iraqi President Saddam Hussein advocated that OPEC push world oil prices up, thereby helping Iraq, and other member states, service debts. But the division of OPEC countries occasioned by the Iraq-Iran War and the Iraqi invasion of

Kuwait marked a low point in the cohesion of OPEC. Once supply disruption fears that accompanied these conflicts dissipated, oil prices began to slide dramatically.

After oil prices slumped at around $15 a barrel in the late 1990s, concerted diplomacy, sometimes attributed to Venezuela's president Hugo Chávez, achieved a coordinated scaling back of oil production beginning in 1998. In 2000, Chávez hosted the first summit of heads of state of OPEC in 25 years. The next year, however, the September 11, 2001 attacks against the United States, the following invasion of Afghanistan, and 2003 invasion of Iraq and subsequent occupation prompted a surge in oil prices to levels far higher than those targeted by OPEC during the preceding period.

Indonesia withdrew from OPEC to protect its oil supply interests. On November 19, 2007, global oil prices reacted strongly as OPEC members spoke openly about potentially converting their cash reserves to the euro and away from the US dollar.

Production Disputes

The economic needs of the OPEC member states often affects the internal politics behind OPEC production quotas.

Various members have pushed for reductions in production quotas to increase the price of oil and thus their own revenues. These demands conflict with Saudi Arabia's stated long-term strategy of being a partner with the world's economic powers to ensure a steady flow of oil that would support economic expansion.

Part of the basis for this policy is the Saudi concern that expensive oil or oil of uncertain supply will drive developed nations to conserve and develop alternative fuels. To this point, former Saudi Oil Minister Sheikh Yamani famously said in 1973: "The stone age didn't end because we ran out of stones."

One such production dispute occurred on September 10, 2008, when the Saudis reportedly walked out of OPEC negotiating session where the organization voted to reduce production.

Although Saudi Arabian OPEC delegates officially endorsed the new quotas, they stated anonymously that they would not observe them. The New York Times quoted one such anonymous OPEC delegate as saying "Saudi Arabia will meet the market's demand. We will see what the market requires and we will not leave a customer without oil. The policy has not changed."

OPEC Aid

OPEC aid dates from well before the 1973/74 oil price explosion. Kuwait has operated a programme since 1961 (through the Kuwait Fund for Arab Economic Development). The OPEC fund became a fully fledged permanent international development agency in May 1980.

Membership

Former members

Country	Region	Joined OPEC	Left OPEC
Gabon	Africa	1975	1994
Indonesia	South East Asia	1962	2009

Current members

OPEC has twelve member countries: six in the Middle East, four in Africa, and two in South America.

Country	Region	Joined OPEC	Population (July 2008)	Area (km^2)
Algeria	Africa	1969	33,779,668	2,381,740
Angola	Africa	2007	12,531,357	1,246,700
Ecuador	South America	2007	13,927,650	283,560
Iran	Middle East	1960	75,875,224	1,648,000
Iraq	Middle East	1960	28,221,180	437,072
Kuwait	Middle East	1960	2,596,799	17,820
Libya	Africa	1962	6,173,579	1,759,540
Nigeria	Africa	1971	158,259,000	923,768
Qatar	Middle East	1961	824,789	11,437
Saudi Arabia	Middle East	1960	28,146,656	2,149,690
United Arab Emirates	Middle East	1967	4,621,399	83,600
Venezuela	South America	1960	26,414,816	912,050
Total			369,368,429	11,854,977 km^2

1. Ecuador initially joined in 1973, left in 1992, and rejoined in 2007.

2. One of five founder members that attended the first OPEC conference, in September 1960.

The United States was a de facto member during its formal occupation of Iraq via the Coalition Provisional Authority.

Indonesia left OPEC in 2008 because it ceased to be a net exporter of oil. It could not fulfill the demand of its own country's needs, as growth in demand outstripped output. The situation was made worse because of weak legal certainty and corruption that deterred foreign investors from investing in new reserves in Indonesia. In recent times, the government has increased financial incentives for foreign firms to invest in exploration and extraction but has found itself forced to import more supplies from the likes of Iran, Saudi Arabia and Kuwait.

Indonesia's departure from OPEC will not likely affect the amount of oil it produces or imports. The country's growing dependence on imports is proving increasingly expensive as global prices soar.

Economics

OPEC is a swing producer and its decisions have had considerable influence on international oil prices. For example, in the 1973 energy crisis OPEC refused to ship oil to western countries that had supported Israel in the Yom Kippur War, which Israel had fought against Egypt and Syria.

This refusal caused a fourfold increase in the price of oil, which lasted five months, starting on October 17, 1973, and ending on March 18, 1974. OPEC nations then agreed, on January 7, 1975, to raise crude oil prices by 10%.

At that time, OPEC nations — including many who had recently nationalized their oil industries —joined the call for a new international economic order to be initiated by coalitions of primary producers. Concluding the First OPEC Summit in Algiers they called for stable and just commodity prices, an international food and agriculture program, technology transfer from North to South, and the democratization of the economic system. Overall, the evidence suggests that OPEC did act as a cartel when it adopted output rationing in order to maintain price.

According to US government, in 2011 OPEC will break above the $1 trillion mark earnings for the first time at $1.034 trillion and it is beating the $965 billion peak set in 2008.

Sustainability

According to Mikael Hook, who researches the life cycles of oil fields, despite technological advances that increase the productivity of oil wells, the rate of decline of oil fields will eventually increase as time continues. Energy policy expert Joyce Dargay accuses OPEC, along with several other institutions, of drastically under predicting future oil demand by 2030 by more than 25%, a difference of 28 million barrels per day (4,500,000 m^3/d) or about twice the current amount supplied by Saudi Arabia.

Quotas circa 2005

***Table:** OPEC Quotas and Production in thousands of barrels per day*

Country	*Quota (7/1/05)*	*Production (1/07)*	*Capacity*
Saudi Arabia	10,099	9,800	12,500
Algeria	894	1,360	1,430
Angola	1,900	1,700	1,700
Ecuador	520	500	500
Iran	4,110	3,700	3,750
Iraq		1,481	
Kuwait	2,247	2,500	2,600
Libya	1,500	1,650	1,700
Nigeria	2,306	2,250	2,250
Qatar	726	810	850
United Arab Emirates	2,444	2,500	2,600
Venezuela	3,225	2,340	2,450
Total	29,971	29,591	30,330

Organization of Arab Petroleum Exporting Countries

The Organization of Arab Petroleum Exporting Countries (OAPEC) is a multi-governmental organization headquartered in Kuwait which coordinates energy policies between oil–producing Arab nations, and whose main purpose is developmental.

History

On 9 January 1968, three of the then–most conservative Arab oil states Kuwait, Libya, and Saudi Arabia agreed at a conference in Beirut, Lebanon to found the Organization of Arab Petroleum Engineering Countries, aiming to separate the production and sale of oil from politics in the wake of the halfhearted 1967 oil embargo in response to the Six Day War.

Such use of the economic weapon of oil embargo in the struggle against Israel had been regularly proposed at Arab Petroleum Congresses, but it took the Six Day War for the embargo happen. However Saudi Arabia's oil production was up by 9% that year, and the main embargo lasted only ten days and was completely ended by the Khartoum Conference.

OAPEC was originally intended to be a conservative Arab political organization which, by restricting membership to countries whose main export was oil, would exclude governments seen as radical such as Egypt and Algeria. This organizational exclusivity was bolstered by an additional rule in the organization's charter requiring the three founders' approval all new members.

The original aim was to control the economic weapon of potential oil embargo and prevent its use caused by popular emotion. Iraq initially declined to join, preferring to work under the umbrella of the Arab League, considering OAPEC too conservative.

Equally the three founders considered Iraq too radical to be desirable as a member. However, by early 1972, the criteria for admission changed to oil being a significant source, rather than the principal source of revenue of a prospective member nation and Algeria, Iraq, Syria and Egypt had been admitted. Consequently the OPAEC became a much more activist organization, contrary to the original intention.

1973 was a turning point for the organization. In October that year, the forces of Egypt and Syria attempted to overwhelm the state of Israel in an offensive later known as the Yom Kippur War. On October 16, ten days after the war's start, Kuwait hosted separate meetings of both OAPEC and the Persian Gulf members of OPEC, including Iran.

OAPEC resolved to cut oil production 5% monthly "until the Israeli forces are completely evacuated from all the Arab territories occupied in the June 1967 war...." The embargo would last for some five months before it was lifted in March 1974 after negotiations at the Washington Oil Summit.

The embargo's aftereffects would linger throughout the rest of the decade. For the oil exporting countries, the embargo was the first instance of the exercise of their ability to leverage their production for political gains. A number of the member nations would use this sense of control to renegotiate the contracts they had made with the companies that had discovered and exploited their resources. Ironically the vastly increased revenues would prove addictive, and a unified OAPEC oil embargo was never again possible.

In 1979, Egypt was expelled from OAPEC for signing the Camp David Accords, although it was readmitted a decade later.

OAPEC is regarded as a regional, specialized international organization focusing on organizing cooperation in oil development, collective projects, and regional integration.

Members

- Saudi Arabia (1968)
- Algeria (1970)
- Bahrain (1970)
- Egypt (1973)
- United Arab Emirates (1970)
- Iraq (1972)
- Kuwait (1968)
- Libya (1968)
- Qatar (1970)
- Syria (1972).

Giant Oil and Gas Fields

The world's 932 giant oil and gas fields are considered those with 500 million barrels (79,000,000 m^3) of ultimately recoverable oil or gas equivalent. Geoscientists believe these giants account for 40 percent of the world's petroleum reserves.

They are clustered in 27 regions of the world, with the largest clusters in the Persian Gulf and Western Siberian Basin. The past three decades reflect declines in discoveries of giant fields. The present decade (2000–2010), however, reflects an upturn in discoveries and appears on track to be the third best for discovery of giant oil and gas fields in the 150 year history of modern oil and gas exploration.

According to analysis led by Paul Mann of the University of Texas' Jackson School of Geosciences, almost all of the 932 giant oil and gas fields cluster within 27 regions, or about 30 percent of Earth's land surface. Since 2003, Mann and colleagues M.K. Horn and Ian Cross have tracked the giants on a map that highlights the tectonic and sedimentary basin maps of the 27 key regions. The map is in the public domain and available as a high-resolution pdf on the Web site of the Jackson School of Geosciences.

Recent work in tracking giant oil and gas fields follows the earlier efforts of the late exploration geologist Michel T. Halbouty, who tracked trends in giant discoveries from the 1960s to 2004.

Tectonic Settings

Geophysicists and exploration geologists who look for oil and gas fields classify the subsurface characteristics, or tectonic setting, of geological structures that contain hydrocarbons. Any one oil and gas field may reflect influences from multiple geological periods and events, but geoscientists often attempt to characterize a field based on the dominant geological event that influenced the structure's ability to trap and contain oil and gas in recoverable quantities.

A majority of the world's giant oil and gas fields exist in two characteristic tectonic settings—passive margin and rift environments. Passive margins are found along the edges of major ocean basins, such as the Atlantic coast of Brazil where oil and gas has been located in large quantities in the Campos basin. Rifts are oceanic ridges formed when tectonic plates separate and a new crust is created. The North Sea is an example of a rift setting associated with prodigious hydrocarbon reserves. Geoscientists theorize that both zones are especially conducive to forming giant oil and gas fields when they are distant from active tectonic areas. Stability appears to be conducive to trapping and retaining hydrocarbons under the subsurface.

Four other common tectonic settings, including collisional margins, strike-slip margins, and subduction margins, are associated with the formation of giant oil and gas fields, though not to the dominant extent of passive margin and rift settings.

Recent and Future Giants

Based on the locations of past giants, Mann et al. predicted new discoveries of giant oil and gas fields would mainly be made in passive margin and rift environments, especially in deepwater basins. They also predicted that existing areas that have produced giant fields would be likely targets for new discoveries of "elephants," as the fields are sometimes known in the oil and gas industry.

Data from 2000-2007 reflect the accuracy of their predictions. The 79 new giant oil and gas fields discovered from 2000-2007 tended to be located in similar tectonic settings as the previously documented giants from 1868–2000, with 36 percent along passive margins, 30 percent in rift zones or overlying sags (structures associated with rifts), and 20 percent in collisional zones.

Despite a recent uptick in the number of giant oil and gas fields, discovery of giants appears to have peaked in the 1960s and 1970s. Looking to the future, geoscientists foresee a continuation of the recent trend of discovering more giant gas fields than oil fields. Two major continental regions—Antarctica and the Arctic—remain largely unexplored. Beyond them, however, trends suggest that remaining giant fields will be discovered in "in-fill" areas where past giants have been clustered and in frontier, or new, areas that correspond to the predominant tectonic settings of past giants.

Giant Field Production Properties and Behaviour

Comprehensive analysis of the production from the majority of the world's giant oil fields has shown their enormous importance for global oil production. For instance, the 20 largest oil fields in the world alone account for roughly 25% of the total oil production. The majority of the world's giants are already in decline and this will have dramatic consequences for future oil supply.

Further analysis shows that giant oil fields typically reach their maximum production before 50% of the ultimate recoverable volume has been extracted. A strong correlation between depletion and the rate of decline was also found in that study, indicating that much new technology has only been able to temporarily decrease depletion at the expense of rapid future decline. This is exactly the case in the Cantarell Field.

Hydrocarbon Exploration

Hydrocarbon exploration (or oil and gas exploration) is the search by petroleum geologists and geophysicists for hydrocarbon deposits beneath the Earth's surface, such as oil and natural gas. Oil and gas exploration are grouped under the science of petroleum geology.

Exploration Methods

Visible surface features such as oil seeps, natural gas seeps, pockmarks (underwater craters caused by escaping gas) provide basic evidence of hydrocarbon generation (be it shallow or deep in the Earth). However, most exploration depends on highly sophisticated technology to detect and determine the extent of these deposits using exploration geophysics. Areas thought to contain hydrocarbons are initially subjected to a gravity survey, magnetic survey, passive seismic or regional seismic reflection surveys to detect large scale features of the sub-surface geology.

Features of interest (known as *leads*) are subjected to more detailed seismic surveys which work on the principle of the time it takes for reflected sound waves to travel through matter (rock) of varying densities and using the process of depth conversion to create a profile of the substructure. Finally, when a prospect has been identified and evaluated and passes the oil company's selection criteria, an exploration well is drilled in an attempt to conclusively determine the presence or absence of oil or gas.

Figure: *Onshore Drilling Rig*

Oil exploration is an expensive, high-risk operation. Offshore and remote area exploration is generally only undertaken by very large corporations or national governments. Typical shallow shelf oil wells (e.g. North Sea) cost USD$10 – 30 million, while deep water wells can cost up to USD$100 million plus. Hundreds of smaller companies search for onshore hydrocarbon deposits worldwide, with some wells costing as little as USD$100,000.

Elements of a Petroleum Prospect

A prospect is a potential trap which geologists believe may contain hydrocarbons. A significant amount of geological, structural and seismic investigation must first be completed to redefine the potential hydrocarbon drill location from a lead to a prospect. Five geological factors have to be present for a prospect to work and if any of them fail neither oil nor gas will be present.

- A source rock - When organic-rich rock such as oil shale or coal is subjected to high pressure and temperature over an extended period of time, hydrocarbons form.

- Migration - The hydrocarbons are expelled from source rock by three density-related mechanisms: the newly-matured hydrocarbons are less dense than their precursors, which causes overpressure; the hydrocarbons are lighter medium, and so migrate upwards due to buoyancy, and the fluids expand as further burial causes increased heating. Most hydrocarbons migrate to the surface as oil seeps, but some will get trapped.
- Trap - The hydrocarbons are buoyant and have to be trapped within a structural (e.g. Anticline, fault block) or stratigraphic trap
- Seal or cap rock - The hydrocarbon trap has to be covered by an impermeable rock known as a seal or cap-rock in order to prevent hydrocarbons escaping to the surface
- Reservoir - The hydrocarbons are contained in a reservoir rock. This is a porous sandstone or limestone. The oil collects in the pores within the rock. The reservoir must also be permeable so that the hydrocarbons will flow to surface during production.

Figure: *Mud log in process, a common way to study the rock types when drilling oil wells.*

Exploration Risk

Hydrocarbon exploration is a high risk investment and risk assessment is paramount for successful exploration portfolio management. Exploration risk is a difficult concept and is usually defined by assigning confidence to the presence of five imperative geological factors, as discussed above. This confidence is based on data and/or models and is usually mapped on Common Risk Segment Maps (CRS Maps). High confidence in the presence of imperative geological factors is usually colored green and low confidence colored red .

Therefore these maps are also called Traffic Light Maps, while the full procedure is often referred to as Play Fairway Analysis . The aim of such procedures is to force the geologist to objectively assess all different geological factors.

Furthermore it results in simple maps that can be understood by non-geologists and managers to base exploration decisions on.

Terms Used in Petroleum Evaluation

- Bright spot - On a seismic section, coda that have high amplitudes due to a formation containing hydrocarbons.
- Chance of success - An estimate of the chance of all the elements within a prospect working, described as a probability. High risk prospects have a less than 10% chance of working, medium risk prospects 10-20%, low risk prospects over 20%. Typically about 40% of wells recently drilled find commercial hydrocarbons.
- Dry hole - A formation that contains brine instead of oil.
- Flat spot - An oil-water contact on a seismic section; flat due to gravity.
- Hydrocarbon in place - amount of hydrocarbon likely to be contained in the prospect. This is calculated using the volumetric equation - GRV x N/G x Porosity x Sh x FVF
    - GRV - Gross rock volume - amount of rock in the trap above the hydrocarbon water contact
    - N/G - net/gross ratio - proportion of the GRV formed by the reservoir rock (range is 0 to 1)
    - Porosity - percentage of the net reservoir rock occupied by pores (typically 5-35%)
    - Sh - hydrocarbon saturation - some of the pore space is filled with water - this must be discounted
    - FVF - formation volume factor - oil shrinks and gas expands when brought to the surface. The FVF converts volumes at reservoir conditions (high pressure and high temperature) to storage and sale conditions
- Lead - a structure which may contain hydrocarbons

- Play - A particular combination of reservoir, seal, source and trap associated with proven hydrocarbon accumulations
- Prospect - a lead which has been fully evaluated and is ready to drill
- Recoverable hydrocarbons - amount of hydrocarbon likely to be recovered during production. This is typically 10-50% in an oil field and 50-80% in a gas field.

Licensing

Petroleum resources are typically owned by the government of the host country. In the USA most onshore (land) oil and gas rights (OGM) are owned by private individuals. Sometimes this is not the same person who owns the surface rights. In this case oil companies must negotiate terms for a lease of these rights with the individual who owns the OGM.

In most nations the government issues licences to explore, develop and produce its oil and gas resources, which are typically administered by the oil ministry. There are several different types of licence. Typically oil companies operate in joint ventures to spread the risk, one of the companies in the partnership is designated the operator who actually supervises the work.

- Tax and Royalty - Companies would pay a royalty on any oil produced, together with a profits tax (which can have expenditure offset against it). In some cases there are also various bonuses and ground rents (license fees) payable to the government - for example a signature bonus payable at the start of the licence. Licences are awarded in competitive bid rounds on the basis of either the size of the work programme (number of wells, seismic etc.) or size of the signature bonus.
- Production Sharing contract (PSA) - A PSA is more complex than a Tax/Royalty system - The companies bid on the percentage of the production that the host government receives (this may be variable with the oil price), There is often also participation by the Government owned National Oil Company (NOC). There are also various bonuses to be paid. Development expenditure is offset against production revenue.
- Service contract - This is when an oil company acts as a contractor for the host government, being paid to produce the hydrocarbons.

Reserves and Resources

Resources are hydrocarbons which may or may not be produced in the future. A resource number may be assigned to an undrilled prospect or an unappraised discovery.

Appraisal by drilling additional delineation wells or acquiring extra seismic data will confirm the size of the field and lead to project sanction. At this point the relevant government body gives the oil company a production licence which enables the field to be developed. This is also the point at which oil reserves can be formally booked.

Definition of Oil Reserves

Oil reserves are primarily a measure of geological risk - of the probability of oil existing and being producible under current economic conditions using current technology. The three categories of reserves generally used are proven, probable, and possible reserves.

- Proven reserves - defined as oil and gas "Reasonably Certain" to be producible using current technology at current prices, with current commercial terms and government consent- also known in the industry as 1P. Some Industry specialists refer to this as P90 - i.e. having a 90% certainty of being produced.
- Probable reserves - defined as oil and gas "Reasonably Probable" of being produced using current or likely technology at current prices, with current commercial terms and government consent - Some Industry specialists refer to this as P50 - i.e. having a 50% certainty of being produced. - This is also known in the industry as 2P or Proven plus probable.
- Possible reserves - i.e. "having a chance of being developed under favourable circumstances" - Some industry specialists refer to this as P10 - i.e. having a 10% certainty of being produced. - This is also known in the industry as 3P or Proven plus probable plus possible.

Reserve Booking

Oil and gas reserves are the main asset of an oil company - booking is the process by which they are added to the Balance sheet. This is done according to a set of rules developed by the Society of Petroleum Engineers (SPE). The Reserves of any company listed on the New York Stock Exchange have to be stated to the U.S. Securities and Exchange Commission. In many cases these reported reserves are audited by external geologists, although this is not a legal requirement. The U.S. Securities and Exchange Commission rejects the probability concept and prohibits companies from mentioning probable and possible reserves in their filings. Thus, official estimates of proven reserves will always be understated compared to what oil companies think actually exists. For practical purposes companies will use proven plus probable estimate (2P), and for long term planning they will be looking primarily at possible reserves. Other countries also have their national hydrocarbon reserves authorities for example, Russia's State Commission on Mineral Reserves (GKZ), to which companies operating in these countries have to report.

Oil Shale Geology

Oil shale geology is a branch of geologic sciences which studies the formation and composition of oil shales–fine-grained sedimentary rocks containing significant amounts of kerogen, and belonging to the group of sapropel fuels. Oil shale formation takes place in a number of depositional settings and has considerable compositional variation. Oil shales can be classified by their composition (carbonate minerals such as calcite or detrital minerals such as quartz and clays) or by their depositional environment (large lakes, shallow marine, and lagoon/ small lake settings). Much of the organic matter in oil shale is of algal origin, but may also include remains of vascular land plants. Three major type of organic matter (macerals) in oil shale are telalginite, lamalginite, and bituminite. Some oil-shale deposits also contain metals which include vanadium, zinc, copper, uranium.

Most oil shale deposits were formed during Middle Cambrian, Early and Middle Ordovician, Late Devonian, Late Jurassic, and Paleogene times through burial by sedimentary loading on top of the algal swamp deposits, resulting in conversion of the organic matter to kerogen by diagenetic processes. The largest deposits are found in the remains of large lakes such as the deposits of the Green River Formation of Wyoming and Utah, USA. Oil-shale deposits formed in the shallow seas of continental shelves generally are much thinner than large lake basin deposits.

Classification and Varieties

There are varying classifications of oil shales depending on their mineral content, type of kerogen, age, depositional history, and organisms from which they are derived. The age of the oil shale deposits ranges from Cambrian to Tertiary age. Lithologies range from shales to marl and carbonate rocks, all of which form a mixture of tightly bound organic and inorganic materials.

Oil shales have been divided into three categories based on mineral composition – carbonate-rich shale, siliceous shale and cannel shale. Carbonate-rich shales derive their name from the large amount of carbonate minerals such as calcite and dolomite. As many as twenty carbonate minerals have been found in oil shale, the majority of which are considered authigenic or diagentic. Carbonate-rich oil shales, particularly that of lacustrine-sourced deposits, have usually the organic-rich layers sandwiched between carbonate-rich layers. These deposits are hard formations that are resistant to weathering and they are difficult to process using *ex-situ* methods. Siliceous oil shales are usually dark brown or black shales. They are not rich in carbonates but rather in siliceous minerals such as quartz, feldspar, clay, chert and opal. Siliceous shales are not as hard and weather-resistant as carbonate-rich shales, and may be better suited for extraction via *ex-situ* methods. Cannel shales are usually dark brown or black shales, which consist of organic matter that completely encloses other mineral grains. They are suitable for extraction via *ex-situ* methods.

Table: *Classification of oil shales by environment of deposition*

Terrestrial	*Lacustrine*	*Marine*
cannel coal	lamosite;torbanite	kukersite; tasmanite; marinite

Figure: *Cannel coal from the Pennsylvanian of NE Ohio.*

Another classification according to the type of kerogen, is based on the hydrogen, carbon, and oxygen content of oil shales' original organic matter. This classification is known as the "van Krevelen diagram". The most used classification of oil shales was developed between 1987 and 1991 by Adrian C. Hutton of the University of Wollongong, adapting petrographic terms from coal terminology.

According to this classification, oil shales are designated as terrestrial, lacustrine (lake-bottom-deposited), or marine (ocean bottom-deposited), based on the environment where the initial biomass was deposited. Hutton's classification scheme has proven useful in estimating the yield and composition of the extracted oil.

Cannel coal (also called *candle coal*) is a type of terrestrial shale, which is hydrogen-rich brown to black coal, sometimes with shaly texture, composed of resins, spores, waxes, cutinaceous and corky materials derived from terrestrial vascular plants as well as varied amounts of vitrinite and inertinite. Lacustrine shales consist of Lamosite and Torbanite. Lamosite is a pale-brown and grayish-brown to dark-gray to black oil shale whose chief organic constituent is lamalginite derived from lacustrine planktonic algae.

Torbanite, named after Torbane Hill in Scotland, is a black oil shale whose organic matter is telalginite derived from lipid-rich *Botryococcus* and related algal forms. Marine shales consist of three varieties, namely Kukersite, Tasmanite, and Marinite. Kukersite, named after Kukruse in Estonia, is a light-brown marine oil shale whose principal organic component is telalginite derived from the green alga, *Gloeocapsomorpha prisca.*

Tasmanite, named after Tasmania, is a brown to black oil shale whose organic matter consists of telalginite derived chiefly from unicellular tasmanitid algae of marine origin. Marinite is a gray to dark-gray to black oil shale of marine origin in which the chief organic components are lamalginite and bituminite derived from marine phytoplankton with varied admixtures of bitumen, telalginite, and vitrinite.

Composition

Photomicrograph showing detail of the varves in a rich Colorado oil shale specimen. The organic laminae are themselves finely laminated. The mineral laminae contain considerable organic matter, but they are readily distinguished by their coarser grain and greater thickness. Note sand grains (white). Enlarged 320 diameters.

As a sapropel fuel, oil shale differs from humus fuels in its lower content of organic matter. The organic matter has an atomic ratio of hydrogen to carbon of about 1.5 – approximately the same as that of crude oil and four to five times higher than coals. The organic matter in oil shales forms a complex macromolecular structure which is insoluble in common organic solvents. It is mixed with varied amounts of mineral matter. For commercial grades of oil shale, the ratio of organic matter to mineral matter is about 0.75:5 to 1.5:5.

The organic portion of oil shale consists largely of prebitumen bituminous groundmass, such as remains of algae, spores, pollen, plant cuticles and corky fragments of herbaceous and woody plants, and cellular debris from other lacustrine, marine, and land plants.

While terrestrial oil shales contain resins, spores, waxy cuticles, and corky tissues of roots and stems of vascular terrestrial plants, lacustrine oil shales include lipid-rich organic matter derived from algae. Marine oil shales are composed of marine algae, acritarchs, and marine dinoflagellates. Organic matter in oil shale also contains organic sulfur (about 1.8 % on average) and a lower proportion of nitrogen.

Three major types of organic matter (macerals) in oil shale are telalginite, lamalginite, and bituminite. Telalginite is defined as structured organic matter composed of large colonial or thick-walled unicellular algae such as Botryococcus and *Tasmanites*. Lamalginite includes thin-walled colonial or unicellular algae that occur as distinct laminae, but display few or no recognizable biologic structures.

Under the microscope, telalginite and lamalginite are easily recognized by their bright shades of yellow under ultraviolet/blue fluorescent light. Bituminite is largely amorphous, lacks recognizable biologic structures, and displays relatively low fluorescence under the microscope. Other organic constituents include vitrinite and inertinite, which are macerals derived from the humic matter of land plants. These macerals are usually found in relatively small amounts in most oil shales.

Formation

Most oil shale formations took place during mid-Cambrian, early and middle Ordovician, late Devonian, late Jurassic and Paleogene periods.

These were formed by the deposition of organic matter in a variety of depositional environments including freshwater to highly saline lakes, epicontinental marine basins and subtidal shelves and were restricted to estuarine areas such as oxbow lakes, peat bogs, limnic and coastal swamps, and muskegs. When plants die in such an anaerobic aquatic environment, low oxygen levels prevent their complete bacterial decay.

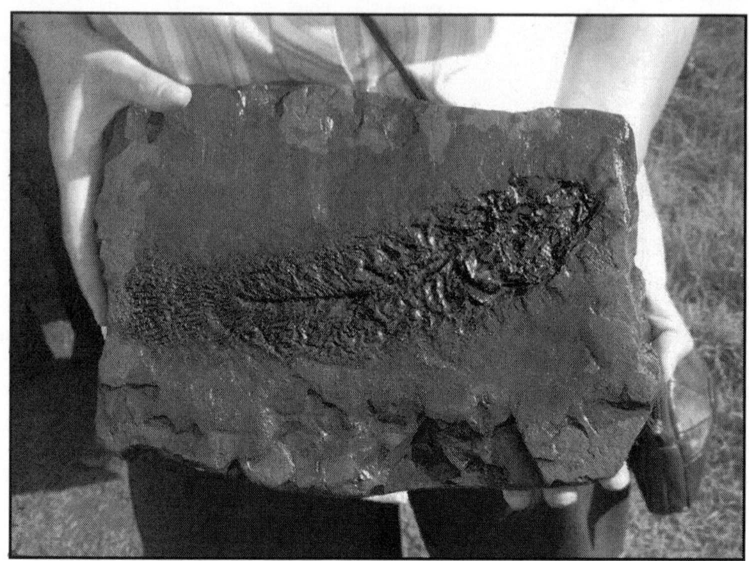

Figure: *Fossil in oil shale from Messel pit, south of Frankfurt am Main, Germany.*

For undecayed organic matter to be preserved and to form oil shale, the environment must remain uniform for prolonged periods of time in order to build up sufficiently thick sequences of algal matter. Eventually, the algal swamp or other restricted environment is disrupted and oil shale accumulation ceases. Burial by sedimentary loading on top of the algal swamp deposits converts the organic matter to kerogen by the following normal diagenetic processes:

- Compaction due to sediment loading on the coal, leading to compression of the organic matter.
- With ongoing heat and compaction, removal of moisture in the peat and from the intracellular structure of fossilized plants, and removal of molecular water.
- Methanogenesis—similar to treating wood in a pressure cooker— results in methane being produced, removing hydrogen, some carbon, and some further oxygen.
- Dehydration, which removes hydroxyl groups from the cellulose and other plant molecules, resulting in the production of hydrogen-reduced coals or oil shales.

Though similar in their formation process, oil shales differ from coals in several distinct ways. The precursors of the organic matter in oil shale and coal differ in a sense that oil shale is of algal origin, but may also include remains of vascular land plants that more commonly compose much of the organic matter in coal. The origin of some of the organic matter in oil shale is obscure because of the lack of recognizable biologic structures that would help identify the precursor organisms. Such materials may be of bacterial origin or the product of bacterial degradation of algae or other organic matter.

Lower temperature and pressure during the diagenesis process compared to other modes of hydrocarbon generation result in a lower maturation level of oil shale. Continuous burial and further heating and pressure could result in the production of oil and gas from the oil shale source rock. The largest deposits are found in the remains of large lakes such as the deposits of the Green River Formation of Wyoming and Utah, USA. Large lake oil shale basins are typically found in areas of block faulting or crustal warping due to mountain building. Deposits such as the Green River may be as much as 2,000 feet (610 m) and yield up to 40 gallons of oil for each ton (166 l/t) of shale.

Oil-shale deposits formed in the shallow seas of continental shelves generally are much thinner than large lake basin deposits. These are typically a few meters thick and are spread over very large areas, extending up to thousands of square kilometres. Of the three lithologic types of oil shales, siliceous oil shales are most commonly found in such environment.

These oil shales are not as organically rich as lake-deposited oil shales, and generally do not contain more than 30 gallons per ton of oil shale. Oil shales deposited in lagoonal or small lake environments are rarely extensive and are often associated with coal-bearing rocks. These oil shales can have high yields– as much as 40 gallons per ton (166 l/t) of oil shale. However, due to their small areal extent, they are considered unlikely candidates for commercial exploitation.

Formations in the United States

The United States has two significant oil-shale deposits which are suited for commercial development due to their size, grade and location. The Eocene Green River Formation covers parts of Colorado, Wyoming and Utah; the second significant deposit is Devonian oil shales in the eastern United States. In both places, there are sub-basins varying in volume and quality of the reserves. Oil shale in the Green River Formation is found in five sedimentary basins namely, Green River, Uinta, Piceance Creek, Sand Wash and Washakie.

The first three have undergone some significant exploration and attempts to commercialize the oil shale reserves since the 1960s. The Green River Formation includes deposits from two large lakes which covered an area of over 65,000 square kilometres (25,100 sq mi) during early to middle Eocene period. These lakes were separated by the Uinta uplift and the Axial Basin anticline. For significant periods during their 10 Ma life, the lakes became closed systems allowing many changes in size, salinity and sediment deposition. Oil shale is a result of abundant blue-green algae that thrived in the lakes.

The oil shale that underlies almost 750,000 square kilometres (289,580 sq mi) in the eastern United States was formed in a marine depositional environment very different from the Green River Basins. These deposits have also undergone commercialization attempts; they are also resources for natural gas and have been mined for low-grade oil shale. These oil shales were formed during the Late Devonian and Early Mississippian periods.

During this time, much of the eastern United States was covered by a large shallow sea. The oil shale is thought to have been the result of slow deposition of planktonic algae. under anoxic conditions. In parts of the basin close to the shoreline, the organic mixture that helped form the oil shale contains organic-rich sediment from the rising Appalachian mountains.

Formations in Brazil

Brazil has nine significant locations of oil shale deposits. The size, location and quality of oil shale deposits in the Paraiba Valley and the Irati Formation have attracted the most attention. These two contain an estimated 1.4 billion barrels of *in-situ* shale oil with total resources as much as more than three billion barrels. While the "Irati formation" deposit is the smaller of the two, containing an estimated 600 million barrels *in-situ* compared to 840 million in the Paraiba valley formation, the former is more economically viable.

The "Irati formation" consists of two oil shale beds separated by 12 metres (40 ft) of limestone and shale. The upper layer is thicker (9 metres (30 ft)) but the thinner lower bed (4 metres (10 ft)) is of greater value; the weight percent of shale oil yield is around 12 % for the lower layer as compared to 7 % for the upper one. The oil shale yield varies laterally, and may be as little as 7 % for the lower layer and 4 % for the upper layer. The formation is a very fine grained and laminated deposit ranging in colour from dark gray to brown to black. While 60-70 % of the shale consists of clay minerals, the balance is made up of organic matter.

No consensus has been reached on the exact depositional nature of the Irati oil shale. One theory suggests that the organic material in the Irati oil shale originated from algae deposited in a lacustrine environment with salinity varying from that of freshwater to brackish water. Other theory suggests that the organic sediment may have been deposited in a shallow, partially restricted marine environment. Hutton's classification describes it as a marine source oil shale.

Formation in Estonia

The kukersite oil shale of Ordovician age in Estonia is part of the Baltic oil shale basin and was deposited in shallow marine basins. The deposit is one of the world's highest-grade deposits with more than 40 % organic content and 66 % conversion ratio into shale oil and gas. The oil shale is located in a single calcareous layer 2.5-3 meters in thickness and is buried at depths from 7 to 100 m. The total area of the basin is about 3,000 km^2.

Oil yield from Kukersite is 30 to 47 %. Most of the organic matter is derived from the fossil green alga, *Gloeocapsomorpha prisca*, which has affinities to the modern cyanobacterium, *Entophysalis major*, an extant species that forms algal mats in inter-tidal to very shallow subtidal waters. Matrix minerals include low-magnesium calcite, dolomite, and siliciclastic minerals. It is not enriched in heavy metals.

Chapter 5

Storage and Marketing

Oil-storage Trade

The oil-storage trade is a trading strategy where oil tank owners and companies that lease storage buy oil for immediate delivery and hold it in their storage tanks, then sell contracts for future delivery at a higher price. When delivery dates approach, they close out existing contracts and sell new ones for future delivery of the same oil.

The oil never moves out of storage. Trading in this fashion is only successful if the forward market is in "contango", that is if the price of oil in the future also known as forward prices are higher than current prices or spot prices. Storing oil became big business in 2008 and 2009, with many participants - including Wall Street giants such as Morgan Stanley, Goldman Sachs or Citicorp - turning sizeable profits simply by sitting on tanks of oil. It has been estimated that one in twelve of the largest oil tankers are being used for the storage, rather than transportation of oil, and that if lined up end to end, the tankers would stretch out for 26 miles.

Oil Refinery

An oil refinery or petroleum refinery is an industrial process plant where crude oil is processed and refined into more useful petroleum products, such as gasoline, diesel fuel, asphalt base, heating oil, kerosene, and liquefied petroleum gas. Oil refineries are typically large sprawling industrial complexes with extensive piping running throughout, carrying streams of fluids between large chemical processing units. In many ways, oil refineries use much of the technology of, and can be thought of as types of chemical plants. The crude oil feedstock has typically been processed by an oil production plant. There is usually an oil depot (tank farm) at or near an oil refinery for storage of bulk liquid products.

An oil refinery is considered an essential part of the downstream side of the petroleum industry.

Figure : *The oil refinery in Haifa, Israel is capable of processing about 9 million tons (66 million barrels) of crude oil a year. Its two cooling towers are landmarks of the city's skyline.*

Operation

Raw or unprocessed crude oil is not generally useful. Although "light, sweet" (low viscosity, low sulfur) crude oil has been used directly as a burner fuel for steam vessel propulsion, the lighter elements form explosive vapours in the fuel tanks and are therefore hazardous, especially in warships.

Instead, the hundreds of different hydrocarbon molecules in crude oil are separated in a refinery into components which can be used as fuels, lubricants, and as feedstock in petrochemical processes that manufacture such products as plastics, detergents, solvents, elastomers and fibers such as nylon and polyesters.

Petroleum fossil fuels are burned in internal combustion engines to provide power for ships, automobiles, aircraft engines, lawn mowers, chainsaws, and other machines. Different boiling points allow the hydrocarbons to be separated by distillation. Since the lighter liquid products are in great demand for use in internal combustion engines, a modern refinery will convert heavy hydrocarbons and lighter gaseous elements into these higher value products. Oil can be used in a variety of ways because it contains hydrocarbons of varying molecular masses, forms and lengths such as paraffins, aromatics, naphthenes (or cycloalkanes), alkenes, dienes, and alkynes. While the molecules in crude oil include different atoms such as sulfur and nitrogen, the hydrocarbons are the most common form of molecules, which are molecules of varying lengths and complexity made of hydrogen and carbon atoms, and a small number of oxygen atoms.

The differences in the structure of these molecules account for their varying physical and chemical properties, and it is this variety that makes crude oil useful in a broad range of applications. Once separated and purified of any contaminants and impurities, the fuel or lubricant can be sold without further processing. Smaller molecules such as isobutane and propylene or butylenes can be recombined to meet specific octane requirements by processes such as alkylation, or less commonly, dimerization. Octane grade of gasoline can also be improved by catalytic reforming, which involves removing hydrogen from hydrocarbons producing compounds with higher octane ratings such as aromatics. Intermediate products such as gasoils can even be reprocessed to break a heavy, long-chained oil into a lighter short-chained one, by various forms of cracking such as fluid catalytic cracking, thermal cracking, and hydrocracking. The final step in gasoline production is the blending of fuels with different octane ratings, vapour pressures, and other properties to meet product specifications.

Oil refineries are large scale plants, processing about a hundred thousand to several hundred thousand barrels of crude oil a day. Because of the high capacity, many of the units operate continuously, as opposed to processing in batches, at steady state or nearly steady state for months to years. The high capacity also makes process optimization and advanced process control very desirable.

Major Products

Petroleum products are usually grouped into three categories: light distillates (LPG, gasoline, naphtha), middle distillates (kerosene, diesel), heavy distillates and residuum (heavy fuel oil, lubricating oils, wax, asphalt). This classification is based on the way crude oil is distilled and separated into fractions (called distillates and residuum) as in the above drawing.

- Liquified petroleum gas (LPG)
- Gasoline (also known as petrol)

- Naphtha
- Kerosene and related jet aircraft fuels
- Diesel fuel
- Fuel oils
- Lubricating oils
- Paraffin wax
- Asphalt and tar
- Petroleum coke.

Oil refineries also produce various intermediate products such as hydrogen, light hydrocarbons, reformate and pyrolysis gasoline. These are not usually transported but instead are blended or processed further on-site. Chemical plants are thus often adjacent to oil refineries. For example, light hydrocarbons are steam-cracked in an ethylene plant, and the produced ethylene is polymerized to produce polyethene.

Flow Diagram of Typical Refinery

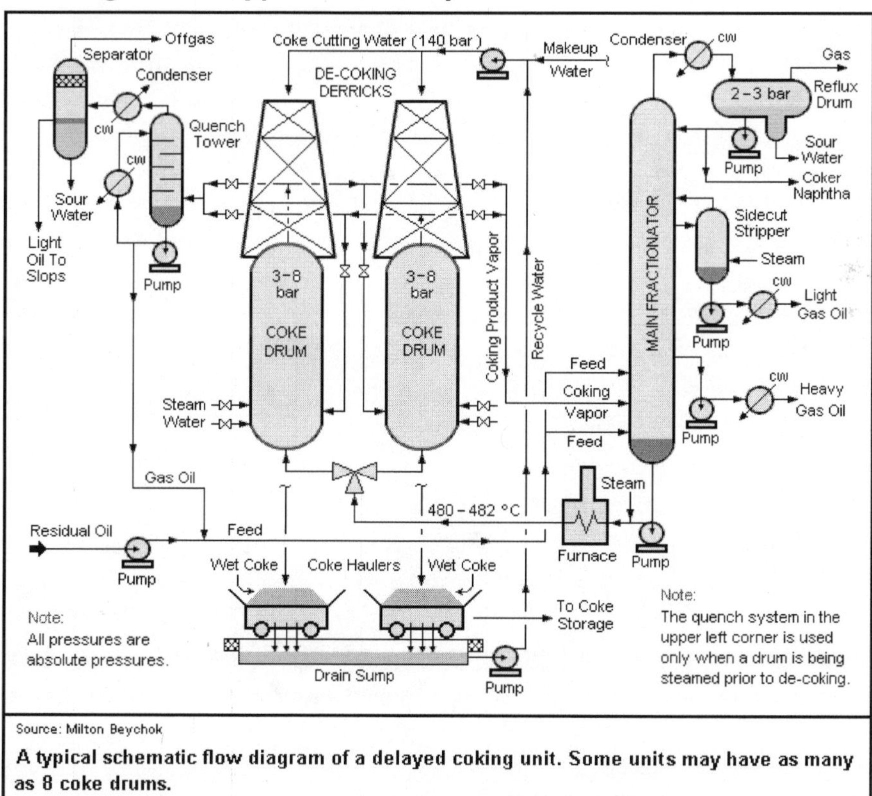

Source: Milton Beychok

A typical schematic flow diagram of a delayed coking unit. Some units may have as many as 8 coke drums.

Figure : *Typical schematic flow diagram*

The diagram depicts only one of the literally hundreds of different oil refinery configurations.

The diagram also does not include any of the usual refinery facilities providing utilities such as steam, cooling water, and electric power as well as storage tanks for crude oil feedstock and for intermediate products and end products.

There are many process configurations other than that depicted above. For example, the vacuum distillation unit may also produce fractions that can be refined into endproducts such as: spindle oil used in the textile industry, light machinery oil, motor oil, and steam cylinder oil. As another example, the vacuum residue may be processed in a coker unit to produce petroleum coke.

Common Process units Found in a Refinery

- Desalter unit washes out salt from the crude oil before it enters the atmospheric distillation unit.
- Atmospheric distillation unit distills crude oil into fractions.
- Vacuum distillation unit further distills residual bottoms after atmospheric distillation.
- Naphtha hydrotreater unit uses hydrogen to desulfurize naphtha from atmospheric distillation. Must hydrotreat the naphtha before sending to a Catalytic Reformer unit.
- Catalytic reformer unit is used to convert the naphtha-boiling range molecules into higher octane reformate (reformer product). The reformate has higher content of aromatics and cyclic hydrocarbons).

  An important byproduct of a reformer is hydrogen released during the catalyst reaction. The hydrogen is used either in the hydrotreaters or the hydrocracker.
- Distillate hydrotreater unit desulfurizes distillates (such as diesel) after atmospheric distillation.
- Fluid catalytic cracker (FCC) unit upgrades heavier fractions into lighter, more valuable products.
- Hydrocracker unit uses hydrogen to upgrade heavier fractions into lighter, more valuable products.
- Visbreaking unit upgrades heavy residual oils by thermally cracking them into lighter, more valuable reduced viscosity products.
- Merox unit treats LPG, kerosene or jet fuel by oxidizing mercaptans to organic disulfides.

- Coking units (delayed coking, fluid coker, and flexicoker) process very heavy residual oils into gasoline and diesel fuel, leaving petroleum coke as a residual product.
- Alkylation unit produces high-octane component for gasoline blending.
- Dimerization unit converts olefins into higher-octane gasoline blending components. For example, butenes can be dimerized into isooctene which may subsequently be hydrogenated to form isooctane. There are also other uses for dimerization.
- Isomerization unit converts linear molecules to higher-octane branched molecules for blending into gasoline or feed to alkylation units.
- Steam reforming unit produces hydrogen for the hydrotreaters or hydrocracker.
- Liquified gas storage units store propane and similar gaseous fuels at pressure sufficient to maintain them in liquid form. These are usually spherical vessels or bullets (horizontal vessels with rounded ends.
- Storage tanks store crude oil and finished products, usually cylindrical, with some sort of vapor emission control and surrounded by an earthen berm to contain spills.
- Slug catcher used when product (crude oil and gas) that comes from a pipeline with two-phase flow, has to be buffered at the entry of the units.
- Amine gas treater, Claus unit, and tail gas treatment convert hydrogen sulfide from hydrodesulfurization into elemental sulfur.
- Utility units such as cooling towers circulate cooling water, boiler plants generates steam, and instrument air systems include pneumatically operated control valves and an electrical substation.
- Wastewater collection and treating systems consist of API separators, dissolved air flotation (DAF) units and further treatment units such as an activated sludge biotreater to make water suitable for reuse or for disposal.
- Solvent refining units use solvent such as cresol or furfural to remove unwanted, mainly aromatics from lubricating oil stock or diesel stock.
- Solvent dewaxing units remove the heavy waxy constituents petrolatum from vacuum distillation products.

Specialty End Products

***Figure:** Sarnia, Ontario is a major Great Lakes refining area for Shell, Imperial Oil, ExxonMobil, Suncor Energy, Dow Chemicals, Bayer, and others.*

These will blend various feedstocks, mix appropriate additives, provide short term storage, and prepare for bulk loading to trucks, barges, product ships, and railcars.

- Gaseous fuels such as propane, stored and shipped in liquid form under pressure in specialized railcars to distributors.
- Liquid fuels blending (producing automotive and aviation grades of gasoline, kerosene, various aviation turbine fuels, and diesel fuels, adding dyes, detergents, antiknock additives, oxygenates, and anti-fungal compounds as required). Shipped by barge, rail, and tanker ship. May be shipped regionally in dedicated pipelines to point consumers, particularly aviation jet fuel to major airports, or piped to distributors in multi-product pipelines using product separators called pipeline inspection gauges ("pigs").
- Lubricants (produces light machine oils, motor oils, and greases, adding viscosity stabilizers as required), usually shipped in bulk to an offsite packaging plant.
- Wax (paraffin), used in the packaging of frozen foods, among others. May be shipped in bulk to a site to prepare as packaged blocks.
- Sulfur (or sulfuric acid), byproducts of sulfur removal from petroleum which may have up to a couple percent

sulfur as organic sulfur-containing compounds. Sulfur and sulfuric acid are useful industrial materials. Sulfuric acid is usually prepared and shipped as the acid precursor oleum.

- Bulk tar shipping for offsite unit packaging for use in tar-and-gravel roofing.
- Asphalt unit. Prepares bulk asphalt for shipment.
- Petroleum coke, used in specialty carbon products or as solid fuel.
- Petrochemicals or petrochemical feedstocks, which are often sent to petrochemical plants for further processing in a variety of ways. The petrochemicals may be olefins or their precursors, or various types of aromatic petrochemicals.

Siting/Locating of Petroleum Refineries

A party searching for a site to construct a refinery or a chemical plant needs to consider the following issues:

- The site has to be reasonably far from residential areas.
- Infrastructure should be available for supply of raw materials and shipment of products to markets.
- Energy to operate the plant should be available.
- Facilities should be available for waste disposal.

Refineries which use a large amount of steam and cooling water need to have an abundant source of water. Oil refineries therefore are often located nearby navigable rivers or on a sea shore, nearby a port. Such location also gives access to transportation by river or by sea. The advantages of transporting crude oil by pipeline are evident, and oil companies often transport a large volume of fuel to distribution terminals by pipeline. Pipeline may not be practical for products with small output, and rail cars, road tankers, and barges are used.

Petrochemical plants and solvent manufacturing (fine fractionating) plants need spaces for further processing of a large volume of refinery products for further processing, or to mix chemical additives with a product at source rather than at blending terminals.

Safety and Environmental Concerns

The refining process releases numerous different chemicals into the atmosphere; consequently, there are substantial air pollution emissions and a notable odor normally accompanies the presence of a refinery. Aside from air pollution impacts there are also wastewater concerns, risks of industrial accidents such as fire and explosion, and noise health effects due to industrial noise. The public has demanded that many governments place restrictions on contaminants that refineries release, and most refineries have installed the equipment needed to comply with the requirements of the pertinent environmental protection regulatory agencies. In the United States, there is strong pressure to prevent the development of new refineries, and no major refinery has been built in the country since Marathon's Garyville, Louisiana facility in 1976.

Figure : *MiRO refinery at Karlsruhe*

However, many existing refineries have been expanded during that time. Environmental restrictions and pressure to prevent construction of new refineries may have also contributed to rising fuel prices in the United States. Additionally, many refineries (over 100 since the 1980s) have closed due to obsolescence and/or merger activity within the industry itself. This activity has been reported to Congress and in specialized studies not widely publicised.

Environmental and safety concerns mean that oil refineries are sometimes located some distance away from major urban areas. Nevertheless, there are many instances where refinery operations are close to populated areas and pose health risks such as in the Campo de Gibraltar, a CEPSA refinery near the towns of Gibraltar, Algeciras, La Linea, San Roque and Los Barrios with a combined population of over 300,000 residents within a 5-mile (8.0 km) radius and the CEPSA refinery in Santa Cruz on the island of Tenerife, Spain which is sited in a densely populated city centre and next to the only two major evacuation routes in and out of the city.

In California's Contra Costa County and Solano County, a shoreline necklace of refineries, built in the early 20th century before this area was populated, and associated chemical plants are adjacent to urban areas in Richmond, Martinez, Pacheco, Concord, Pittsburg, Vallejo and Benicia, with occasional accidental events that require "shelter in place" orders to the adjacent populations.

Corrosion Problems and Prevention

Petroleum refineries run as efficiently as possible to reduce costs. One major factor that decreases efficiency is corrosion of the metal components found throughout the process line of the hydrocarbon refining process. Corrosion causes the failure of parts in addition to dictating the cleaning schedule of the refinery, during which the entire production facility must be shut down and cleaned. The cost of corrosion in the petroleum industry has been estimated at US$3.7 billion.

Corrosion occurs in various forms in the refining process, such as pitting corrosion from water droplets, embrittlement from hydrogen, and stress corrosion cracking from sulfide attack. From a materials standpoint, carbon steel is used for upwards of 80% of refinery components, which is beneficial due to its low cost. Carbon steel is resistant to the most common forms of corrosion, particularly from hydrocarbon impurities at temperatures below 205 °C, but other corrosive chemicals and environments prevent its use everywhere. Common replacement materials are low alloy steels containing chromium and molybdenum, with stainless steels containing more chromium dealing with more corrosive environments. More expensive materials commonly used are nickel, titanium, and copper alloys. These are primarily saved for the most problematic areas where extremely high temperatures or very corrosive chemicals are present.

Corrosion is fought by a complex system of monitoring, preventative repairs and careful use of materials. Monitoring methods include both off-line checks taken during maintenance and on-line monitoring. Off-line checks measure corrosion after it has occurred, telling the engineer when equipment must be replaced based on the historical information he has collected. This is referred to as preventative management.

On-line systems are a more modern development, and are revolutionizing the way corrosion is approached. There are several types of on-line corrosion monitoring technologies such as linear polarization resistance, electrochemical noise and electrical resistance. On-Line monitoring has generally had slow reporting rates in the past (minutes or hours) and been limited by process conditions and sources of error but newer technologies can report rates up to twice per minute with much higher accuracy (referred to as real-time monitoring).

This allows process engineers to treat corrosion as another process variable that can be optimized in the system. Immediate responses to process changes allow the control of corrosion mechanisms, so they can be minimized while also maximizing production output. In an ideal situation having on-line corrosion information that is accurate and real-time will allow conditions that cause high corrosion rates to be identified and reduced. This is known as predictive management.

Materials methods include selecting the proper material for the application. In areas of minimal corrosion, cheap materials are preferable, but when bad corrosion can occur, more expensive but longer lasting materials should be used. Other materials methods come in the form of protective barriers between corrosive substances and the equipment metals. These can be either a lining of refractory material such as standard Portland cement or other special acid-resistant cements that are shot onto the inner surface of the vessel. Also available are thin overlays of more expensive metals that protect cheaper metal against corrosion without requiring lots of material.

History

The first oil refineries in the world were built by Ignacy £ukasiewicz near Jas³o, Poland from 1854 to 1856, but they were initially small as there was no real demand for refined fuel. As £ukasiewicz's kerosene lamp gained popularity, the refining industry grew in the area.

The world's first large refinery opened at Cîmpina, Romania, in 1856-1857, with United States investment. After being taken over by Nazi Germany, the Cîmpina refineries were bombed in Operation Tidal Wave by the Allies during the Oil Campaign of World War II. Another early large refinery is Oljeon, Sweden (1875) (Swedish name means *The Petroleum Isle*), now preserved as a museum near Engelsberg Ironworks, a UNESCO World Heritage Site, and part of the Ekomuseum Bergslagen.

At one point, the refinery in Ras Tanura, Saudi Arabia owned by Saudi Aramco was claimed to be the largest oil refinery in the world. For most of the 20th century, the largest refinery was the Abadan Refinery in Iran. This refinery suffered extensive damage during the Iran-Iraq war. The world's largest refinery complex is the Jamnagar Refinery Complex, consisting of two refineries side by side operated by Reliance Industries Limited in Jamnagar, India with a combined production capacity of 1,240,000 barrels per day (197,000 m^3/d) (J-1 660,000 bbl/d (105,000 m^3/d), J-2 580,000 bbl/d (92,000 m^3/d). PDVSA's Paraguana refinery complex in Venezuela with a capacity of 956,000 bbl/d (152,000 m^3/d) and SK Energy's Ulsan in South Korea with 840,000 bbl/d (134,000 m^3/d) are the second and third largest, respectively.

Oil Refining in the United States

In the 19th century, refineries in the U.S. processed crude oil primarily to recover the kerosene. There was no market for the more volatile fraction, including gasoline, which was considered waste and was often dumped directly into the nearest river. The invention of the automobile shifted the demand to gasoline and diesel, which remain the primary refined products today. Today, national and state legislation requires refineries to meet stringent air and water cleanliness standards. In fact, oil companies in the U.S. perceive obtaining a permit to build a modern refinery to be so difficult and costly that no new refineries have been built (though many have been expanded) in the U.S. since 1976.

More than half the refineries that existed in 1981 are now closed due to low utilization rates and accelerating mergers. As a result of these closures total US refinery capacity fell between 1981 to 1995, though the operating capacity stayed fairly constant in that time period at around 15,000,000 barrels per day (2,400,000 m^3/d). Increases in facility size and improvements in efficiencies have offset much of the lost physical capacity of the industry. In 1982 (the earliest data provided), the United States operate 301 refineries with a combined capacity of 17.9 million barrels (2,850,000 m^3) of crude oil each calendar day. In 2010, there were 149 operable U.S. refineries with a combined capacity of 17.6 million barrels (2,800,000 m^3) per calendar day.

In 2009 through 2010, as revenue streams in the oil business dried up and profitability of oil refineries fell due to lower demand for product and high reserves of supply preceding the economic recession, oil companies began to close or sell refineries. Due to EPA regulations, the costs associated with closing a refinery are very high, meaning that many former refineries are re-purposed.

K Factor Crude Oil Refining

In the oil and gas engineering industry, the K-factor formula is used to calculate pressure drop across fittings or a set of fittings in a piping system. K-factor, when multiplied by ρv2/2, gives pressure drop across the fittings. K-factor can also be used to find out the equivalent length of all the fittings in a piping system. When the total pressure drop across a line (straight line + fittings) is divided by pressure drop per unit length for that line, the result is equivalent straight length of that piping system accounting for all the bends and fittings.

List of Oil Refineries

This is a list of oil refineries. The Oil and Gas Journal also publishes a worldwide list of refineries annually in a country-by-country tabulation that includes for each refinery: location, crude oil daily processing capacity, and the size of each process unit in the refinery. For the U.S., the refinery list is further categorized state-by-state. The list usually appears in one of their December issues. It is about 45 pages in length and is updated each year with additions, deletions, name changes, capacity changes, etc.

World's largest refineries

Name of Refinery	*Location*	*Barrels per Day*
Jamnagar Refinery (Reliance Industries Limited)	Jamnagar, Gujarat, India	1,300,000
Paraguana Refinery Complex (PDVSA)	Paraguana, Falcon, Venezuela	940,000
Baytown Refinery (ExxonMobil)	Baytown, TX, USA	572,500
Baton Rouge Refinery (ExxonMobil)	Baton Rouge, LA, USA	503,000
Hovensa LLC (PDVSA) (Hess Corporation)	Virgin Islands, USA	500,000
Marathon Petroleum Company	Garyville LA, USA	464,000
BP Texas City	Texas City,TX USA	460,000
Abadan Refinery	Iran	450,000
BP Whiting Refinery	Whiting, IN	440,000
Citgo Petroleum Corporation	Lake Charles LA, USA	427,800
Royal Dutch Shell Pernis Refinery	Netherlands	416,000
Fawley Southampton Refinery (ExxonMobil)	Southampton, United Kingdom	347,000
Kirishi Refinery (Surgutneftegas)	Kirishi, Russia	337,000
Flint Hills Resources	Corpus Christi TX, USA	288,000
Chevron Richmond Refinery	Richmond CA, USA	240,000
Saudi Aramco Yanbu Refinery	Yanbu, KSA	235,000

Africa

Algeria:

- Adrar Refinery (CNPC), 12,500 bbl/d (1,990 m^3/d)
- Alger Refinery (Sonatrach), 55,000 bbl/d (8,700 m^3/d)
- Arzew Refinery (Sonatrach), 50,000 bbl/d (7,900 m^3/d)
- Hassi Messaoud Refinery (Sonatrach), 25,000 bbl/d (4,000 m^3/d)
- Skikda Refinery (Sonatrach), 356,000 bbl/d (56,600 m^3/d).

Angola:

- Cabinda Refinery (Chevron Corporation), 16,000 bbl/d (2,500 m^3/d)
- Luanda Refinery (Sonangol), 56,000 bbl/d (8,900 m^3/d)

Cameroon:

- Limbé Refinery (SoNaRa), 42,600 bbl/d (6,770 m^3/d).

Chad:

- N'Djamena Refinery (Société de Raffinage de N'Djamena), 20,000 bbl/d (3,200 m^3/d).

Congo:

- Pointe Noire Refinery (CORAF), 21,000 bbl/d (3,300 m^3/d).

Côte d'Ivoire:

- Abidjan Refinery (SIR), 68,000 bbl/d (10,800 m^3/d)
- Abidjan Bitumen Refinery (SMB), 10,000 bbl/d (1,600 m^3/d).

Egypt:

- Alexandria Ameriya Refinery (EGPC), 81,000 bbl/d (12,900 m^3/d)
- Alexandria El Mex Refinery (EGPC), 117,000 bbl/d (18,600 m^3/d)
- Alexandria MIDOR Refinery (EGPC), 100,000 bbl/d (16,000 m^3/d)
- Asyut Refinery (EGPC), 47,000 bbl/d (7,500 m^3/d)
- Cairo Mostorod Refinery (EGPC), 142,000 bbl/d (22,600 m^3/d)
- El Nasr Refinery (EGPC), 132,000 bbl/d (21,000 m^3/d)
- El Suez Refinery (EGPC), 70,000 bbl/d (11,000 m^3/d)
- Tanta Refinery (EGPC), 35,000 bbl/d (5,600 m^3/d)
- Wadi Feran Refinery (EGPC), 8,550 bbl/d (1,359 m^3/d).

Gabon:

- Port Gentil Refinery (Sogara), 25,000 bbl/d (4,000 m^3/d).

Ghana:

- Tema Oil Refinery (TOR), 45,000 bbl/d (7,200 m^3/d).

Kenya:

- Mombasa Refinery (KPRL), 70,000 bbl/d (11,000 m^3/d).

Libya:

- Zawiya Refinery (NOC), 120,000 bbl/d (19,000 m^3/d)
- Ra's Lanuf Refinery (NOC), 220,000 bbl/d (35,000 m^3/d)
- El-Brega Refinery (NOC), 10,000 bbl/d (1,600 m^3/d)
- Sarir Refinery (AGOC), 10,000 bbl/d (1,600 m^3/d)
- Tobruk Refinery (AGOC), 20,000 bbl/d (3,200 m^3/d).

Morocco:

- Mohammedia Refinery (SAMIR), 127,000 bbl/d (20,200 m^3/d)

Nigeria:

- Kaduna Refinery (NNPC), 110,000 bbl/d (17,000 m^3/d)
- Port Harcourt Refinery (NNPC), 210,000 bbl/d (33,000 m^3/d)
- Warri Refinery (NNPC), 125,000 bbl/d (19,900 m^3/d).

Senegal:

- Dakar Refinery (SAR), 127,000 bbl/d (20,200 m^3/d).

South Africa:

- Cape Town Refinery (Chevron Corporation), 110,000 bbl/d (17,000 m^3/d)
- Durban Engen Refinery (Petronas), 122,000 bbl/d (19,400 m^3/d)
- Durban Sapref Refinery (Sapref), 125,000 bbl/d (19,900 m^3/d)
- Sasolburg Refinery (Sasol), 125,000 bbl/d (19,900 m^3/d).

Sudan:

- El Obeid Refinery (ERC), 15,000 bbl/d (2,400 m^3/d)
- Khartoum Refinery (KRC), 100,000 bbl/d (16,000 m^3/d).

Tunisia:

- Bizerte Refinery (STIR), 34,000 bbl/d (5,400 m^3/d).

Zambia:

- Ndola Refinery (Indeni), 34,000 bbl/d (5,400 m^3/d).

Asia

Bangladesh:

- Eastern Refinery.

China:

- Fushun Petrochemical Refinery (CNPC), 160,000 bbl/d (25,000 m^3/d).

India:

- Assam
  - Digboi Refinery, Assam (IOC), 13,000 bbl/d (2,100 m^3/d)
  - Guwahati Refinery, Assam (IOC), 20,000 bbl/d (3,200 m^3/d)
  - Bongaigaon Refinery, (IOC), 48,000 bbl/d (7,600 m^3/d)
  - Numaligarh Refinery Limited, Assam (NRL), 58,000 bbl/d (9,200 m^3/d)
- Bihar
  - Barauni Refinery (IOC), 116,000 bbl/d (18,400 m^3/d)
- Punjab
  - Guru Gobind Singh Refinery Bhatinda (HPCL and Mittal energy limited -HMEL)Template:14 MMTPA
- Gujarat
  - Jamnagar Refinery (Reliance Industries), 1,240,000 bbl/d (197,000 m^3/d)
  - Essar Refinery (Essar Oil), 300,000 bbl/d (48,000 m^3/d)
  - Gujarat Refinery (IOC), 170,000 bbl/d (27,000 m^3/d)
- Haryana
  - Panipat Refinery (IOC), 300,000 bbl/d (48,000 m^3/d)
- Karnataka
  - Mangalore Refinery (MRPL), 199,000 bbl/d (31,600 m^3/d)
- Madhya Pradesh
  - Bina Refinery (BORL), 116,000 bbl/d (18,400 m^3/d)
- West Bengal
  - Haldia Refinery (IOC), 116,000 bbl/d (18,400 m^3/d)
- Uttar Pradesh
  - Mathura Refinery (IOC), 156,000 bbl/d (24,800 m^3/d)
- Maharashtra
  - Mumbai Refinery (HPCL), 107,000 bbl/d (17,000 m^3/d)
  - Mumbai Refinery Mahaul (BPCL), 135,000 bbl/d (21,500 m^3/d)
- Andhra Pradesh
  - Visakhapatnam Refinery (HPCL), 150,000 bbl/d (24,000 m^3/d)

  - o Tatipaka Refinery (ONGC), 1,600 bbl/d (250 m^3/d)
- Kerala
  - o Kochi Refinery (BPCL), 172,000 bbl/d (27,300 m^3/d)
- Tamil Nadu
  - o Chennai Refinery (IOC), 185,000 bbl/d (29,400 m^3/d)
  - o Nagapattnam Refinery (CPCL), 20,000 bbl/d (3,200 m^3/d).

Indonesia:

- Musi Refinery (Pertamina), 135,200 bbl/d (21,500 m^3/d)
- Balongan Refinery (Pertamina), 125,000 bbl/d (19,900 m^3/d)
- Dumai Refinery (Pertamina), 120,000 bbl/d (19,000 m^3/d)
- Cilacap Refinery (Pertamina), 348,000 bbl/d (55,300 m^3/d)
- Balikpapan Refinery (Pertamina), 260,000 bbl/d (41,000 m^3/d)
- Sungai Pakning Refinery (Pertamina), 50,000 bbl/d (7,900 m^3/d)
- Pangkalan Brandan Refinery (Pertamina), 5,000 bbl/d (790 m^3/d)
- Cepu Refinery (Pertamina), 3,800 bbl/d (600 m^3/d)
- Kasim Refinery (Pertamina), 10,000 bbl/d (1,600 m^3/d)
- Tuban Refinery (PT TPPI), 100,000 bbl/d (16,000 m^3/d).

Iran:

- Abadan Refinery (NIOC), 450,000 bbl/d (72,000 m^3/d)
- Arak Refinery (NIOC), 150,000 bbl/d (24,000 m^3/d)
- Tehran Refinery (NIOC), 225,000 bbl/d (35,800 m^3/d)
- Isfahan Refinery (NIOC), 265,000 bbl/d (42,100 m^3/d)
- Tabriz Refinery (NIOC), 112,000 bbl/d (17,800 m^3/d)
- Shiraz Refinery (NIOC), 40,000 bbl/d (6,400 m^3/d)
- Lavan Refinery (NIOC), 20,000 bbl/d (3,200 m^3/d)
- Bandar Abbas Refinery (NIOC), 232,000 bbl/d (36,900 m^3/d)
- Kermanshah refinery (NIOC),21,000 bpd.

Iraq:

- Basrah Refinery (INOC), 126,000 bbl/d (20,000 m^3/d)
- Daurah Refinery (INOC), 100,000 bbl/d (16,000 m^3/d)
- Kirkuk Refinery (INOC), 270,000 bbl/d (43,000 m^3/d)
- Baiji Salahedden Refinery (INOC), 140,000 bbl/d (22,000 m^3/d)
- Baiji North Refinery (INOC), 150,000 bbl/d (24,000 m^3/d)
- Khanaqin/Alwand Refinery (INOC), 10,500 bbl/d (1,670 m^3/d)

- Samawah Refinery (INOC), 27,000 bbl/d (4,300 m³/d)
- Haditha Refinery (INOC), 14,000 bbl/d (2,200 m³/d)
- Muftiah Refinery (INOC), 4,500 bbl/d (720 m³/d)
- Gaiyarah Refinery (INOC), 4,000 bbl/d (640 m³/d)
- Irbel Refinery (INOC), 40,000 bbl/d (6,400 m³/d).

Japan:

- Chiba Refinery (Cosmo Oil) (Cosmo Oil), 240,000 bbl/d (38,000 m³/d)
- Yokkaichi Refinery (Cosmo Oil), 175,000 bbl/d (27,800 m³/d)
- Sakai Refinery (Cosmo Oil) (Cosmo Oil), 80,000 bbl/d (13,000 m³/d)
- Sakaide Refinery (Cosmo Oil), 140,000 bbl/d (22,000 m³/d)
- Muroran Refinery (Nippon Oil Corporation (NOC)), 180,000 bbl/d (29,000 m³/d)
- Sendai Refinery (Nippon Oil Corporation (NOC)), 145,000 bbl/d (23,100 m³/d)
- Negishi Yokahama Refinery (Nippon Oil Corporation (NOC)), 340,000 bbl/d (54,000 m³/d)
- Osaka Refinery (Nippon Oil Corporation (NOC)) 115,000 bpd
- Mizushima Refinery (Nippon Oil Corporation (NOC)), 250,000 bbl/d (40,000 m³/d)
- Marifu Refinery (Nippon Oil Corporation (NOC)) 127,000 bpd
- Toyama Refinery (Nihonkai Oil/Nippon Oil Corporation (NOC)), 60,000 bbl/d (9,500 m³/d)
- Kubiki Refinery (Teikoku Oil), 4,410 bbl/d (701 m³/d)
- Chiba Refinery (Kyokuto) (Kyokuto Petroleum/ExxonMobil), 175,000 bbl/d (27,800 m³/d)
- Kawasaki Refinery (TonenGeneral Sekiyu/ExxonMobil), 335,000 bbl/d (53,300 m³/d)
- Wakayama Refinery (TonenGeneral Sekiyu/ExxonMobil), 170,000 bbl/d (27,000 m³/d)
- Sakai Refinery (TonenGeneral) (TonenGeneral Sekiyu/ExxonMobil), 156,000 bbl/d (24,800 m³/d)
- Nishihara Refinery (Nansei sekiyu/Petrobras), 100,000 bbl/d (16,000 m³/d)
- Keihin Refinery (Toa Oil/Shell), 185,000 bbl/d (29,400 m³/d)

- Showa Yokkaichi Refinery (Showa Yokkaichi/Shell), 210,000 bbl/d (33,000 m^3/d)
- Yamaguchi Refinery (Seibu Oil/Shell), 120,000 bbl/d (19,000 m^3/d)
- Sodegaura Refinery (Fuji Oil Campany), 192,000 bbl/d (30,500 m^3/d)
- Kashima Refinery (Kashima Oil Campany/Japan Energy), 210,000 bbl/d (33,000 m^3/d)
- Mizushima Refinery (Japan Energy) (Japan Energy), 205,200 bbl/d (32,620 m^3/d)
- Shikoku Refinery (Taiyo Oil), 120,000 bbl/d (19,000 m^3/d)
- Ohita Refinery (Kyusyu Oil), 160,000 bbl/d (25,000 m^3/d)
- Hokkaido Refinery (Idemitsu Kosan), 140,000 bbl/d (22,000 m^3/d)
- Chiba Refinery (Idemitsu) (Idemitsu Kosan), 220,000 bbl/d (35,000 m^3/d)
- Aichi Refinery (Idemitsu Kosan), 160,000 bbl/d (25,000 m^3/d)
- Tokuyama Refinery (Idemitsu Kosan), 120,000 bbl/d (19,000 m^3/d).

Jordan:

- Jordan Refinery, Zarqa, Az Zarqa, (Jordan Petroleum Refinery Company), 65,000 bbl/d (10,300 m^3/d).

Kazakhstan:

- Shymkent Refinery (PetroKazakhstan), 160,000 bbl/d (25,000 m^3/d)
- Pavlodar Refinery (KazMunayGas), 162,600 bbl/d (25,850 m^3/d)
- Atyrau Refinery (KazMunayGas), 104,400 bbl/d (16,600 m^3/d)

Kuwait:

- Mina Al-Ahmadi Refinery (KNPC), 470,000 bbl/d (75,000 m^3/d)
- Shuaiba Refinery (KNPC), 200,000 bbl/d (32,000 m^3/d)
- Mina Abdullah Refinery (KNPC), 270,000 bbl/d (43,000 m^3/d)

Malaysia:

- Melaka I Refinery (Petronas), 100,000 bbl/d (16,000 m^3/d)[3]
- Melaka II Refinery (Petronas/ConocoPhillips), 100,000 bbl/d (16,000 m^3/d)[4]
- Kertih Refinery (Petronas), 40,000 bbl/d (6,400 m^3/d)
- Port Dickson Refinery (Royal Dutch Shell), 156,000 bbl/d (24,800 m^3/d)[5]

- Lutong Refinery (Royal Dutch Shell), 45,000 bbl/d (7,200 m^3/d). Has been closed.
- Esso Port Dickson Refinery (ExxonMobil), 88,000 bbl/d (14,000 m^3/d).

Oman:

- Mina Al Fahal Oman Refinery Company (ORC) 85,000 bbl/d (13,500 m^3/d)
- Sohar Refinery Company (SRC) 116,000 bbl/d (18,400 m^3/d)
- Dukum Refinery Company (DRC) 200,000 bpd (Proposed).

Pakistan:

- six oil refrenies
- Pakistan Refinery Limited (PRL), 15,000 bbl/d (2,400 m^3/d)
- National Refinery Limited (NRL),64,000 bpd
- Attock Refinery Limited (ARL), 46,000 bbl/d (7,300 m^3/d)
- Enar Petroleum Refining Facility (EPRF), 3,000 bbl/d (480 m^3/d)
- TransAisa Refinery Limited (TRL), 96,000 bbl/d (15,300 m^3/d)
- Taba Refinery Limited (TRL), 76,000 bbl/d (12,100 m^3/d).

Papua New Guinea:

- InterOil Refinery, Port Moresby (InterOil), 32,500 bbl/d (5,170 m^3/d).

Philippines:

- Limay Refinery (Petron), 180,000 bbl/d (29,000 m^3/d)
- Tabangao Refinery (Royal Dutch Shell), 120,000 bbl/d (19,000 m^3/d)
- Batangas Refinery (Caltex(Chevron)), 86,000 bbl/d (13,700 m^3/d).

Qatar:

- Um Said Refinery (QP Refinery 100%), 147,000 bbl/d (23,400 m^3/d)
- Lafan Refinery (Qatar Petroleum 51%, ExxonMobil 10%, Total 10%, Idemitsu 10%, Cosmo 10%, Mitsui 4.5%, Marubeni 4.5%), 146,000 bbl/d (23,200 m^3/d)
- AL-Shahene Refinery (2012), 250,000 bbl/d (40,000 m^3/d).

Saudi Arabia:

- Riyadh Refinery (Saudi Aramco), 120,000 bbl/d (19,000 m^3/d)

- Rabigh Refinery (PetroRabigh), 400,000 bbl/d (64,000 m^3/d)
- Jeddah Refinery (Saudi Aramco), 100,000 bbl/d (16,000 m^3/d)
- Ras Tanura Refinery (Saudi Aramco), 550,000 bbl/d (87,000 m^3/d)
- Yanbu' Refinery (Saudi Aramco), 225,000 bbl/d (35,800 m^3/d)
- Yanbu' Refinery (SAMREF) (Saudi Aramco/Exxon Mobil), 400,000 bbl/d (64,000 m^3/d)
- Yanbu' Refinery (Saudi Aramco/ConocoPhillips), 400,000 bbl/d (64,000 m^3/d)
- Jubail Refinery (SASREF) (Saudi Aramco/Shell), 305,000 bbl/d (48,500 m^3/d)
- Jubail Refinery (Saudi Aramco/TOTAL), 400,000 bbl/d (64,000 m^3/d).

Singapore:

- ExxonMobil Jurong Island Refinery (ExxonMobil), 605,000 bbl/d (96,200 m^3/d)
- SRC Jurong Island Refinery (Singapore Refining Corporation), 285,000 bbl/d (45,300 m^3/d)
- Shell Pulau Bukom Refinery (Royal Dutch Shell), 458,000 bbl/d (72,800 m^3/d)

Sri Lanka:

- Sapugaskanda Oil Refinery [cpc], 51,000 bbl/d (8,100 m^3/d)

South Korea:

- SK Energy Co., Ltd. Ulsan Refinery (SK Energy), 850,000 bbl/d (135,000 m^3/d)
- S-Oil Ulsan Refinery (S-Oil), 560,000 bbl/d (89,000 m^3/d)
- GS-Caltex Yeosu Refinery (GS-Caltex), 730,000 bbl/d (116,000 m^3/d)
- SK Energy Co., Ltd. Inchon Refinery (SK Energy), 275,000 bbl/d (43,700 m^3/d)
- Hyundai Daesan Refinery (Hyundai), 275,000 bbl/d (43,700 m^3/d)

Taiwan:

- Talin Refinery (CPC), 100,000 bbl/d (16,000 m^3/d)
- Kaohsiung Refinery (CPC), 270,000 bbl/d (43,000 m^3/d)
- Taoyuan Refinery (CPC), 200,000 bbl/d (32,000 m^3/d)
- Mailiao Refinery (*Formosa*), 450,000 bbl/d (72,000 m^3/d).

Thailand:

- Thai Oil Refinery (Thai Oil Company of PTT), 220,000 bbl/d (35,000 m^3/d)
- IRPC Refinery (IRPC PLC of PTT), 215,000 bbl/d (34,200 m^3/d)
- Rayong Refinery (Rayong Refinery PLC of PTT), 145,000 bbl/d (23,100 m^3/d)
- SPRC Refinery (Star Petroleum Refining Company of PTT), 150,000 bbl/d (24,000 m^3/d)
- Bangchak Refinery (Bangchak Petroleum of PTT), 120,000 bbl/d (19,000 m^3/d)
- Sri Racha Refinery (ExxonMobil), 170,000 bbl/d (27,000 m^3/d)
- Rayong Purifier Refinery (Rayong Purifier Company), 17,000 bbl/d (2,700 m^3/d)

Turkmenistan:

- Seidi, 120,000 bbl/d (19,000 m^3/d)
- Turkmenbashi, 116,000 bbl/d (18,400 m^3/d)

United Arab Emirates:

- Al-Ruwais Refinery (Abu Dhabi Oil Refining Company), 280,000 bbl/d (45,000 m^3/d)
- Umm Al-Narr Refinery (Abu Dhabi Oil Refining Company), 90,000 bbl/d (14,000 m^3/d)
- Jebel Ali Refinery (ENOC), 120,000 bbl/d (19,000 m^3/d)
- Hamriyah Sharjah Refinery (Sharjah Oil), 71,300 bbl/d (11,340 m^3/d)

Vietnam:

- Dung Quat Refinery (Petrovietnam), 148,000 bbl/d (23,500 m^3/d)

Yemen:

- Aden Refinery, (Aden Refinery Company), 120,000 bbl/d (19,000 m^3/d)
- Marib Refinery, (Yemen Hunt Oil Company), 10,000 bbl/d (1,600 m^3/d).

Europe

Austria:

- Schwechat Refinery, (OMV), 176,000 bbl/d (28,000 m^3/d)

Azerbaijan:

- Haydar Aliev Refinery (SOCAR), 220,000 bbl/d (35,000 m^3/d)
- Azerineftyag Refinery (SOCAR), 239,000 bbl/d (38,000 m^3/d)

Bosnia and Herzegovina:

- Bosanski Brod Refinery.

Belarus:

- Mozyr Refinery, (Slavneft),[7] 95,000 bbl/d (15,100 m^3/d)
- Novopolotsk Refinery, (Naftan), [8] 88,000 bbl/d (14,000 m^3/d)

Belgium:

- Total Antwerp Refinery, (Total), 360,000 bbl/d (57,000 m^3/d)
- ExxonMobil Antwerp Refinery, (ExxonMobil), 333,000 bbl/d (52,900 m^3/d)
- Antwerp N.V. Refinery, (Vitol), 35,000 bbl/d (5,600 m^3/d)
- BRC Antwerp (Petroplus), 115,000 bbl/d (18,300 m^3/d).

Bulgaria:

- LUKOIL Neftochim Burgas, (LUKOIL), 208,000 bbl/d (33,100 m^3/d)

Croatia:

- Rijeka Refinery, (INA), 90,000 bbl/d (14,000 m^3/d)
- Sisak Refinery, (INA), 60,000 bbl/d (9,500 m^3/d)

Czech Republic:

- Kralupy Refinery, (Ceska Rafinerska), 55,000 bbl/d (8,700 m^3/d)
- Litvinov Refinery, (Ceska Rafinerska), 120,000 bbl/d (19,000 m^3/d)
- Pardubice Refinery, (PARAMO), 15,000 bbl/d (2,400 m^3/d).

Denmark:

- Kalundborg Refinery, (Statoil), 110,000 bbl/d (17,000 m^3/d)
- Fredericia Refinery, (Royal Dutch Shell), 68,000 bbl/d (10,800 m^3/d).

Finland:

- Porvoo Refinery, (Neste Oil Oyj), 206,000 bbl/d (32,800 m^3/d)
- Naantali Refinery, (Neste Oil Oyj), 58,000 bbl/d (9,200 m^3/d)

France:

- Provence Refinery, (Total), 155,000 bbl/d (24,600 m^3/d)
- Normandy Refinery, (Total), 350,000 bbl/d (56,000 m^3/d)

- Flandres Refinery, (Total), 160,000 bbl/d (25,000 m^3/d) going to be closed
- Donges Refinery, (Total), 231,000 bbl/d (36,700 m^3/d).
- Feyzin Refinery, (Total), 119,000 bbl/d (18,900 m^3/d)
- Grandpuits Refinery, (Total), 99,000 bbl/d (15,700 m^3/d)
- Port Jérôme-Gravenchon Refinery, (ExxonMobil), 270,000 bbl/d (43,000 m^3/d)
- Fos-sur-Mer Refinery, (ExxonMobil), 140,000 bbl/d (22,000 m^3/d)
- Reichstett Refinery, (Petroplus), 77,000 bbl/d (12,200 m^3/d)
- Petit Couronne Refinery, (Petroplus), 142,000 bbl/d (22,600 m^3/d)
- Berre L'Etang Refinery, (LyondellBasell), 80,000 bbl/d (13,000 m^3/d)
- Lavera Marseilles Refinery, (Ineos), 220,000 bbl/d (35,000 m^3/d)
- Fort de France Refinery, (Total), 17,000 bbl/d (2,700 m^3/d).

Germany:

- Schwedt Refinery (PCK Raffinerie(Shell/PDVSA/BP/AET), 210,000 bbl/d (33,000 m^3/d)
- Ingolstadt Refinery (Bayernoil(OMV/Agip/PDVSA/BP)), 262,000 bbl/d (41,700 m^3/d)
- Ingolstadt Refinery (Petroplus), 110,000 bbl/d (17,000 m^3/d)
- Ruhr Ol Refinery (Rosneft/BP), 266,000 bbl/d (42,300 m^3/d)
- Buna SOW Leuna Refinery (Total), 222,000 bbl/d (35,300 m^3/d)
- Wilhelmshaven Refinery (ConocoPhillips), 300,000 bbl/d (48,000 m^3/d)
- Rheinland Werk Godorf Cologne Refinery (Royal Dutch Shell), 190,000 bbl/d (30,000 m^3/d)
- Rheinland Werk Wesseling Cologne Refinery (Royal Dutch Shell), 160,000 bbl/d (25,000 m^3/d)
- Mineralolraffinerie Karlsruhe Refinery (MiRo(Shell/ExxonMobil/PDVSA/BP/Conoco)) 285,000 bpd
- Burghausen Refinery (OMV) 70,000 bpd
- Mitteldeutschland Spergau Refinery (Total) 227,000 bpd
- Emsland Lingen Refinery (BP) 80,000 bpd
- Elbe Mineralolwerke Hamburg-Harburg Refinery (Royal Dutch Shell)
- Holborn Europa Raffinerie GmbH Hamburg (Holborn) 100,000 bpd.

Greece:

- Aspropyrgos Refinery, (Hellenic Petroleum), 135,000 bbl/d (21,500 m^3/d)
- Elefsina Refinery, (Hellenic Petroleum), 100,000 bbl/d (16,000 m^3/d)
- Thessaloniki Refinery, (Hellenic Petroleum), 66,500 bbl/d (10,570 m^3/d)

Hungary:

- Szazhalombatta Refinery, (MOL), 161,000 bbl/d (25,600 m^3/d)

Ireland:

- Whitegate Refinery, (ConocoPhillips), 71,000 bbl/d (11,300 m^3/d).

Italy:

- Esso Trecate, Novara Refinery, (ExxonMobil 74.1%/ERG 25.9%), 200,000 bbl/d (32,000 m^3/d)
- Esso Augusta Refinery, (ExxonMobil), 190,000 bbl/d (30,000 m^3/d)
- Sarroch Refinery, (Saras SPA), 300,000 bbl/d (48,000 m^3/d)
- Rome Refinery, (Total 77.5%/ERG 22.5%), 90,000 bbl/d (14,000 m^3/d)
- Falconara Marittima Ancona Refinery, (APIOIL), 85,000 bbl/d (13,500 m^3/d)
- Mantova Refinery, (IESItaliana), 55,000 bbl/d (8,700 m^3/d)
- Impianti Sud Refinery, (ISAB ERG), 214,000 bbl/d (34,000 m^3/d)
- Impianti Nord Refinery, (ISAB ERG), 160,000 bbl/d (25,000 m^3/d)
- Milazzo Refinery, (Eni/KNPC) 80,000 bpd
- Sannazzaro de' Burgondi Refinery, (Eni) 160,000 bpd
- Gela Refinery, (Eni) 100,000 bpd
- Taranto Refinery, (Eni) 90,000 bpd
- Livorno Refinery, (Eni) 84,000 bpd
- Porto Marghera Venice Refinery, (Eni) 70,000 bpd
- Cremona Refiney, (Tamoil) 80,000 bpd
- Iplom [9] Busalla, Genoa.

Lithuania:

- Mazeikiu Refinery, (Mazeikiu Nafta - PKN Orlen), 263,000 bbl/d (41,800 m^3/d)

Macedonia:

- OKTA Skopje Refinery, (Hellenic Petroleum), 50,000 bbl/d (7,900 m^3/d)

Netherlands:

- Shell Pernis Refinery, (Royal Dutch Shell), 416,000 bbl/d (66,100 m^3/d)
- Botlek (ExxonMobil) Rotterdam, 195,000 bbl/d (31,000 m^3/d)
- Total Refinery Netherlands - Vlissingen, (Total/LUKoil), 158,000 bbl/d (25,100 m^3/d)
- Europoort, (BP), 400,000 bbl/d (64,000 m^3/d)
- Q8-KPE Refinery Europoort, (Q8-Kuwait Petroleum Company), 80,000 bbl/d (13,000 m^3/d).

Norway:

- Slagen Refinery, (ExxonMobil), 110,000 bbl/d (17,000 m^3/d)
- Mongstad Refinery, (Statoil), 200,000 bbl/d (32,000 m^3/d).

Poland:

- Plock Refinery, (PKN Orlen), 276,000 bbl/d (43,900 m^3/d)
- Gdansk Refinery, (Grupa LOTOS), 210,000 bbl/d (33,000 m^3/d), (processing capacity after second distillation startup in 1Q2010).
- Czechowice Refinery, (Grupa LOTOS), 12,000 bbl/d (1,900 m^3/d), crude oil processing terminated 1Q2006.
- Trzebinia Refinery, (PKN Orlen), 4,000 bbl/d (640 m^3/d)
- Jaslo Oil Refinery , (Grupa LOTOS), 3,000 bbl/d (480 m^3/d), crude oil processing terminated 4Q2008.
- Jedlicze Refinery, (PKN Orlen), 2,800 bbl/d (450 m^3/d).
- Glimar Refinery, (Hudson Oil), 3,400 bbl/d (540 m^3/d), all operations (incl. crude oil processing) terminated 2005. Acquired 2011.

Portugal:

- Porto Refinery, (Galp Energia), 100,000 bbl/d (16,000 m^3/d)
- Sines Refinery, (Galp Energia), 200,000 bbl/d (32,000 m^3/d)

Romania:

- Arpechim Refinery Pite°ti, (Petrom/OMV), 70,000 bbl/d (11,000 m^3/d)
- Astra Refinery, (Interagro), closed for preservation , 20,000 bbl/d (3,200 m^3/d)

- Petrobrazi Refinery Ploie°ti, (Petrom/OMV), 90,000 bbl/d (14,000 m^3/d)
- Petromidia Constanþa Refinery, (Rompetrol), 100,000 bbl/d (16,000 m^3/d)
- Petrotel Lukoil Refinery Ploie°ti, (LUKOIL), 68,000 bbl/d (10,800 m^3/d)
- Petrolsub Suplacu de Barcãu Refinery, (Petrom/OMV), 15,000 bbl/d (2,400 m^3/d)
- RAFO One°ti, (Calder A), 70,000 bbl/d (11,000 m^3/d)
- Steaua Romanã Câmpina Refinery, (Omnimpex Chemicals), 15,000 bbl/d (2,400 m^3/d)
- Vega Ploie°ti Refinery, (Rompetrol), 20,000 bbl/d (3,200 m^3/d).

Kosovo:

- Kulla Exim Refinery, (KER), 101,000 bbl/d (16,100 m^3/d).

Russia:

Refineries with capacity more than 20,000 bbl/d (3,200 m^3/d)

Europe:

- Syzran Refinery, (Rosneft), 213,400 bbl/d (33,930 m^3/d)
- Novokuibyshevsk Refinery, (Rosneft), 191,500 bbl/d (30,450 m^3/d)
- Kuibyshev Oil Refinery, (Rosneft), 139,800 bbl/d (22,230 m^3/d)
- Salavatnefteorgsintez Refinery, (Gazprom, Salavat), 250,000 bbl/d (40,000 m^3/d)
- Volgograd Refinery, (LUKOIL), 193,000 bbl/d (30,700 m^3/d)
- Ukhta Refinery, (LUKOIL), 72,000 bbl/d (11,400 m^3/d)
- Perm Refinery, (LUKOIL), 235,000 bbl/d (37,400 m^3/d)
- NORSI-oil, (LUKOIL, Kstovo), 292,000 bbl/d (46,400 m^3/d)
- Ryazan Refinery, (TNK-BP), 253,000 bbl/d (40,200 m^3/d)
- Orsk Refinery, (Russneft), 159,000 bbl/d (25,300 m^3/d)
- Saratov Refinery, (TNK-BP), 108,000 bbl/d (17,200 m^3/d)
- Moscow Refinery, (Gazprom Neft/Central Fuel Company/ Tatneft), 213,000 bbl/d (33,900 m^3/d)
- Kirishi Refinery, (Surgutneftegas), 337,000 bbl/d (53,600 m^3/d)
- YaNOS Yaroslavl Refinery, (Slavneft), 132,000 bbl/d (21,000 m^3/d)

- Krasnodar Refinery, (Russneft), 58,000 bbl/d (9,200 m^3/d)
- Tuapse Refinery, (Rosneft), 85,000 bbl/d (13,500 m^3/d)
- Nizhnekamsk Refinery, (TAIF), 14,000 bbl/d (2,200 m^3/d)
- Ufa Refinery, (Bashneft), 190,000 bbl/d (30,000 m^3/d)
- Novo-Ufa Refinery, (Bashneft), 380,000 bbl/d (60,000 m^3/d)
- Ufaneftekhim Refinery, (Bashneft), 250,000 bbl/d (40,000 m^3/d)

Asia:

- Achinsk Refinery, (Rosneft), 131,000 bbl/d (20,800 m^3/d)
- Angarsk Petrochemical Refinery, (Rosneft), 384,000 bbl/d (61,100 m^3/d)
- Khabarovsk Refinery, (Alliance), 85,000 bbl/d (13,500 m^3/d)
- Komsomolsk Refinery, (Rosneft), 120,000 bbl/d (19,000 m^3/d)
- Nizhnevartovsk Refinery, (TNK-BP), 25,100 bbl/d (3,990 m^3/d)
- Omsk Refinery, (Gazprom Neft), 380,000 bbl/d (60,000 m^3/d).

Serbia:

- Panèevo Refinery (Naftna Industrija Srbije),
- Novi Sad Refinery (Naftna Industrija Srbije),
- Hemco Refinery

Slovakia:

- Slovnaft Bratislava Refinery, (MOL), 110,000 bbl/d (17,000 m^3/d)
- Petrochema Dubova Refinery, (russian investors),

Spain:

- Bilbao Refinery, (Repsol YPF), 220,000 bbl/d (35,000 m^3/d)
- Puertollano Refinery, (Repsol YPF), 140,000 bbl/d (22,000 m^3/d)
- Tarragona Refinery, (Repsol YPF), 160,000 bbl/d (25,000 m^3/d)
- A Coruña Refinery, (Repsol YPF), 120,000 bbl/d (19,000 m^3/d)
- Cartagena Refinery, (Repsol YPF), 220,000 bbl/d (35,000 m^3/d)
- Tenerife Refinery, (CEPSA), 90,000 bbl/d (14,000 m^3/d)
- Palos de la Frontera Refinery, (CEPSA), 100,000 bbl/d (16,000 m^3/d)
- Gibraltar-San Roque Refinery, (CEPSA), 240,000 bbl/d (38,000 m^3/d)
- Castellon Refinery, (BP), 100,000 bbl/d (16,000 m^3/d).

Switzerland:

- Cressier Refinery, (Petroplus), 68,000 bbl/d (10,800 m^3/d)
- Collombey-Muraz Refinery, (Tamoil), 45,000 bbl/d (7,200 m^3/d).

Turkey:

- Central Anatolian Refinery, (Tüpra°), 100,000 bbl/d (16,000 m^3/d)
- Izmit Refinery, (Tüpra°), 226,000 bbl/d (35,900 m^3/d)
- Aliaga Refinery, (Tüpra°), 200,000 bbl/d (32,000 m^3/d)
- Batman Refinery, (Tüpra°) 22,000 bbl/d (3,500 m^3/d)
- Akdeniz Refinery, (Petrol Ofisi) (still under construction)
- Dopu Akdeniz Petrol Refinery, (still under construction)
- Ýzmir Petrol Refinery, (Turcas-Socar) (still under construction)

Ukraine:

- Odessa Refinery, (LUKOIL), 70,000 bbl/d (11,000 m^3/d)
- LINOS Refinery, (TNK-BP), 320,000 bbl/d (51,000 m^3/d)
- Kherson Refinery, (Alliance), 36,000 bbl/d (5,700 m^3/d)
- Kremenchug Refinery, (Ukrtatnafta) 368,500 bpd
- Drogobych Refinery, (Pryvat) 40,000 bpd
- Neftekhimik Prikarpatya Nadvirna Refinery, (Pryvat) 39,000 bpd.

United Kingdom:

- Lindsey Oil Refinery, (Total), 223,000 bbl/d (35,500 m^3/d)
- Milford Haven Refinery, (Murco), 140,000 bbl/d (22,000 m^3/d)
- Pembroke Refinery, (Chevron), 220,000 bbl/d (35,000 m^3/d)
- Stanlow Refinery, (Essar Energy), 246,000 bbl/d (39,100 m^3/d)
- Teesside Refinery, (Petroplus), 117,000 bbl/d (18,600 m^3/d)
- Fawley Southampton Refinery, (ExxonMobil), 347,000 bbl/d (55,200 m^3/d)
- Humber Refinery, (ConocoPhillips), 221,000 bbl/d (35,100 m^3/d)
- Coryton Refinery, (Petroplus), 208,000 bbl/d (33,100 m^3/d)
- Grangemouth Refinery, (Ineos), 205,000 bbl/d (32,600 m^3/d)

North America

Aruba:

- Aruba Refinery (Valero) 275,000 bpd.

Canada:

Newfoundland and Labrador:

- North Atlantic Refinery, located in Come by Chance, (North Atlantic Refining), 115,000 bbl/d (18,300 m^3/d).

Nova Scotia:

- Imperial Oil Refinery - Dartmouth, (Imperial Oil), 89,000 bbl/d (14,100 m^3/d).

New Brunswick:

- Saint John, (Irving Oil), 300,000 bbl/d (48,000 m^3/d).

Quebec:

- Montreal-East, (Shell Canada), 161,000 bbl/d (25,600 m^3/d). Montreal East Refinery (Shell Canada). On June 4, 2010, Shell Canada officially announced the commencement to downgrade the refinery into a terminal, following the unsuccessful attempt to find a buyer to take over the plant.
- Montreal, (Suncor Energy), 160,000 bbl/d (25,000 m^3/d). Formerly Petro-Canada (before Aug 2009) and historically a Petrofina refinery. Montreal Refinery
- Montreal, Gulf Canada Oil, 70,000 bbl/d (11,000 m^3/d) Closed in 1985 and restarted in 2003. Montreal East Refinery (Gulf Oil Canada)
- Lévis, (Ultramar(Valero)), 215,000 bbl/d (34,200 m^3/d).

Ontario:

- Nanticoke Refinery, Nanticoke - (Imperial Oil), 112,000 bbl/d (17,800 m^3/d)
- Sarnia, (Imperial Oil), 115,000 bbl/d (18,300 m^3/d)
- Sarnia, (Suncor Energy), 85,000 bbl/d (13,500 m^3/d)
- Corunna, (Shell Canada), 72,000 bbl/d (11,400 m^3/d)

Lubricant Refinery:

- Mississauga, (Suncor Energy), 15,600 bbl/d (2,480 m^3/d) - aka Clarkson Refinery - base oil production is 13,600 bpd of API Group II capacity and 2,000 bpd of API Group III capacity. Formerly Petro-Canada (before Aug 2009) and historically a Gulf refinery.

Saskatchewan:

- CCRL Refinery Complex, Regina (Consumers' Co-operative Refineries Limited (CCRL)), 100,000 bbl/d (16,000 m^3/d)

Upgraders (improve the quality of crude for sale at a higher price)

- Husky Lloydminster Refinery, Lloydminster, (Husky Energy), 25,000 bbl/d (4,000 m^3/d)
- Husky Lloydminster Upgrader Lloydminster, (Husky Energy), 75,000 bbl/d (11,900 m^3/d).

Alberta:

- Strathcona Refinery, Edmonton, (Imperial Oil), 187,000 bbl/d (29,700 m^3/d)
- Scotford Refinery, Scotford, (Shell Canada), 100,000 bbl/d (16,000 m^3/d)
- Edmonton, (Suncor Energy), 135,000 bbl/d (21,500 m^3/d). Formerly Petro-Canada (before Aug 2009).
- Scotford Upgrader, Scotford, (AOSP - Shell Canada 60%, Chevron Corporation 20%, Marathon Oil 20%), 250,000 bpd (located next to Shell Refinery) raw bitumen
- Horizon Oil Sands, Fort McMurray, (Canadian Natural Resources Limited), 110,000 bbl/d (17,000 m^3/d) raw bitumen
- Long Lake, Fort McMurray, (OPTI Canada Inc. 35% and Nexen Inc. 65%), 70,000 bbl/d (11,000 m^3/d) raw bitumen
- Syncrude, Fort McMurray, (Canadian Oil Sands Trust, Imperial Oil, Suncor, Nexen, Conoco Phillips, Mocal Energy and Murphy Oil), 350,000 bbl/d (56,000 m^3/d) raw bitumen
- Suncor, Fort McMurray, (Suncor), 350,000 bbl/d (56,000 m^3/d) raw bitumen.

British Columbia:

- Burnaby Refinery, Burnaby, (Chevron Corporation), 52,000 bbl/d (8,300 m^3/d)
- Prince George Refinery, Prince George, (Husky Energy), 12,000 bbl/d (1,900 m^3/d)

Cuba:

- Nico Lopez Refinery (Cupet) 122,000 bpd
- Hermanos Diaz Refinery (Cupet) 102,500 bpd
- Cienfuegos Refinery (Cupet) 76,000 bpd.

Curaçao:

- Isla Refinery (PDVSA) 320,000 bpd.

Costa Rica:

- Puerto Limon Refinery (Recope), 8,000 bpd (start-up 1967) 2006, 25,000 bbl/d (4,000 m^3/d)

Dominican Republic:

- Haina Refinery (REFIDOMSA) 33,000 bpd (start-up 1973).

El Salvador:

- Refineria Petrolera de Acajutla S.A. de C.V. (RASA) (ExxonMobil) 22,000 bpd (start-up 1962).

Jamaica:

- Kingston Refinery (PCJ & PDVSA) 50,000 bpd.

Mexico:

- Reynosa Refinery (Pemex) Reynosa, Tamaulipas
- Minatitlan Refinery (Pemex) Minatitlan 167,000 bpd
- Cadereyta Refinery (Pemex) Cadereyta Jiménez, Nuevo Leon 217,000 bpd
- Tula Refinery (Pemex) Tula, Hidalgo 290,000 bpd
- Salamanca Refinery (Pemex) Salamanca, Guanajuato 192,000 bpd
- Ciudad Madero Refinery (Pemex) Ciudad Madero 152,000 bpd
- Salina Cruz Refinery (Pemex) Salina Cruz 227,000 bpd

Nicaragua:

- Cuesta del Plomo-Managua (ExxonMobil) 20,900 bpd (start-up 1962).

Trinidad and Tobago:

- Pointe-à-Pierre Refinery (Petrotrin) 165,000 bpd.

United States

Alabama:

- Tuscaloosa Refinery (Hunt Refining Company), Tuscaloosa 52,000 bbl/d (8,300 m^3/d)
- Saraland Refinery (Shell Oil Company), Saraland 80,000 bbl/d (13,000 m^3/d)
- Mobile Refinery (Gulf Atlantic Refining & Marketing), Mobile 16,700 bbl/d (2,660 m^3/d)

Alaska:

- Kenai Refinery (Tesoro), Kenai 72,000 bbl/d (11,400 m^3/d)

- Valdez Refinery (Petro Star), Valdez 50,000 bbl/d (7,900 m^3/d)
- North Pole Refinery (Petro Star), North Pole 17,000 bbl/d (2,700 m^3/d)
- Kuparuk Refinery (ConocoPhillips), Kuparuk 14,400 bbl/d (2,290 m^3/d).
- North Pole Refinery (Flint Hills Resources), North Pole 210,000 bbl/d (33,000 m^3/d)
- Prudhoe Bay Refinery (BP), Prudhoe Bay 12,500 bbl/d (1,990 m^3/d).

Arkansas:

- El Dorado Refinery (Lion Oil), El Dorado 70,000 bbl/d (11,000 m^3/d)
- Smackover Refinery (Cross Oil), Smackover 6,800 bbl/d (1,080 m^3/d).

California:

- Bakersfield Refinery (Alon USA), Bakersfield, 66,000 bbl/d (10,500 m^3/d)
- Bakersfield Refinery (Kern Oil), Bakersfield, 25,000 bbl/d (4,000 m^3/d)
- Bakersfield Refinery (San Joaquin Refining Company), Bakersfield, 24,300 bbl/d (3,860 m^3/d)
- Benicia Refinery (Valero), Benicia, 144,000 bbl/d (22,900 m^3/d)
- Carson Refinery (BP), Carson, 265,000 bbl/d (42,100 m^3/d)
- El Segundo Refinery (Chevron), El Segundo, 265,500 bbl/d (42,210 m^3/d)
- Golden Eagle Refinery (Tesoro), near Martinez, 166,000 bbl/d (26,400 m^3/d)
- Long Beach Refinery (Alon USA), Long Beach, 26,000 bbl/d (4,100 m^3/d)
- Martinez Refinery (Shell Oil Company), Martinez, 154,900 bbl/d (24,630 m^3/d)
- Oxnard Refinery (Tenby Inc), Oxnard, 2,800 bbl/d (450 m^3/d)
- Paramount Refinery (Paramount Petroleum), Paramount, 50,000 bbl/d (7,900 m^3/d)
- Richmond Refinery (Chevron), Richmond, 242,901 bbl/d (38,618.2 m^3/d)
- Rodeo San Francisco Refinery (ConocoPhillips), Rodeo, 100,000 bbl/d (16,000 m^3/d)

- Santa Maria Refinery (ConocoPhillips), Santa Maria, 41,800 bbl/d (6,650 m^3/d).
- Santa Maria Refinery (Greka Energy), Santa Maria, 9,500 bbl/d (1,510 m^3/d)
- South Gate Refinery (Lunday Thagard), South Gate, 8,500 bbl/d (1,350 m^3/d)
- Torrance Refinery (ExxonMobil), Torrance, 149,000 bbl/d (23,700 m^3/d)
- Wilmington Asphalt Refinery (Valero), Wilmington, 5,900 bbl/d (940 m^3/d)
- Wilmington Refinery (Tesoro), Wilmington, 133,100 bbl/d (21,160 m^3/d)
- Wilmington Refinery (Shell Oil Company), Wilmington, 98,500 bbl/d (15,660 m^3/d)
- Wilmington Refinery (Valero), Wilmington, 149,000 bbl/d (23,700 m^3/d).

Colorado:

- Commerce City Refinery (Suncor Energy (U.S.A.) Inc.), Commerce City, 100,000 bbl/d (16,000 m^3/d)

Delaware:

- Delaware City Refinery (idle in 2010; purchased by PBF Energy Partners from Valero in April 2010; currently up and processing crude oil).

Georgia

- Savannah Refinery (NuStar Energy), Savannah (Asphalt Refinery) 28,000 bpd
- Douglasville Refinery (Young Refining), Douglasville — shutdown 07/04

Hawaii:

- Kapolei Refinery (Tesoro), Kapolei 93,500 bbl/d (14,870 m^3/d)
- Hawaii Refinery (Chevron), Kapolei 54,000 bbl/d (8,600 m^3/d).

Illinois:

- Lemont Refinery (Citgo), Lemont 160,000 bbl/d (25,000 m^3/d)
- Joliet Refinery (ExxonMobil), Joliet 238,000 bbl/d (37,800 m^3/d)
- Robinson Refinery (Marathon Petroleum Company), Robinson 215,000 bbl/d (34,200 m^3/d)

- Wood River Refinery (ConocoPhillips), Wood River 306,000 bbl/d (48,700 m^3/d)

Indiana:

- Whiting Refinery (BP), Whiting 405,000 bbl/d (64,400 m^3/d)
- Mount Vernon Refinery (Countrymark Co-op), Mount Vernon 23,000 bbl/d (3,700 m^3/d)

Kansas:

- Coffeyville Refinery (Coffeyville Resources LLC), Coffeyville 112,000 bbl/d (17,800 m^3/d)
- El Dorado Refinery (Frontier Oil), El Dorado 120,000 bbl/d (19,000 m^3/d)
- McPherson Refinery (NCRA), McPherson 81,200 bbl/d (12,910 m^3/d)

Kentucky:

- Catlettsburg Refinery (Marathon Petroleum Company), Catlettsburg 222,000 bbl/d (35,300 m^3/d)
- HDG International Group Refinery, Perry 195,500 bbl/d (31,080 m^3/d)
- Somerset Refinery, Somerset 5,500 bbl/d (870 m^3/d).

Louisiana:

- Alliance Refinery (ConocoPhillips), Belle Chasse 247,000
- Baton Rouge Refinery (ExxonMobil), Baton Rouge 503,000 bbl/d (80,000 m^3/d)
- Chalmette Refinery (Chalmette Refining LLC, joint venture of ExxonMobil and PDVSA), Chalmette 193,000 bbl/d (30,700 m^3/d)
- Convent Refinery (Motiva Enterprises), Convent 255,000 bbl/d (40,500 m^3/d)
- Cotton Valley Refinery (Calumet Lubricants), Cotton Valley 13,000 bbl/d (2,100 m^3/d)
- Garyville Refinery (Marathon Petroleum Company), near Garyville 436,000 bbl/d (69,300 m^3/d)
- Krotz Springs Refinery (Alon), Krotz Springs 85,000 bbl/d (13,500 m^3/d)
- Lake Charles Refinery (Calcasieu Refining), Lake Charles 30,000 bbl/d (4,800 m^3/d)
- Lake Charles Refinery (Citgo), Lake Charles 427,800

- Lake Charles Refinery (ConocoPhillips), Westlake 247,000
- Meraux Refinery (Murphy Oil), Meraux 125,000 bbl/d (19,900 m^3/d)
- Norco Refinery (Motiva Enterprises), Norco 242,000 bbl/d (38,500 m^3/d)
- Port Allen Refinery (Placid Refining), Port Allen 48,500 bbl/d (7,710 m^3/d)
- Princeton Refinery (Calumet Lubricants), Princeton 8,300 bbl/d (1,320 m^3/d)
- Shreveport Refinery (Calumet Lubricants), Shreveport 35,000 bbl/d (5,600 m^3/d)
- St. Charles Refinery (Valero), Norco 260,000 bbl/d (41,000 m^3/d).

Michigan:

- Detroit Refinery (Marathon Petroleum Company), Detroit 180,000 bbl/d (29,000 m^3/d).

Minnesota:

- Pine Bend Refinery (Flint Hills Resources), Rosemount 320,000 bbl/d (51,000 m^3/d)
- St. Paul Park Refinery (Northern Tier Energy), St. Paul Park 70,000 bbl/d (11,000 m^3/d).

Mississippi:

- Lumberton Refinery (Hunt Southland Refining), Lumberton 5,800 bbl/d (920 m^3/d)
- Pascagoula Refinery (Chevron), Pascagoula 325,000 bbl/d (51,700 m^3/d)
- Vicksburg Refinery (Ergon), Vicksburg 23,000 bbl/d (3,700 m^3/d)
- Rogerslacy Refinery (Hunt Southland Refining), Sandersville 11,000 bbl/d (1,700 m^3/d)
- Greenville Refinery, Scott Petroleum, Biodiesel Oil Refinery

Montana:

- Billings Refinery (ConocoPhillips), Billings 58,000 bbl/d (9,200 m^3/d)
- Billings Refinery (ExxonMobil), Billings 60,000 bbl/d (9,500 m^3/d)
- Montana Refining Company (Connacher Oil & Gas Limited), Great Falls 9,500 bbl/d (1,510 m^3/d)
- Laurel Refinery (Cenex), Laurel 55,000 bbl/d (8,700 m^3/d)

Nevada:

- Eagle Springs Refinery (Foreland Refining), Currant 1,700 bbl/d (270 m^3/d).

New Jersey:

- Bayway Refinery (ConocoPhillips), Linden 230,000 bbl/d (37,000 m^3/d)
- Eagle Point Refinery (Sunoco), Westville closed 2010 145,000 bbl/d (23,100 m^3/d)
- Paulsboro Asphalt Refinery (NuStar), Paulsboro 51,000 bbl/d (8,100 m^3/d)
- Paulsboro Refinery (PBF Energy Corporation), Paulsboro 160,000 bbl/d (25,000 m^3/d)
- Perth Amboy Refinery (Chevron), Perth Amboy 80,000 bbl/d (13,000 m^3/d)
- Port Reading Refinery (Hess), Port Reading 62,000 bbl/d (9,900 m^3/d).

New Mexico:

- Artesia Refinery (Holly Corporation via Navajo Refining), Artesia 100,000 bbl/d (16,000 m^3/d)
- Bloomfield Refinery (Western Refining), Bloomfield 16,800 bbl/d (2,670 m^3/d)
- Ciniza Refinery (Western Refining), Gallup 26,000 bbl/d (4,100 m^3/d)
- Lovington Refinery (Holly Corporation), Lovington.

North Dakota:

- Mandan Refinery (Tesoro), Mandan 60,000 bbl/d (9,500 m^3/d)

Ohio:

- Canton Refinery (Marathon Petroleum Company), Canton 73,000 bbl/d (11,600 m^3/d)
- Lima Refinery (Husky Energy), Lima 158,400 bbl/d (25,180 m^3/d)
- Toledo Refinery (BP/Husky Oil), Toledo 160,000 bbl/d (25,000 m^3/d)
- Toledo Refinery (PBF Energy), Toledo 160,000 bbl/d (25,000 m^3/d).

Oklahoma:

- Ardmore Refinery (Valero), Ardmore 74,700 bbl/d (11,880 m^3/d)

- Ponca City Refinery (ConocoPhillips), Ponca City 194,000 bbl/d (30,800 m^3/d)
- Tulsa Refinery (Sinclair Oil), Tulsa 70,300 bbl/d (11,180 m^3/d)
- Tulsa Refinery (Holly Corporation), Tulsa 83,200 bbl/d (13,230 m^3/d)
- Wynnewood Refinery, Wynnewood 71,700 bbl/d (11,400 m^3/d)
- Ventura Refining and Transmission, Thomas 14,000 bbl/d (2,200 m^3/d).

Pennsylvania:

- Bradford Refinery (American Refining Group), Bradford 10,000 bbl/d (1,600 m^3/d)
- Marcus Hook Refinery (Sunoco), Marcus Hook 175,000 bbl/d (27,800 m^3/d)
- Philadelphia Refinery (Sunoco), Philadelphia 335,000 bbl/d (53,300 m^3/d)
- Penreco (Calumet), Karns City
- Trainer Refinery (ConocoPhillips), Trainer 185,000 bbl/d (29,400 m^3/d)
- Warren Refinery, United Refining Company, Warren 70,000 bbl/d (11,000 m^3/d)
- Wamsutta Oil Refinery (historical), McClintocksville
- Hess oil Refinery.

Tennessee:

- Memphis Refinery (Valero), Memphis 180,000 bbl/d (29,000 m^3/d).

Texas:

- Baytown Refinery (ExxonMobil), Baytown 560,640 bbl/d (89,135 m^3/d)
- Big Spring Refinery (Alon USA), Big Spring 61,000 bbl/d (9,700 m^3/d)
- Beaumont Refinery (ExxonMobil), Beaumont 348,500 bbl/d (55,410 m^3/d)
- Borger Refinery (ConocoPhillips/Cenovus), Borger 146,000 bbl/d (23,200 m^3/d)
- Corpus Christi Complex (Flint Hills Resources), Corpus Christi 288,000 bbl/d (45,800 m^3/d)
- Corpus Christi Refinery (Citgo), Corpus Christi 156,000 bbl/d (24,800 m^3/d)

- Corpus Christi West Refinery (Valero), Corpus Christi 142,000 bbl/d (22,600 m^3/d)
- Corpus Christi East Refinery (Valero), Corpus Christi 115,000 bbl/d (18,300 m^3/d)
- Deer Park Refinery (Shell Oil Company), Deer Park 333,700 bbl/d (53,050 m^3/d)
- El Paso Refinery (Western Refining), El Paso 120,000 bbl/d (19,000 m^3/d)
- Houston Refinery (Lyondell), Houston 270,200 bbl/d (42,960 m^3/d)
- Houston Refinery (Valero), Houston 83,000 bbl/d (13,200 m^3/d)
- Independent Refinery (Stratnor), Houston 100,000 bbl/d (16,000 m^3/d)
- McKee Refinery (Valero), Sunray 158,300 bbl/d (25,170 m^3/d)
- Pasadena Refinery (Petrobras), Pasadena 100,000 bbl/d (16,000 m^3/d)
- Port Arthur Refinery (Total), Port Arthur 174,000 bbl/d (27,700 m^3/d)
- Port Arthur Refinery (Motiva Enterprises), Port Arthur 285,000 bbl/d (45,300 m^3/d).
- Port Arthur Refinery (Valero), Port Arthur 325,000 bbl/d (51,700 m^3/d)
- Penreco (Calumet), Houston
- San Antonio Refinery (NuStar Energy), San Antonio 10,300 bbl/d (1,640 m^3/d)
- Sweeny Refinery (ConocoPhillips), Sweeny 229,000 bbl/d (36,400 m^3/d)
- Texas City Refinery (BP), Texas City 460,000 bbl/d (73,000 m^3/d)
- Texas City Refinery (Marathon Petroleum Company), Texas City 72,000 bbl/d (11,400 m^3/d)
- Texas City Refinery (Valero), Texas City 210,000 bbl/d (33,000 m^3/d)
- Three Rivers Refinery (Valero), Three Rivers 90,000 bbl/d (14,000 m^3/d)
- Tyler Refinery (Delek Refining Ltd.), Tyler 62,000 bbl/d (9,900 m^3/d).

Utah:

- North Salt Lake Refinery (Big West Oil), North Salt Lake 35,000 bbl/d (5,600 m^3/d)
- Salt Lake City Refinery (Chevron), Salt Lake City 45,000 bbl/d (7,200 m^3/d)
- Salt Lake City Refinery (Tesoro), Salt Lake City 58,000 bbl/d (9,200 m^3/d)
- Woods Cross Refinery (Holly Corporation), Woods Cross 26,000 bbl/d (4,100 m^3/d)
- Woods Cross Refinery (Silver Eagle Refining), Woods Cross 10,200 bbl/d (1,620 m^3/d).

Virginia:

- Yorktown Refinery (Western Refining), Yorktown 58,600 bbl/d (9,320 m^3/d)

Washington:

- Tesoro Anacortes Refinery (Tesoro), Anacortes 108,000 bbl/d (17,200 m^3/d)
- Shell Anacortes Refinery (Shell Oil Company), Anacortes 145,000 bbl/d (23,100 m^3/d)
- Cherry Point Refinery (BP), Blaine 225,000 bbl/d (35,800 m^3/d)
- ConocoPhillips Ferndale Refinery (ConocoPhillips), Ferndale 105,000 bbl/d (16,700 m^3/d)
- Tacoma Refinery (U.S. Oil and Refining), Tacoma 35,000 bbl/d (5,600 m^3/d).

West Virginia:

- Newell Refinery (Ergon), Newell 19,400 bbl/d (3,080 m^3/d).

Wisconsin:

- Superior Refinery (Murphy Oil), Superior 33,000 bbl/d (5,200 m^3/d).

Wyoming:

- Cheyenne Refinery (Frontier Oil), Cheyenne 52,000 bbl/d (8,300 m^3/d)
- Evanston Refinery (Silver Eagle Refining), Evanston 3,000 bbl/d (480 m^3/d)
- Evansville Refinery (Little America Refining), Evansville 24,500 bbl/d (3,900 m^3/d)

- Newcastle Refinery (Wyoming Refining), Newcastle 12,500 bbl/d (1,990 m^3/d)
- Sinclair Refinery (Sinclair Oil), Sinclair 66,000 bbl/d (10,500 m^3/d)

US Virgin Islands:

- St Croix Refinery (HOVENSA) 494,000 bpd.

New South Wales:

- Kurnell Refinery, (Caltex), 124,500 bbl/d (19,790 m^3/d), Botany Bay
- Clyde Refinery, (Royal Dutch Shell), 100,000 bbl/d (16,000 m^3/d), Clyde.

Victoria:

- Geelong Refinery, (Royal Dutch Shell), 130,000 bbl/d (21,000 m^3/d), Geelong
- Altona Refinery, (ExxonMobil), ~75,000 bpd, Altona North (refinery reduced from 2 trains to 1 train between 2000–2004)

Queensland:

- Bulwer Island Refinery, (BP), 90,000 bbl/d (14,000 m^3/d), Bulwer Island
- Lytton Refinery, (Caltex), 104,000 bbl/d (16,500 m^3/d), Lytton

South Australia:

- Port Stanvac Refinery, (ExxonMobil), 100,000 bbl/d (16,000 m^3/d), Lonsdale (mothballed since 2003 - 239 ha site to be cleaned up and redeveloped for housing)

Western Australia:

- Kwinana Refinery, (BP), 138,000 bbl/d (21,900 m^3/d), Kwinana

New Zealand:

- Marsden Point Oil Refinery (NZRC), 96,000 b.

Papua New Guinea:

- InterOil Refinery (InterOil), 32,500 hi.

South America

Argentina:

- La Plata Refinery (Repsol YPF) 189,000 bpd
- Buenos Aires Refinery (Royal Dutch Shell) 110,000 bpd
- Luján de Cuyo Refinery (Repsol YPF) 105,500 bpd
- Esso Campana Refinery (ExxonMobil) 84,500 bpd

- San Lorenzo Refinery (Refisan S.A.) 38,000 bpd (start-up 1938)
- Plaza Huincul Refinery (Repsol YPF) 37,190 bpd (start-up 1919)
- Campo Duran Refinery (Refinor) 32,000 bpd
- Bahia Blanca Refinery (Petrobras) 28,975 bpd.

Bolivia:

- Gualberto Villarael Cochabamba Refinery (YPFB) 40,000 bpd
- Guillermo Elder Bell Santa Cruz Refinery (YPFB) 20,000 bpd
- Carlos Montenegro Sucre Refinery (Refisur SA) 3,000 bpd
- Reficruz 2,000 bbl/d (320 m^3/d)
- Refineria Oro Negro SA 2,000 bbl/d (320 m^3/d).

Brazil:

- REFAP (Petrobras), Canoas 189,000 bbl/d (30,000 m^3/d)
- RECAP (Petrobras), Mauá 53,000 bbl/d (8,400 m^3/d)
- REPLAN (Petrobras), Paulinia 365,000 bbl/d (58,000 m^3/d)
- REVAP (Petrobras), São José dos Campos 251,000 bbl/d (39,900 m^3/d)
- RPBC (Petrobras), Cubatão 170,000 bbl/d (27,000 m^3/d)
- REDUC (Petrobras), Duque de Caxias 242,000 bbl/d (38,500 m^3/d)
- REMAN (Petrobras), Manaus 46,000 bbl/d (7,300 m^3/d)
- Lubnor (Petrobras), Fortaleza 6,000 bbl/d (950 m^3/d)
- REGAP (Petrobras), Betim 151,000 bbl/d (24,000 m^3/d)
- REPAR (Petrobras), Araucária 189,000 bbl/d (30,000 m^3/d)
- RLAM (Petrobras), São Francisco do Conde 323,000 bbl/d (51,400 m^3/d)
- Refinaria Ipiranga (Refinaria Riograndense), Pelotas 12,500 bbl/d (1,990 m^3/d)
- Refinaria Manguinhos (Grupo Peixoto de Castro and Repsol YPF), Rio de Janeiro 14,000 bbl/d (2,200 m^3/d).

Chile:

- BioBio Refinery (Empresa Nacional de Petroleo), 113,000 bbl/d (18,000 m^3/d)
- Aconcagua Concon Refinery (Empresa Nacional de Petroleo), 97,650 bbl/d (15,525 m^3/d)
- Gregorio Refinery (Empresa Nacional de Petroleo), 14,750 bbl/d (2,345 m^3/d).

Colombia:

- Barrancabermeja-Santander Refinery (Ecopetrol), 252,000 bpd (start-up 1922), in process to expansion to 300,000 bpd and increase the conversion.
- Cartagena Refinery (Reficar S.A.), 80,000 bpd (start-up 1957), in process expansion to 140,000 bpd.
- Apiay Refinery (Ecopetrol), 2,250 bbl/d (358 m^3/d)
- Orito Refinery (Ecopetrol), 1,800 bbl/d (290 m^3/d)
- Tibu Refinery (Ecopetrol), 1,800 bbl/d (290 m^3/d).

Ecuador:

- Esmeraldas Refinery (Petroecuador), 110,000 bpd (start-up 1978)
- La Libertad Refinery (Petroecuador), 45,000 bbl/d (7,200 m^3/d)
- Shushufindi Refinery (Petroecuador), 20,000 bbl/d (3,200 m^3/d)

Paraguay:

- Villa Elisa Refinery (Petropar) 7,500 bpd.

Peru:

- Refineria La Pampilla Lima (Repsol YPF) 102,000 bpd
- Refineria de Talara (Petroperú) 65,000 bpd (start-up 1917) with FCC unit
- Refineria Iquitos Loreto (Petroperú) 12,000 bpd (start-up 1982)
- Refineria Conchan (Petroperú) 15,000 bpd (start-up 1961)
- Refineria Pucallpa (Maple Gas) 3,250 bpd
- Refineria El Milagro (Petroperú) 1,500 bpd (start-up 1994)
- Refineria Shiviyacu (Pluspetrol) 2,000 bpd (start-up 1950).

Surinam:

- Paramaribo (Staatsolie) 7,000 bpd.

Uruguay:

- La Teja Montevideo Refinery (ANCAP) 40,000 bpd (start-up 1937)

Venezuela:

- Paraguana Refinery Complex (CRP) (PDVSA) 956,000 bdp (Amuay-Cardon-Bajo Grande) (start-up 1997)
    - o Amuay Refinery (CRP) (PDVSA) 635,000 bpd (start-up 1950)
    - o Cardon Refinery (CRP) (PDVSA) 305,000 bpd (start-up 1949)

  - o Bajo Grande Refinery (CRP) (PDVSA) 16,000 bpd (start-up 1956)
- Puerto La Cruz Refinery (PDVSA) 200,000 bpd (start-up 1948)
- El Palito Refinery (PDVSA) 140,000 bpd (start-up 1954)
- San Roque Refinery (PDVSA) 5,200 bpd.
- Upgraders (Extra Heavy Oil Joint Ventures with PDVSA at Jose)
  - o Petrozuata (PDVSA) 140,000 bpd (start-up 2000)
  - o Operadora Cerro Negro (ExxonMobil, Aral AG, and PDVSA) 120,000 bpd (start-up 2001)
  - o Sincor (Total S.A., Statoil, and PDVSA) 180,000 bpd (start-up 2001)
  - o Ameriven (ConocoPhillips, ChevronTexaco, and PDVSA) 190,000 bpd (start-up 2004).

Oil India

Oil India (OIL) is a public sector oil and gas company in India under the administrative control of the Ministry of Petroleum and Natural Gas of the Government of India. OIL is engaged in the business of exploration, development and production of crude oil and natural gas, transportation of crude oil and production of liquid petroleum gas.

The story of Oil India Limited (OIL) traces and symbolizes the development and growth of the Indian petroleum industry. From the discovery of crude oil in the far east of India at Digboi, Assam in 1889 to its present status as a fully integrated upstream petroleum company, OIL has come far, crossing many milestones.

The Company presently produces over 3.2 MMTPA (million tons per annum) of crude oil, over 5 MMSCMD of Natural Gas and over 50,000 Tones of LPG annually. Most of this emanates from its traditionally rich oil and gas fields concentrated in the Northeastern part of India and contribute to over 65% of total Oil&Gas produced in the region.

The search for newer avenues has seen OIL spreading out its operations in onshore / offshore Orissa and Andaman, deserts of Rajasthan, plains of Uttar Pradesh, riverbeds of Brahmaputra and offshore Saurashtra. In Rajasthan, OIL discovered gas in 1988, heavy oil / bitumen in 1991 and started production of gas in 1996. The company has accumulated over a hundred years of experience in the field of oil and gas production, since the discovery of Digboi oilfield in 1889. It is possibly the only company to do so. From well completion to wellbore servicing, installation, operation and maintenance of modern surface handling facilities, the company has the skill and expertise to manage the entire range of operations required for onshore oil and gas production.

The company has over 100,000 square kilometres of license areas for oil and gas exploration. It has emerged as a consistently profitable international company with exploration blocks as far as Libya and sub-Saharan Africa.

In recent years, OIL has stepped up E & P activities significantly including Gas monetization in the North-East India. OIL has set up the NEF (North East Frontier) project to intensify its exploration activities in the frontier areas in North East, which are logistically very difficult and geologically complex. Presently, seismic surveys are being carried out in Manbhum, Pasighat and other Trust Belt areas. The Company operates a crude oil pipeline in the North East for transportation of crude oil produced by both OIL and ONGCL in the region to feed Numaligarh, Guwahati, Bongaigaon and Barauni refineries and a branch line to feed Digboi refinery.

Oil India Pipeline History

A 1157 kilometres long fully automated telemetric pipeline with 212 kilometres of looping having a total capacity to transport over 6.0 MMTPA remains the lifeline of the Company. Commissioned in 1962, the double skinned crude oil pipeline traverses 78 river crossings including the mighty Brahmaputra River meandering through paddy fields,. forests and swamps. There are 9 pumping stations, 17 Repeater stations and a terminal at Barauni. The engines that drive the giant pumps along the pipeline have crossed over two hundred thousand hours of service and established a world record of machine run - hours. The Company is currently in the process of constructing a 660 KM long Product Pipeline from Numaligarh to Siliguri. The Pipeline is expected to be completed by mid 2007. OIL also sells its produced gas to different customers in Assam viz. BVFCL, ASEB, NEEPCO, IOC (AOD), and APL and to RSEB in Rajasthan. The company also produces Liquefied Gas (LPG) in its plant at Du.

Oil India Limited

Oil India Limited (OIL) is a premier Indian National oil company under the administrative control of Ministry of Petroleum and Natural Gas, Govt. of India. OIL is engaged in the business of Exploration,

Development and Production of Crude Oil and Natural Gas, Transportation of Crude Oil and Production of LPG. The Company has over 1 lakh sq. km. of license areas. Oil India Limited is the pioneer in exploration and production of hydrocarbon in India, has been serving the nation for over four decades. Oil India is an integrated upstream petroleum company performing the following main activities:

- o Exploration for hydrocarbons.
- o Production of crude oil and natural gas.
- o Transportation of crude oil to refineries.
- o Supply of gas to consumers.
- o Extraction and bottling of LPG.

Oil India owns and operates a wide array of facilities and equipment to carry out seismic and geodetic work, 2D and 3D data acquisition, processing and analysis, onshore and offshore drilling, oil and gas field development and production, LPG production and other ancillary services to make it a fully integrated E&P company.

The Company has been steadily improving its performance year after year in the areas of production, sales, accretion to reserves, etc. The physical and financial performances in the last three years are as follows:

Oil India, which has traditionally been producing around 3 MMTPA of crude and 5 MMSCMD of natural gas, has recently embarked on an overall performance-improvement exercise. It has been successful in arresting the declining trend in production of crude oil from its ageing fields in the North-East region by application of latest technology land equipment. It has, in fact, recorded a growth of 20 per cent in the last 18 months. It is worth mentioning that over the years the Reserve Accretion Ratio for Oil India has consistently been over 1. The company is optimistic of continuing with its growth plan and expects to achieve 4.00 MMTPA of crude oil and 7 MMSCM of natural gas in the next financial year, i.e.2006-07.

Asia's first cross-country Pipeline is owned and operated by Oil India. This 1157 KM long pipeline traverses through three states, viz. Assam, West Bengal and Bihar, is the lifeline of the North-East as it carries the crude oil, which is very vital for the survival of the four Refineries in the region.

The Company is currently in the process of constructing a 660 KM long Product Pipeline from Numaligarh to Siliguri. The Pipeline, when commissioned in early 2006, is expected to solve the product evacuation problem of the modern and state-of-the-art Numaligarh Refinery which has been set up under the Assam Accord with the objective of creating all-round socio-economic development in the State.

The Company's operational areas are spread in the states of Assam, Arunachal Pradesh, Orissa, Rajasthan, Uttar Pradesh and Uttaranchal. Active participation in the NELP bids has helped the Company to acquire interests in 13 Blocks and with Operatorship in five of them.

Out of the balance eight Blocks, five Blocks are in deep sea, wherein ONGCL is the operator with participating interest in the range of 15-20%. The Company is determined to aggressively bid for Blocks offered in the NELP-V Rounds which is due for closure on 31.5.2005.

Oil India has identified acquisition of overseas exploration and production ventures as an essential requirement for fast growth. The Company already has participating interests in various overseas projects, such as, in Iran, Cote d'lvoire, and Sudan.

It has recently formed a 50:50 strategic alliance with Indian Oil Corporation Limited (IOC) to jointly pursue exploration and production opportunities abroad and to achieve synergy in the downstream sector. T

his consortium has achieved a major breakthrough in its maiden attempt by winning a Block in the highly prospective Sirte Basin in Libya with the Operatorship for Oil India, against competitive bidding.

Petroleum Product

Petroleum products are useful materials derived from crude oil (petroleum) as it is processed in oil refineries.

According to crude oil composition and demand, refineries can produce different shares of petroleum products. The largest share of oil products is used as energy carriers: various grades of fuel oil and gasoline. These energy-carrying fuels include or can be blended to give gasoline, jet fuel, diesel fuel, heating oil, and heavier fuel oils.

Heavier (less volatile) fractions can also be used to produce asphalt, tar, paraffin wax, lubricating and other heavy oils. Refineries also produce other chemicals, some of which are used in chemical processes to produce plastics and other useful materials.

Since petroleum often contains a couple of percent sulfur, sulfur is also often produced as a petroleum product. Hydrogen and carbon in the form of petroleum coke may also be produced as petroleum products. The hydrogen produced is often used as an intermediate product for other oil refinery processes such as hydrogen catalytic cracking (hydrocracking) and hydrodesulfurization.

Figure: *A petrochemical refinery in Grangemouth, Scotland.*

Major Products of Oil Refineries

- Asphalt
- Diesel fuel
- Fuel oils
- Gasoline
- Jet fuel
- Kerosene
- Liquefied petroleum gas (LPG)
- Lubricating oils
- Paraffin wax
- Tar
- Petrochemicals.

Specialty End Products

Oil refineries will blend various feedstocks, mix appropriate additives, provide short term storage, and prepare for bulk loading to trucks, barges, product ships, and railcars.

- Gaseous fuels such as propane, stored and shipped in liquid form under pressure in specialized railcars to distributors.
- Liquid fuels blending (producing automotive and aviation grades of gasoline, kerosene, various aviation turbine fuels, and diesel fuels, adding dyes, detergents, antiknock additives, oxygenates, and anti-fungal compounds as required). Shipped by barge, rail, and tanker ship.

  May be shipped regionally in dedicated pipelines to point consumers, particularly aviation jet fuel to major airports, or piped to distributors in multi-product pipelines using product separators called pipeline inspection gauges ("pigs").

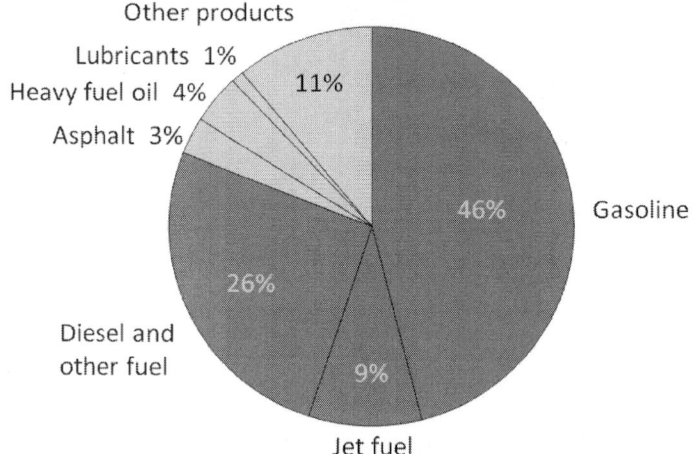

Figure : *A breakdown of the products made from a typical barrel of US oil.*

- Lubricants (produces light machine oils, motor oils, and greases, adding viscosity stabilizers as required), usually shipped in bulk to an offsite packaging plant.
- Wax (paraffin), used in the packaging of frozen foods, among others. May be shipped in bulk to a site to prepare as packaged blocks.
- Sulfur (or sulfuric acid), byproducts of sulfur removal from petroleum which may have up to a couple percent sulfur as organic sulfur-containing compounds. Sulfur and sulfuric acid are useful industrial materials. Sulfuric acid is usually prepared and shipped as the acid precursor oleum.
- Bulk tar shipping for offsite unit packaging for use in tar-and-gravel roofing or similar uses.

- Asphalt - used as a binder for gravel to form asphalt concrete, which is used for paving roads, lots, etc. An asphalt unit prepares bulk asphalt for shipment.
- Petroleum coke, used in specialty carbon products such as certain types of electrodes, or as solid fuel.
- Petrochemicals or petrochemical feedstocks, which are often sent to petrochemical plants for further processing in a variety of ways. The petrochemicals may be olefins or their precursors, or various types of aromatic petrochemicals.

Petrochemicals have a vast variety of uses. They are commonly used as monomers or feedstocks for monomer production. Olefins such as alpha-olefins and dienes are often used as monomers, although aromatics can also be used as monomer precursors.

The monomers are then polymerized in various ways to form polymers. Polymer materials can be used as plastics, elastomers, or fibres, or possibly some intermediate form of these material types. Some polymers are also used as gels or lubricants.

Petrochemicals can also be used as solvents or as feedstock for producing solvents. Petrochemicals can also be used as precursors for a wide variety of chemicals and substances such as vehicle fluids, surfactants for cleaners, etc.

Crude Oil Products

In the international petroleum industry, crude oil products are traded on various oil bourses based on established chemical profiles, delivery locations, and financial terms. The chemical profiles, or crude oil assays, specify important properties such as the oil's API gravity. The delivery locations are usually sea ports close to the oil fields from which the crude was obtained (and new fields are constantly being explored), and the pricing is usually quoted based on F.O.B. (*free on board*, without consideration of final delivery costs).

Benchmarks

The three most quoted oil products are North America's West Texas Intermediate crude (WTI), North Sea Brent Crude, and the UAE Dubai Crude, and their pricing is used as a barometer for the entire petroleum industry, although, in total, there are 46 key oil exporting countries. Brent Crude is typically priced at about $2 dollars over the WTI Spot price, which is typically priced $5 to $6 dollars above the EIA's Imported Refiner Acquisition Cost (IRAC) and OPEC Basket prices. WTI and Brent are quoted F.O.B specific locations, not F.O.B. the oilfields. For

WTI, the delivery point is Cushing, OK; for Brent, it is Sullom Voe, an island north of Scotland.

Although crude oil assays evaluate various chemical properties of the oil, the two most important properties determining a crude's value are its density (measured as API specific gravity) and its sulphur content (measured per mass).

Crude oil is considered "heavy" if it is high in wax content, or "light" if low in wax content: an API gravity of 34 or higher is "light", between 31-33 is "medium", and 30 or below is "heavy". Crude is considered "sweet" if it is low in sulphur content (< 0.5%/weight), or "sour" if high (> 1.0%/weight). Generally, the higher the API gravity (the "lighter" it is), the more valuable the crude.

Chapter 6

Strategy and Management of Oil Reserves

The Strategic Petroleum Reserve (SPR) is an emergency fuel store of oil maintained by the United States Department of Energy.

United States

The US SPR is the largest emergency supply in the world with the current capacity to hold up to 727 million barrels (115,600,000 m^3). The current inventory is displayed on the SPR's website. As of May 31, 2011, the current inventory was 726.5 million barrels (115,500,000 m^3). This equates to 34 days of oil at current daily US consumption levels of 21 million barrels per day (3,300,000 m^3/d). At recent market prices ($65 a barrel as of October 2008) the SPR holds over $34.3 billion in sweet crude and approximately $51.2 billion in sour crude (assuming a $15/barrel discount for sulfur content). The total value of the crude in the SPR is approximately $85.5 billion USD. The price paid for the oil is $20.1 billion (an average of $28.42 per barrel).

Purchases of crude oil resumed in January 2009 using revenues available from the 2005 Hurricane Katrina emergency sale. The DOE purchased 10,700,000 barrels (1,700,000 m^3) at a cost of $553 million.

The United States started the petroleum reserve in 1975 after oil supplies were cut off during the 1973-74 oil embargo, to mitigate future temporary supply disruptions. According to the World Factbook, the United States imports a net 12 million barrels (1,900,000 m^3) of oil a day (MMbd), so the SPR holds about a 58-day supply. However, the maximum total withdrawal capability from the SPR is only 4.4 million barrels (700,000 m^3) per day, making it a 160 + day supply.

Facilities

The SPR management office is located in New Orleans, Louisiana. The reserve is stored at four sites on the Gulf of Mexico, each located near a major center of petrochemical refining and processing. Each site contains a number of artificial caverns created in salt domes below the surface. Individual caverns within a site can be up to 1000 m below the surface, average dimensions are 60 m wide and 600 m deep, and capacity ranges from 6 to 37 million barrels (950,000 to 5,900,000 m^3). Almost $4 billion was spent on the facilities.

The decision to store in caverns was made in order to reduce costs; the Department of Energy claims it is roughly 10 times cheaper to store oil below surface with the added advantages of no leaks and a constant natural churn of the oil due to a temperature gradient in the caverns. The caverns were created by drilling down and then dissolving the salt with water.

Existing:

- Bryan Mound - Freeport, Texas. 20 caverns with a storage capacity of 254 million barrels (40,400,000 m^3) with a drawdown capacity of 1.5 million barrels (240,000 m^3) per day.
- Big Hill - Winnie, Texas. Has a capacity of 160 million barrels (25,000,000 m^3) with a drawdown capacity of 1.1 million barrels (170,000 m^3) per day. This facility is planned to be expanded by 250 million barrels (40,000,000 m^3) with a new drawdown capacity of 1.5 million barrels (240,000 m^3) per day.
- West Hackberry - Lake Charles, Louisiana. Has a capacity of 227 million barrels (36,100,000 m^3) with a drawdown capacity of 1.3 million barrels (210,000 m^3) per day.
- Bayou Choctaw - Baton Rouge, Louisiana. Has a capacity of 76 million barrels (12,100,000 m^3) with a maximum drawdown rate of 550,000 barrels (87,000 m^3). This facility is planned to be expand to 109 million barrels (17,300,000 m^3) with a new drawdown capacity of 600,000 barrels (95,000 m^3) per day.

Future:

- Richton, Mississippi. This facility, if built as planned, will have a capacity of 160 million barrels (25,000,000 m^3) with a drawdown capacity of 1 million barrels (160,000 m^3) per day. The Secretary of the Energy Department, Samuel Bodman, announced the creation of this site in February 2007. This new site is currently facing some opposition.

Retired:

- Weeks Island - Iberia Parish, Louisiana (Decommissioned 1999) Capacity of 72 million barrels (11,400,000 m^3). This facility was a conventional room and pillar near-surface salt mine, formerly owned by Morton Salt. In 1993, a sinkhole formed on the site, allowing fresh water to intrude into the mine. Because of the mine's construction in salt deposits, fresh water would erode the ceiling, potentially causing the structure to fail. The mine was backfilled with salt-saturated brine. This process, which allowed for recovery of 98% of the petroleum stored in the facility, reduced the risk of further freshwater intrusion, and helped prevent the remaining oil from leaking into the aquifer that is located over the salt dome.

History

Background: Access to the reserve is determined by the conditions written into the 1975 Energy Policy and Conservation Act (EPCA), primarily to counter a severe supply interruption. The maximum removal rate, by physical constraints, is 4.4 million barrels per day (700,000 m^3/d). Oil could begin entering the marketplace 13 days after a Presidential order.

The Dept. of Energy says that it has about 59 days of import protection in the SPR. This, combined with private sector inventory protection, is estimated to equal 115 days of imports. The SPR was created following the 1973 energy crisis. The EPCA of December 22, 1975, made it policy for the U.S. to establish a reserve up to one billion barrels (159 million m^3) of petroleum.

A number of existing storage sites were acquired in 1977. Construction of the first surface facilities began in June 1977. On July 21, 1977, the first oil—approximately 412,000 barrels (65,500 m^3) of Saudi Arabian light crude—was delivered to the SPR. Fill was suspended in FY 1995 to devote budget resources to refurbishing the SPR equipment and extending the life of the complex. The current SPR sites are expected to be usable until around 2025. Fill was resumed in 1999.

Filling and Suspending the SPR

On November 13, 2001, President George W. Bush announced that the SPR would be filled, saying, "The Strategic Petroleum Reserve is an important element of our Nation's energy security. To maximize long-term protection against oil supply disruptions, I am directing the Secretary of Energy to fill the SPR up to its 700 million barrel [111,000,000 m^3] capacity."

The highest prior level was reached in 1994 with 592 million barrels (94,100,000 m^3). At the time of President Bush's directive, the SPR contained about 545 million barrels (86,600,000 m^3). Since the directive in 2001, the capacity of the SPR increased by 27 million barrels (4,300,000 m^3) due to natural enlargement of the salt caverns in which the reserves are stored. The Energy Policy Act of 2005 has since directed the Secretary of Energy to fill the SPR to the full 1-billion-barrel (160,000,000 m^3) authorized capacity, a process which will require a physical expansion of the Reserve's facilities.

On August 17, 2005, the SPR reached its goal of 700 million barrels (110,000,000 m^3), or about 96% of its now-increased 727-million-barrel (115,600,000 m^3) capacity. Approximately 60% of the crude oil in the reserve is the less desirable sour (high sulfur content) variety.

The oil delivered to the reserve is "royalty-in-kind" oil—royalties owed to the U.S. government by operators who acquire leases on the federally owned Outer Continental Shelf in the Gulf of Mexico. These royalties were previously collected as cash, but in 1998 the government began testing the effectiveness of collecting royalties "in kind" - or in other words, acquiring the crude oil itself. This mechanism was adopted when refilling the SPR began, and once filling is completed, revenues from the sale of future royalties will be paid into the federal treasury.

On April 25, 2006, President Bush announced a temporary halt to petroleum deposits to the SPR as part of a four point program to alleviate high fuel prices. On January 23, 2007, President Bush suggested in his State of the Union speech that Congress should approve expansion of the current reserve capacity to twice its current level.

In April 2008, Speaker Pelosi called on President Bush to suspend purchases of oil for the Strategic Petroleum Reserve (SPR) temporarily.

On May 12, 2008, Rep. Peter Welch (D, Vermont) and 63 co-sponsors introduced the Strategic Petroleum Reserve Fill Suspension and Consumer Protection Act bill (H.R.6022), to suspend the acquisition of petroleum for the Strategic Petroleum Reserve.

On May 16, 2008, the U.S. Department of Energy said it would halt all deliveries to the Strategic Petroleum Reserve sometime in July. This announcement came days after Congress voted to direct the Bush administration to do the same. The U.S. Department of Energy did not state when the shipments would resume.

On May 19, 2008, President Bush signed the Act passed by the Congress, which he previously opposed.

On January 2, 2009, the U.S. Energy Department said that it would begin buying approximately 12,000,000 barrels (1,900,000 m^3) of crude oil to fill the Strategic Petroleum Reserve, replenishing supplies that were sold after hurricanes Katrina and Rita in 2005. The purchase will be funded by the roughly $600 million received in 2005 from the emergency sales.

Emergency sales to Israel

According to the 1975 Second Sinai withdrawal document signed by the United States and Israel, in an emergency the U.S. is obligated to make oil available for sale to Israel for up to 5 years.

Limitations

The Strategic Petroleum Reserve is exclusively a crude petroleum reserve, not a stockpile of refined petroleum fuels, such as gasoline, diesel and kerosene. Although there are small-scale (2,000,000 barrels) heating oil reserves in Connecticut, Rhode Island and New Jersey under the aegis of the Department of Energy (DOE), the federal government maintains no gasoline reserves on anything like the scale of the SPR. Consequently, while the US enjoys some protection from disruptions in oil supplies, it would have to depend on other stockpiling members of the International Energy Agency for relief from any major disruption to refinery operations. Since no new refineries have been constructed in the US for thirty years, there is little excess refining capacity. This was illustrated during Hurricane Katrina, when many of the Gulf coast oil refining complexes were disrupted for some time.

There have been suggestions that the DOE should stockpile both gasoline and jet fuel, to rectify this weakness. Some countries and zones, such as Australia, have a strategic reserve of both petroleum and petroleum products. In some cases, this includes a strategic reserve of jet fuel.

The former Secretary of Energy, Samuel Bodman, has said the Department will consider refined products as part of the expansion of between 1 billion and 1.5 billion barrels (240,000,000 m^3).

SPR Drawdowns

Petroleum Sales:

- 1985 - Test sale - 1.1 million barrels (170,000 m^3)
- 1990/91 - Desert Storm sale - 21 million barrels (3,300,000 m^3)

  - o 4 million in August 1990 test sale
  - o 17 million in January 1991 Presidentially-ordered drawdown
- 1996-97 total non-emergency sales for deficit reduction - 28 million barrels (4,500,000 m^3)
- 2005 - Hurricane Katrina sale - 11 million barrels (1,700,000 m^3) Katrina shut down 95% of crude production and 88% of natural gas output in the Gulf of Mexico. This amounted to a quarter of total U.S. output. About 735 oil and natural gas rigs and platforms had been evacuated due to the hurricane.
- 2011 - Arab Spring sale - 30 million barrels (4,800,000 m^3) to offset disruptions caused by political upheaval in Libya and elsewhere in the Middle East. The amount was matched by IEA countries, for a total of 60 million barrels (9,500,000 m^3) released from stockpiles around the world.

Petroleum Exchanges and Loans

- April–May 1996 - 900,000 barrels (140,000 m^3) lent to ARCO to alleviate pipeline blockage.
- August 1998 - 11 million barrels (1,700,000 m^3) lent to PEMEX in return for 8.5 million barrels (1,350,000 m^3) of higher quality crude.
- June 2000 - 1 million barrels (160,000 m^3) lent to Citgo and Conoco in response to shipping channel blockage.
- July–August 2000 - 2.8 million barrels (450,000 m^3) to supply the Northeast Home Heating Oil Reserve.
- September–October 2000 - 30 million barrels (4,800,000 m^3) in response to a concern over low distillate levels in the North-eastern U.S.
- October 2002 - 296,000 barrels (47,100 m^3) lent to Shell Pipeline Company in advance of Hurricane Lili.
- September–October 2004 - 5.4 million barrels (860,000 m^3) lent to Astra Oil, ConocoPhillips, Placid Refining, Shell Oil Company, and Premcor after Hurricane Ivan.
- September–October 2005 - 9.8 million barrels (1,560,000 m^3) lent to ExxonMobil, Placid Refining, Valero, BP, Marathon Oil, and Total S.A. after Hurricane Katrina.
- January–February 2006 - 767,000 barrels (121,900 m^3) lent to Total Petrochemicals USA due to closure of the Sabine Neches ship channel to deep-draft vessels after a barge accident in the channel.

- June 2006 - 750,000 barrels (119,000 m^3) of sour crude lent to ConocoPhillips and Citgo due to the closure for several days of the Calcasieu Ship Channel caused by the release of a mixture of storm water and oil. Repaid in early October 2006.
- September 2008 - 250,000 barrels (40,000 m^3) loaned to Citgo because it could not secure crude oil in the aftermath of Hurricane Gustav.
- September 2008 - 130,000 barrels (21,000 m^3) loaned to Placid Refining's Port Allen refinery and 250,000 barrels (40,000 m^3) loaned to Marathon Oil due to disruptions from Hurricane Gustav.

Northeast Home Heating Oil Reserve

The Northeast Home Heating Oil Reserve was created in July 2000 to provide a reserve of heating oil for the approximately 5.3 million households in the Northeast region of the United States that use heating oil for their homes.

History

On July 10, 2000, President of the United States Bill Clinton directed Energy Secretary Bill Richardson to establish a 2-million-barrel home heating oil component of the Strategic Petroleum Reserve in the Northeast. The intent was to create a buffer large enough to allow commercial companies to compensate for interruptions in supply or severe winter weather, but not so large as to dissuade suppliers from responding to increasing prices as a sign that more supply is needed.

Unproven Reserves

Unproven reserves are based on geological and/or engineering data similar to that used in estimates of proven reserves, but technical, contractual, or regulatory uncertainties preclude such reserves being classified as proven. Unproven reserves may be used internally by oil companies and government agencies for future planning purposes but are not routinely compiled. They are sub-classified as *probable* and *possible*.

Probable reserves are attributed to known accumulations and claim a 50% confidence level of recovery. Industry specialists refer to them as P50 (i.e., having a 50% certainty of being produced). These reserves are also referred to in the industry as 2P (proven plus probable).

Possible reserves are attributed to known accumulations that have a less likely chance of being recovered than probable reserves. This term is often used for reserves which are claimed to have at least a 10% certainty of being produced (P10). Reasons for classifying reserves as possible include varying interpretations of geology, reserves not producible at commercial rates, uncertainty due to reserve infill (seepage from adjacent areas) and projected reserves based on future recovery methods. They are referred to in the industry as 3P (proven plus probable plus possible).

Strategic Petroleum Reserves

Many countries maintain government-controlled oil reserves for both economic and national security reasons. According to the United States Energy Information Administration, approximately 4.1 billion barrels (650,000,000 m^3) of oil are held in strategic reserves, of which 1.4 billion is government-controlled. These reserves are generally not counted when computing a nation's oil reserves.

Resources

A more sophisticated system of evaluating petroleum accumulations was adopted in 2007 by the Society of Petroleum Engineers (SPE), World Petroleum Council (WPC), American Association of Petroleum Geologists (AAPG), and Society of Petroleum Evaluation Engineers (SPEE). It incorporates the 1997 definitions for reserves, but adds categories for *contingent resources* and *prospective resources.*

Contingent resources are those quantities of petroleum estimated, as of a given date, to be potentially recoverable from *known* accumulations, but the applied project(s) are not yet considered mature enough for commercial development due to one or more contingencies. Contingent resources may include, for example, projects for which there are currently no viable markets, or where commercial recovery is dependent on technology under development, or where evaluation of the accumulation is insufficient to clearly assess commerciality.

Prospective resources are those quantities of petroleum estimated, as of a given date, to be potentially recoverable from *undiscovered* accumulations by application of future development projects. Prospective resources have both an associated chance of discovery and a chance of development.

The United States Geological Survey uses the terms *technically* and *economically* recoverable resources when making its petroleum resource assessments. Technically recoverable resources represent that proportion of assessed in-place petroleum that may be recoverable using current recovery technology, without regard to cost. Economically recoverable resources are technically recoverable petroleum for which the costs of discovery, development, production, and transport, including a return to capital, can be recovered at a given market price.

Unconventional resources exist in petroleum accumulations that are pervasive throughout a large area. Examples include extra heavy oil, natural bitumen, and oil shale deposits.

Unlike conventional resources, in which the petroleum is recovered through wellbores and typically requires minimal processing prior to sale, unconventional resources require specialized extraction technology to produce. For example, steam and/or solvents are used to mobilize bitumen for in-situ recovery. Moreover, the extracted petroleum may require significant processing prior to sale (e.g., bitumen upgraders). The total amount of unconventional oil resources in the world considerably exceeds the amount of conventional oil reserves, but are much more difficult and expensive to develop.

Estimation Techniques

The amount of oil in a subsurface reservoir is called *oil in place* (OIP). Only a fraction of this oil can be recovered from a reservoir. This fraction is called the *recovery factor*. The portion that can be recovered is considered to be a reserve. The portion that is not recoverable is not included unless and until methods are implemented to produce it. There are a number of different methods of calculating oil reserves. These methods can be grouped into three general categories: volumetric, material balance, and production performance. Each method has its advantages and drawbacks.

Volumetric Method

Volumetric methods attempt to determine the amount of oil in place by using the size of the reservoir as well as the physical properties of its rocks and fluids. Then a recovery factor is assumed, using assumptions from fields with similar characteristics. OIP is multiplied by the recovery factor to arrive at a reserve number.

Current recovery factors for oil fields around the world typically range between 10 and 60 percent; some are over 80 percent. The wide variance is due largely to the diversity of fluid and reservoir characteristics for different deposits. The method is most useful early in the life of the reservoir, before significant production has occurred.

Materials Balance Method

The *materials balance method* for an oil field uses an equation that relates the volume of oil, water and gas that has been produced from a reservoir and the change in reservoir pressure to calculate the remaining oil. It assumes that, as fluids from the reservoir are produced, there will be a change in the reservoir pressure that depends on the remaining volume of oil and gas.

The method requires extensive pressure-volume-temperature analysis and an accurate pressure history of the field. It requires some production to occur (typically 5% to 10% of ultimate recovery), unless reliable pressure history can be used from a field with similar rock and fluid characteristics.

Production Decline Curve Method

The *decline curve method* uses production data to fit a decline curve and estimate future oil production. The three most common forms of decline curves are exponential, hyperbolic, and harmonic. It is assumed that the production will decline on a reasonably smooth curve, and so allowances must be made for wells shut in and production restrictions.

The curve can be expressed mathematically or plotted on a graph to estimate future production. It has the advantage of (implicitly) including all reservoir characteristics. It requires a sufficient history to establish a statistically significant trend, ideally when production is not curtailed by regulatory or other artificial conditions.

Reserves Growth

Experience shows that initial estimates of the size of newly discovered oil fields are usually too low. As years pass, successive estimates of the ultimate recovery of fields tend to increase. The term *reserve growth* refers to the typical increases in estimated ultimate recovery that occur as oil fields are developed and produced.

Estimated Reserves by Country

Summary of Reserve Data as of 2011

Country	*Reserves*		*Production*		*Reserve life*[1]
	10^9 bbl	*10^9 m^3*	*10^6 bbl/d*	*10^3 m^3/d*	*years*
Saudi Arabia	264.52	42.055	8.9	1,410	81
Venezuela	211.5	33.63	2.1	330	129
Canada	175	27.8	2.7	430	178
Iran	151.2	24.04	4.1	650	101

Contd...

Country	***Reserves***		***Production***		***Reserve life***[1]
	10^9 bbl	***10^9 m^3***	***10^6 bbl/d***	***10^3 m^3/d***	***years***
Iraq	143.1	22.75	2.4	380	163
Kuwait	101.5	16.14	2.3	370	121
United Arab Emirates	97.8	15.55	2.4	380	112
Russia	74.2	11.80	9.7	1,540	21
Libya	47	7.5	1.7	270	76
Nigeria	37	5.9	2.5	400	41
Kazakhstan	30	4.8	1.5	240	55
Qatar	25.41	4.040	1.1	170	63
China	20.35	3.235	4.1	650	14
United States	19.12	3.040	5.5	870	10
Angola	13.5	2.15	1.9	300	19
Algeria	13.42	2.134	1.7	270	22
Brazil	13.2	2.10	2.1	330	17
Total of top seventeen reserves	1,324	210.5	56.7	9,010	64

Notes: 1 Reserve to Production ratio (in years), calculated as reserves / annual production. Although the IEA insists on Canada's Reserves as being listed as 178 billion barrels, many experts including CEO of Shell Canada, Clive Mather estimate it to actually be 2 Trillion barrels or more, essentially 8 times more than Saudi Arabia.3 Iraq is estimated to be the first oil reserve in the world with more than 360 billion barrels.4 Most of oil reserves on Venezuela are extra-heaby petrolium, with high amounts of sulfur.

OPEC Countries

There are doubts about the reliability of official OPEC reserves estimates, which are not provided with any form of audit or verification that meet external reporting standards. Since a system of country production quotas was introduced in the 1980s, partly based on reserves levels, there have been dramatic increases in reported reserves among OPEC producers. In 1983, Kuwait increased its proven reserves from 67 Gbbl ($10.7\times10^{\triangle 9}$ m^3) to 92 Gbbl ($14.6\times10^{\triangle 9}$ m^3). In 1985–86, the UAE almost tripled its reserves from 33 Gbbl ($5.2\times10^{\triangle 9}$ m^3) to 97 Gbbl ($15.4\times10^{\triangle 9}$ m^3). Saudi Arabia raised its reported reserve number in 1988 by 50%. In 2001–02, Iran raised its proven reserves by some 30% to 130 Gbbl ($21\times10^{\triangle 9}$ m^3), which advanced it to second place in reserves and ahead of Iraq. Iran denied accusations of a political motive behind the readjustment, attributing the increase instead to a combination of new discoveries and improved recovery. No details were offered of how any of the upgrades were arrived at.

***Table:** OPEC Annual Statistical Bulletin 2010/2011*

Year	*Iran*	*Iraq*	*Kuwait*	*Saudi Arabia*	*UAE*	*Venezuela*	*Libya*	*Nigeria*
1980	58.3	30.0	67.9	168.0	30.4	19.5	20.3	16.7
1981	57.0	32.0	67.7	167.9	32.2	19.9	22.6	16.5
1982	56.1	*59.0*	67.2	165.5	32.4	24.9	22.2	16.8
1983	55.3	65.0	67.0	168.8	32.3	25.9	21.8	16.6
1984	58.9	65.0	*92.7*	171.7	32.5	28.0	21.4	16.7
1985	59.0	65.0	92.5	171.5	33.0	*54.5*	21.3	16.6
1986	*92.9*	72.0	94.5	169.7	*97.2*	55.5	22.8	16.1
1987	92.9	*100.0*	94.5	169.6	98.1	58.1	22.8	16.0
1988	92.9	100.0	94.5	*255.0*	98.1	58.5	22.8	16.0
1989	92.9	100.0	97.1	260.1	98.1	59.0	22.8	16.0
1990	92.9	100.0	97.0	260.3	98.1	60.1	22.8	17.1
1991	92.9	100.0	96.5	260.9	98.1	62.6	22.8	20.0
1992	92.9	100.0	96.5	261.2	98.1	63.3	22.8	21.0
1993	92.9	100.0	96.5	261.4	98.1	64.4	22.8	21.0
1994	94.3	100.0	96.5	261.4	98.1	64.9	22.8	21.0
1995	93.7	100.0	96.5	261.5	98.1	66.3	29.5	20.8
1996	92.6	112.0	96.5	261.4	97.8	72.7	29.5	20.8
1997	92.6	112.5	96.5	261.5	97.8	74.9	29.5	20.8
1998	93.7	112.5	96.5	261.5	97.8	76.1	29.5	22.5
1999	93.1	112.5	96.5	262.8	97.8	76.8	29.5	29.0
2000	99.5	112.5	96.5	262.8	97.8	76.8	36.0	29.0
2001	99.1	115.0	96.5	262.7	97.8	77.7	36.0	31.5
2002	*130.7*	115.0	96.5	262.8	97.8	77.3	36.0	34.3
2003	133.3	115.0	99.0	262.7	97.8	77.2	39.1	35.3
2004	132.7	115.0	101.5	264.3	97.8	79.7	39.1	35.9
2005	137.5	115.0	101.5	264.2	97.8	80.0	41.5	36.2
2006	138.4	115.0	101.5	264.3	97.8	87.3	41.5	36.2
2007	138.2	115.0	101.5	264.2	97.8	99.4	43.7	36.2
2008	137.6	115.0	101.5	264.1	97.8	172.3	43.7	36.2
2009	137.0	115.0	101.5	264.6	97.8	211.1	46.4	36.2
2010	151.2	143.1	101.5	264.5	97.8	296.5	47.1	36.2

The sudden revisions in OPEC reserves, totalling nearly 300 bn barrels, have been much debated. Some of it is defended partly by the shift in ownership of reserves away from international oil companies, some of whom were obliged to report reserves under conservative US Securities and Exchange Commission rules. The most prominent explanation of the revisions is prompted by a change in OPEC rules which set production quotas (partly) on reserves. In any event, the revisions in official data had little to do with the actual discovery of new reserves.

Total reserves in many OPEC countries hardly changed in the 1990s. Official reserves in Kuwait, for example, were unchanged at 96.5 Gbbl ($15.34\times10^{\triangle 9}$ m^3) (including its share of the Neutral Zone) from 1991 to 2002, even though the country produced more than 8 Gbbl ($1.3\times10^{\triangle 9}$ m^3) and did not make any important new discoveries during that period. The case of Saudi Arabia is also striking, with proven reserves estimated at between 260 and 264 billion barrels (4.20×10^{10} m^3) in the past 18 years, a variation of less than 2%, while extracting approximately 60 billion barrels (9.5×10^{9} m^3) during this period.

Sadad al-Huseini, former head of exploration and production at Saudi Aramco, estimates 300 Gbbl ($48\times10^{\triangle 9}$ m^3) of the world's 1,200 Gbbl ($190\times10^{\triangle 9}$ m^3) of proven reserves should be recategorized as speculative resources, though he did not specify which countries had inflated their reserves.

Dr. Ali Samsam Bakhtiari, a former senior expert of the National Iranian Oil Company, has estimated that Iran, Iraq, Kuwait, Saudi Arabia and the United Arab Emirates have overstated reserves by a combined 320–390bn barrels and has said, "As for Iran, the usually accepted official 132 billion barrels (2.10×10^{10} m^3) is almost one hundred billion over any realistic assay." *Petroleum Intelligence Weekly* reported that official confidential Kuwaiti documents estimate reserves of Kuwait were only 48 billion barrels ($7.6\times10^{\triangle 9}$ m^3), of which half were proven and half were possible. The combined value of proven and possible is half of the official public estimate of proven reserves.

In July 2011, OPEC's Annual Statistical Review showed Venezuela's reserves to be larger than Saudi Arabia's.

Prospective Resources

Arctic Prospective Resources: A 2008 United States Geological Survey estimates that areas north of the Arctic Circle have 90 billion barrels (1.4×10^{10} m^3) of undiscovered, technically recoverable oil and 44 billion barrels (7.0×10^{9} m^3) of natural gas liquids in 25 geologically defined areas thought to have potential for petroleum. This represented 13% of the expected undiscovered oil in the world.

Of the estimated totals, more than half of the undiscovered oil resources were estimated to occur in just three geologic provinces—Arctic Alaska, the Amerasia Basin, and the East Greenland Rift Basins. More than 70% of the mean undiscovered oil resources was estimated to occur in five provinces: Arctic Alaska, Amerasia Basin, East Greenland Rift Basins, East Barents Basins, and West Greenland–East Canada. It was further estimated that approximately 84% of the oil and gas would occur offshore. The USGS did not consider economic factors such as the effects of permanent sea ice or oceanic water depth in its assessment of undiscovered oil and gas resources. This assessment was lower than a 2000 survey, which had included lands south of the Arctic Circle.

Miscellaneous Prospective Resources

In October 2009, the USGS updated the Orinoco tar sands (Venezuela) value to 513 billion barrels (8.16×10^{10} m^3).

The Exclusive Economic Zone is a delineated offshore area, mostly to the west and north of Cuba, which, under international agreements, is owned by Cuba. This 112,000-square-kilometer zone has been divided into 59 exploration blocks. A 2004 joint partnership between a Spanish oil company and Cuba's state oil company (CUPET) estimated Cuba's offshore reserves to be able to produce ultimately between 4.6 and 9.3 billion barrels of crude oil.

The US Geological Survey (USGS) estimates that Cuba has resources up to 9 billion barrels (1.4×10^9 m^3) of oil. In October 2008, the Cuban government announced that it had discovered oil basins that would double its total oil resources to 20 billion barrels (3.2×10^9 m^3). Note that, consistent with the definitions of reserves and resources as given in the above sections, at this stage (June 2009), given no commercial discoveries to date, all recoverable oil estimates in the Exclusive Economic Zone (EEZ) are prospective resources estimates and not reserves estimates.

Global Strategic Petroleum Reserves

Global strategic petroleum reserves ("GSPR") refer to crude oil inventories (or stockpiles) held by the government of a particular country, as well as private industry, for the purpose of providing economic and national security during an energy crisis. According to the United States Energy Information Administration, approximately 4.1 billion barrels (650,000,000 m^3) of oil are held in strategic reserves, of which 1.4 billion is government-controlled. The remainder is held by private industry. At the moment the US Strategic Petroleum Reserve is one of the largest strategic reserves, with much of the remainder held by the other 26 members of the International Energy Agency. Other non-IEA countries have begun creating their own strategic petroleum reserves, with China being the largest of these new reserves. Since current consumption levels are neighbouring 0.1 billion barrels (16,000,000 m^3) per day, in the case of a dramatic worldwide drop in oil field output as suggested by some peak oil analysts, the strategic petroleum reserves are unlikely to last for more than a few months.

International Energy Agency Reserves

According to a March 2001 agreement, all 28 members of the International Energy Agency must have a strategic petroleum reserve equal to 90 days of prior year's net oil imports for their respective country. Only net-exporter members of the IEA are exempt from the reserve requirement. The exempt countries are Canada, Denmark, Norway, and the United Kingdom. However, Denmark and the UK have both recently created strategic reserves due to their requirements as European Union members.

Forward Commercial Storage Agreements

To allow oil-exporting countries increased flexibility in their production quotas, there has been an increased movement towards forward commercial storage agreements. These agreements allow petroleum to be stored at an oil-importing country, however the reserves are technically under the control of the oil-exporting country. Oil importing countries benefit from the close access to the commercial reserves, while reducing the costs of access.

Emergency Oil Sharing Agreements

In addition to maintaining a domestic stockpile of petroleum, several countries also have agreements to share their stockpiles in the event of an emergency.

The Japan, New Zealand and South Korea Agreement

In mid-2007 Japan announced a program to share its strategic reserve with other countries in its region. Negotiations are currently underway with New Zealand on an emergency oil-sharing program whereby Japan would make available for purchase its strategic reserves. In an emergency New Zealand would pay the market price plus negotiated option fees for the amount of oil previously held for them by Japan.

South Korea and Japan have also agreed to share their oil reserves in case of an emergency.

The United States and Israel Agreement

According to the 1975 Second Sinai withdrawal document signed by the United States and Israel, in an emergency the U.S. is obligated to make oil available for sale to Israel for up to 5 years.

The France, Germany, and Italy Agreement

France, Germany and Italy have an oil-sharing agreement to allow each other to purchase their strategic reserves in the event of an emergency.

Africa

South Africa has an SPR. It is managed by PetroSA and the primary facility is the Saldanha Bay oil storage facility, which is a major transit point for oil shipping. Saldanha Bay's six in-ground concrete storage tanks give the facility a storage capacity of 45,000,000 barrels (7,200,000 m^3).

Malawi is considering creating a 21-day reserve of fuel, which is an expansion from the current five day reserve. The government has begun planning for storage facilities in the provinces of Chipoka and Mchinji as well as Kamuzu International Airport.

Kenya is setting up a Strategic Fuel Reserve, similar to that of cereals. The strategic stocks would be procured by the National Oil Corporation of Kenya and stored by the Kenya Pipeline Company Limited.

Asia

China: In 2007 China announced an expansion of their crude reserves into a two part system. Chinese reserves would consist of a government-controlled strategic reserve complemented by mandated commercial reserves. The government-controlled reserves are being completed in three phases. Phase one consisted of a 101,900,000 barrels (16,200,000 m^3) reserve, mostly completed by the end of 2008.

The second phase of the government-controlled reserves with an additional 170,000,000 barrels (27,000,000 m^3) will be completed by 2011. Recently, Zhang Guobao the head of the National Energy Administration also stated that there will be a third phase that will expand reserves by 204,000,000 barrels (32,400,000 m^3) with the goal of increasing China's SPR to 90 days of supply by 2020.

The planned state reserves of 475,900,000 barrels (75,660,000 m^3) plus the planned enterprise reserves of 209,440,000 barrels (33,298,000 m^3) will provide around 90 days of consumption or a total of 684,340,000 barrels (108,801,000 m^3).

India: India has begun the development of a strategic crude oil reserve sized at 37,400,000 barrels (5,950,000 m^3), enough for two weeks of consumption. Petroleum stocks have been transferred from the Indian Oil Corporation (IndianOil) to the Oil Industry Development Board (OIDB). The OIDB then created the Indian Strategic Petroleum Reserves Ltd (ISPRL) to serve as the controlling government agency for the strategic reserve.

The facilities are:

- Mangalore, State of Karnataka. Capacity of 11.22 million barrels (1,784,000 m^3).
- Padur village, Udipi in the state of Karnataka. Capacity of 18.7 million barrels (2,970,000 m^3).
- Visakhapatnam, State of Andhra Pradesh. Capacity of 7.48 million barrels (1,189,000 m^3).

Japan: As of 2010 Japan has an SPR composed of the following three types of stockpiles:

Figure: *Japan Shibushi Oil Stockpile Site*

- State controlled reserves of petroleum at eleven different locations totalling 324,000,000 barrels (51,500,000 m^3). *All numbers, unless otherwise cited, come from p. 177 of this document:*

- o Tomakomai Eastern Oil Reserve Storage Base, 55 storage tanks, total capacity 34 million barrels (5,400,000 m^3).
- o Mutsu-Ogawara Storage Base, 53 storage tanks, total capacity 31 million barrels (4,900,000 m^3).
- o Kuji Storage Base, 3 storage tanks, total capacity 10.5 million barrels (1,670,000 m^3).
- o Akita Storage Base, 15 storage tanks, total capacity 23.4 million barrels (3,720,000 m^3).
- o Fukui Storage Base, 27 storage tanks, total capacity 17.9 million barrels (2,850,000 m^3).
- o Kikuma Underground Petroleum Storage Facility, 8 storage tanks, total capacity 8.9 million barrels (1,410,000 m^3).
- o Shirashima Storage Facility, 8 tankers (4,400,000 barrels (700,000 m^3) each), total capacity 35.2 million barrels (5,600,000 m^3).
- o Kamigotou Storage Base, 7 storage tanks, total capacity 21.45 million barrels (3,410,000 m^3).
- o Kushikino Storage Base, 3 storage tanks, total capacity 10.5 million barrels (1,670,000 m^3).
- o Shibushi Storage Base, 40 storage tanks, total capacity 27.6 million barrels (4,390,000 m^3).
- o Kagoshima former Nippon Oil facility, 4,000,000 barrels (640,000 m^3). This is a forward commercial storage facility with Abu Dhabi.

- Privately held reserves of petroleum held "in accordance with the Petroleum Stockpiling Law" of 129,000,000 barrels (20,500,000 m^3).
- Privately held reserves of petroleum products for another 130,000,000 barrels (21,000,000 m^3).

The state stockpile and the privately held stockpiles total about 583,000,000 barrels (92,700,000 m^3). The Japanese SPR is run by the Japan Oil, Gas and Metals National Corporation.

South Korea: As part of the government's energy security efforts, South Korea holds strategic oil reserves to protect against oil supply disruptions. The country's strategic oil reserve program is managed by the Korea National Oil Corporation, which reports that its system has the capacity to store 116,000,000 barrels (18,400,000 m^3) of oil. As of April 2007, KNOC held 76,000,000 barrels (12,100,000 m^3) of oil in its strategic stockpiles, 64,000,000 barrels (10,200,000 m^3) of crude oil and 12,000,000 barrels (1,900,000 m^3) of petroleum products.

This total amounts to approximately 34 days of net import cover, according to 2006 estimates of demand. KNOC has plans to expand the country's strategic storage capacity from 116,000,000 barrels (18,400,000 m^3) to 146,000,000 barrels (23,200,000 m^3) by 2009, and to fill the emergency reserves to 141,000,000 barrels (22,400,000 m^3) by 2010.

Others: The Philippines has begun plans for a National Petroleum Strategic Reserve by 2010 with an approximate size of 30,000,000 barrels (4,800,000 m^3).

Russia has begun plans for a strategic petroleum reserve. Analysts estimate the size of the Russian SPR would be around 78,000,000 barrels (12,400,000 m^3).

Singapore has an SPR composed of 31.8 million barrels (5,060,000 m^3) of crude oil with an additional 64.5 million barrels (10,250,000 m^3) of oil products for a total of 96,300,000 barrels (15,310,000 m^3).

Taiwan has an SPR with a 1999 reported size of 13,000,000 barrels (2,100,000 m^3). Taiwan's refiners (Kaohsiung 270,000 bbl/d (43,000 m^3/d); Ta-Lin 300,000 bbl/d (48,000 m^3/d); Tao-Yuan 200,000 bbl/d (32,000 m^3/d); Mailiao 150,000 bbl/d) are also required to store at least 30 days of petroleum stocks. As of 2005, these mandated commercial reserves total 27,600,000 barrels (4,390,000 m^3) of strategic petroleum stocks.

Thailand has increased the size of its SPR from 60 days to 70 days of consumption in 2006.

Pakistan has begun plans for a 20 day emergency reserve.

Europe

European Union: In the European Union, according to Council Directive 68/414/EEC of 20 December 1968, all 27 members must have a strategic petroleum reserve within the territory of the E.U. equal to at least 90 days average daily internal consumption.

The Czech Republic has a four tank SPR facility in Nelahozeves run by the company CR Mero. The Czech SPR is equal to 100 days of consumption or 20,300,000 barrels (3,230,000 m^3).

Denmark has a reserve of 81 days of consumption, equal to about 1,4 million tonnes of oil products. Not counting reserves held by the military defence.

Finland has an SPR with an approximate size of 62,400,000 barrels (9,920,000 m^3). France has an SPR with an approximate size of 65,000,000 barrels (10,300,000 m^3).

As of 2000 jet fuel stocks were required for at least 55 days of consumption, with half of those stocks controlled by the *Société Anonyme de Gestion des Stocks de Sécurité* (SAGESS) and the other half controlled by producers.

Germany created the Federal Oil Reserve in 1970, stored in the Etzel salt caverns near Wilhelmshaven in northern Germany, with an initial size of 70 million barrels (11,000,000 m^3). The current German Federal Oil Reserve and the Erdolbevorratungsverband (EBV) (the German stockholding company) mandates that refiners must keep 90 days of stock on hand, giving Germany an approximate reserve size of 250,000,000 barrels (40,000,000 m^3) as of 1997. The German SPR is the largest in Europe.

Hungary has an SPR with approximately 90 days of consumption or 11,880,000 barrels (1,889,000 m^3).

Ireland has approximately 31 days of oil stocks in Ireland and another 9 days of oil stocks held in fellow EU members states.

Additionally, they have stock tickets (contracts with a 3rd party where the government has the option to purchase in the event of an emergency) and stocks held by large industry or large consumers. On average Ireland has approximately 100 days of oil available.

Poland has an SPR with approximately 70 days of consumption. Another facility holding 20 additional days of consumption is scheduled to be completed in 2008. Poland also requires oil companies to maintain reserves sufficient for 73 days of production.

Portugal has an SPR with an approximate size of 22,440,000 barrels (3,568,000 m^3). Slovakia has an SPR with an approximate size of 748,000 barrels (118,900 m^3).

Spain has an SPR with an approximate size of 120,000,000 barrels (19,000,000 m^3). Sweden has an SPR with an approximate size of 13,290,000 barrels (2,113,000 m^3).

The United Kingdom has created a strategic reserve, the size is unknown.

Russia: Russia has begun accumulating strategic reserves of refined products which will be held by Rosneftegaz, the state-owned company.

The reserves will be held at commercial refineries, Transneft facilities, and state reserve facilities. The current planned size is 14,665,982 barrels (2,331,704.8 m^3).

Switzerland: Switzerland has SPRs consisting of gas, diesel, jet fuel and heating oil for 4.5 months of consumption. The reserves were created in the 1940s and were used for the first time in 2005 following Hurricane Katrina.

Middle East

Iran: In April 2006 the Fars News Agency reported that Iran has begun plans to create an SPR.

The National Iranian Oil Company (NIOC) has begun construction of 15 crude oil storage tanks with a planned capacity of 10,000,000 barrels (1,600,000 m^3). In August 2008, Iran announced plans to expand their SPR with a new facility on Kharg Island containing 4 tanks holding 1,000,000 barrels (160,000 m^3) each. Iran's SPR facilities are:

- Ahwaz. 4 storage tanks, total capacity 2 million barrels (320,000 m^3).
- Omidiyeh. 3 storage tanks, total capacity 3 million barrels (480,000 m^3).
- Goureh. 6 storage tanks, total capacity 4 million barrels (640,000 m^3).
- Sirri Island. 1 storage tank, total capacity 500,000 barrels (79,000 m^3).
- Bahregansar. 1 storage tank, total capacity 500,000 barrels (79,000 m^3).
- Kharg Island. 4 storage tanks, total capacity 4 million barrels (640,000 m^3). Planned facility, not operational yet.

Kuwait: Kuwait has a joint stockpile held in South Korea. The deal gives South Korea first rights to purchase the oil. The current size of the stockpile is 2 million barrels (320,000 m^3).

Others: As of 1975 Israel is believed to have a strategic oil reserve equal to 270 days of consumption.

Jordan has strategic oil reserves equal to 60 days of consumption or 6,240,000 barrels (992,000 m^3).

North America

United States: The United States has the largest reported Strategic Petroleum Reserve with a total capacity of 727,000,000 barrels (115,600,000 m^3).

If completely filled, the US SPR could theoretically replace about 60 days of oil imports as the US is estimated to import approximately 12,000,000 barrels per day (1,900,000 m^3/d) of crude oil.

According to the US Department of Energy the facilities maximum flow rate is limited to approximately 4,400,000 barrels per day (700,000 m^3/d) when filled to maximum, with flow rate declining as the reserve is drawn down.

The U.S. facilities are in salt caverns with locations in:

- Bryan Mound - located near Freeport, Texas. Capacity of 226,000,000 barrels (35,900,000 m^3).
- Big Hill - located near Winnie, Texas. Capacity of 160,000,000 barrels (25,000,000 m^3).
- West Hackberry - located near Lake Charles, Louisiana. Capacity of 219,000,000 barrels (34,800,000 m^3).
- Bayou Choctaw - located near Baton Rouge, Louisiana. Capacity of 72,000,000 barrels (11,400,000 m^3).
- Richton, Mississippi. A planned facility.

The US has also organized the 2-million-barrel (320,000 m^3) Northeast Home Heating Oil Reserve to supply northeast homeowners during shortages.

California: The state of California is considering the creation of Strategic Fuels Reserve.

Oceania: New Zealand has a strategic reserve with a 2008 size of 170,000 tons or 1,200,000 barrels (190,000 m^3). Much of this reserve is based on ticketed option contracts with Australia, Japan, the United Kingdom and the Netherlands, which allow for guaranteed purchases of petroleum in the event of an emergency.

Chapter 7

International Pressure and Pricing

Alternative Propulsion

Alternative Fuels

Economists say that the substitution effect will spur demand for alternate fossil fuels, such as coal or liquefied natural gas and for renewable energies, such as solar power, wind power, and advanced biofuels.

For example, China and India are currently heavily investing in natural gas and coal liquefaction facilities. Nigeria is working on burning natural gas to produce electricity instead of simply flaring the gas, where all non-emergency gas flaring will be forbidden after 2008. Outside the U.S., more than 50% of oil is consumed for stationary, non-transportation purposes such as electricity production where it is relatively easy to substitute natural gas for oil.

Ironically, oil companies including the supermajors have begun to fund research into alternative fuel. BP has invested half a billion dollars for research over the next several years. The motivations behind such moves are to acquire the patent rights as well as understanding the technology so vertical integration of the future industry could be achieved.

Bioplastics and Bioasphalt

Another major factor in petroleum demand is the widespread use of petroleum products such as plastic. These could be partially replaced by bioplastics, which are derived from renewable plant feedstocks such as vegetable oil, cornstarch, pea starch, or microbiota. They are used either as a direct replacement for traditional plastics or as blends with traditional plastics. The most common end use market is for packaging materials. Japan has also been a pioneer in bioplastics, incorporating them into electronics and automobiles. Also bioasphalt can be used as a replacement of petroleum asphalt.

United States Strategic Fuel Reserve

The United States Strategic Petroleum Reserve could, on its own, supply current U.S. demand for about a month in the event of an emergency, unless it were also destroyed or inaccessible in the emergency. This could potentially be the case if a major storm were to hit the Gulf of Mexico, where the reserve is located.

While total consumption has increased, the western economies are less reliant on oil than they were twenty-five years ago, due both to substantial growth in productivity and the growth of sectors of the economy with little oil dependence such as finance and banking, retail, etc. The decline of heavy industry and manufacturing in most developed countries has reduced the amount of oil per unit GDP; however, since these items are imported anyway, there is less change in the oil dependence of industrialized countries than the direct consumption statistics indicate.

Fuel Taxes

One recourse used and discussed in the past to avoid the negative impacts of oil shocks in the many developed countries which have high fuel taxes has been to temporarily or permanently suspend these taxes as fuel costs rise.

France, Italy, and the Netherlands lowered taxes in 2000 in response to protests over high prices, but other European nations resisted this option because public service financiation is partly based on energy taxes. The issue came up again in 2004, when oil reached $40 a barrel causing a meeting of 25 EU finance ministers to lower economic growth forecasts for that year. Because of budget deficits in several countries, they decided to pressure OPEC to lower prices instead of lowering taxes. In 2007, European truckers, farmers, and fishermen again raised concerns over record oil prices cutting into their earnings, hoping to have taxes lowered.

In the United Kingdom, where fuel taxes were raised in October and are scheduled to rise again in April 2008, there was talk of protests and roadblocks if the tax issue was not addressed. On April 1, 2008, a 25 yen per liter fuel tax in Japan was allowed to lapse temporarily.

This method of softening price shocks is even less viable to countries with much lower gas taxes, such as the United States.

Demand Management

Transportation demand management has the potential to be an effective policy response to fuel shortages or price increases and has a greater probability of long term benefits than other mitigation options.

There are major differences in energy consumption for private transport between cities; an average U.S. urban dweller uses 24 times more energy annually for private transport as a Chinese urban resident. These differences cannot be explained by wealth alone but are closely linked to the rates of walking, cycling, and public transport use and to enduring features of the city including urban density and urban design.

For individuals, telecommuting provides alternatives to daily commuting and long-distance air travel for business. Technologies for telecommuting, such as videoconferencing, e-mail, and corporate wikis, continue to improve, in keeping with the overall improvement in information technologies ascribed to Moore's law.

As the cost of moving information by moving human workers continues to rise, while the cost of moving information electronically continues to fall, presumably market forces should cause more people to substitute virtual travel for physical travel. Matthew Simmons explicitly calls for "liberating the workforce" by changing the corporate mindset from paying people to show up physically to work every day, to paying them instead for the work they do, from any location.

This would allow many more information workers to work from home either part-time or full-time, or from satellite offices or Internet cafes near to where they live, freeing them from long daily commutes to central offices. However, even full adoption of telecommuting by all eligible workers might only decrease energy consumption by about 1% (with present energy savings estimated at 0.01-0.04%). By comparison, a 20% increase in automobile fuel economy would save 5.4%.

High energy prices and a slowed economy caused petroleum consumption to reach a three year low in crude oil imports to the United States in December 2008.

Political Action against Market Speculation

The price rises of mid-2008 led to a variety of proposals to change the rules governing energy markets and energy futures markets, in order to prevent rises due to market speculation.

On July 26, 2008, the United States House of Representatives passed the Energy Markets Emergency Act of 2008 (H.R. 6377), which directs the Commodity Futures Trading Commission (CFTC) "to utilize all its authority, including its emergency powers, to curb immediately the role of excessive speculation in any contract market within the jurisdiction and control of the Commodity Futures Trading Commission, on or through which energy futures or swaps are traded, and to eliminate excessive speculation, price distortion, sudden or unreasonable fluctuations or unwarranted changes in prices, or other unlawful activity causing major market disturbances that prevent the market from accurately reflecting the forces of supply and demand for energy commodities.

Seven Sisters (Oil Companies)

The "Seven Sisters" was a term coined in the 1950s by businessman Enrico Mattei, then-head of the Italian state oil company Eni, to describe the seven oil companies which formed the "Consortium for Iran" and dominated the global petroleum industry from the mid-1940s to the 1970s. The group comprised Standard Oil of New Jersey and Standard Oil Company of New York (now ExxonMobil); Standard Oil of California (now Chevron), Gulf Oil (acquired by Chevron in 1985) and Texaco; Royal Dutch Shell; and Anglo-Persian Oil Company (now BP).

In 1973 the members of the Seven Sisters controlled 85% of the world's petroleum reserves but in recent decades the dominance of them and their successor companies has been reduced by the increasing influence of the OPEC cartel and state-owned oil companies in emerging-market economies.

Composition and History

In 1951 Iran nationalised its oil industry, then controlled by the Anglo-Iranian Oil Company (now BP), and Iranian oil was subjected to an international embargo. In an effort to bring Iranian oil production back to international markets, the U.S. State Department suggested the creation of a "Consortium" of major oil companies. The "Consortium for Iran" was subsequently formed by the following companies:

- *Anglo-Persian Oil Company* (United Kingdom). This subsequently became Anglo-Iranian Oil Company and then British Petroleum. Following the acquisition of Amoco (which in turn was formerly Standard Oil of Indiana) and Atlantic Richfield it shortened its name to BP in 2000.

- *Gulf Oil* (United States) In 1985 most of Gulf was acquired by Chevron, with smaller parts acquired by BP and Cumberland Farms. A network of service stations in the northeastern United States still bears the Gulf name.
- *Royal Dutch Shell* (Netherlands/United Kingdom)
- *Standard Oil of California ("Socal")* (United States) This subsequently became Chevron.
- *Standard Oil of New Jersey (Esso)* (United States) This subsequently became Exxon, which renamed itself ExxonMobil following the acquisition of Mobil in 1999.
- *Standard Oil Co. of New York ("Socony")* (United States) This subsequently became Mobil, which was acquired by Exxon in 1999.
- *Texaco* (United States). This was acquired by Chevron in 2001.

The head of the Italian state oil company, Enrico Mattei sought membership for the Italian oil company AGIP, but was rejected by what he dubbed the "Seven Sisters" to describe the Anglo-Saxon companies that controlled the Middle East's oil production after World War II. British writer Anthony Sampson took over the term when he wrote the book *The Seven Sisters* in 1975, to describe the shadowy oil cartel, which tried to eliminate competitors and control the world's oil resource.

Being well-organized and able to negotiate as a cartel, the Seven Sisters were initially able to exert considerable power over Third World oil producers. In recent decades the dominance of the Seven Sisters and their successor companies has been challenged by the increasing influence of the OPEC cartel (formed in 1960), OECD countries' share of world oil production declining, and the emergence of powerful state-owned oil companies in emerging-market economies. As of 2010, the surviving companies from the Seven Sisters are BP, Chevron, ExxonMobil and Royal Dutch Shell, which form four members of the "supermajors" group.

The "New Seven Sisters"

The *Financial Times* has used the label the "New Seven Sisters" to describe a group of what it argues are the most influential national oil and gas companies based in countries outside of the OECD. According to the *Financial Times* this group comprises:

- China National Petroleum Corporation (China)
- Gazprom (Russia)

- National Iranian Oil Company (Iran)
- Petrobras (Brazil)
- PDVSA (Venezuela)
- Petronas (Malaysia)
- Saudi Aramco (Saudi Arabia).

Greater than the sum of its parts: Knowledge Management in British Petroleum. The biggest single source of sustainable competitive advantage in the future will be our ability to create and mobilize knowledge in the interest of new products and services."

The words of Kent Greenes, who leads BP's Knowledge Management effort with a dedicated team of ten staff. His multi-disciplinary team, drawn from across the range of BP's business activities, is supporting a range of knowledge management initiatives underway in business units, as well as developing new tools and processes to support the approach.

The establishment of such a team underwrites a commitment to knowledge management made by BP's CEO, John Browne, who sees it as key to helping the multinational "separate itself from the pack". BP's flat organizational structure revolves around a "federation" of 87 business units. Each has a high degree of autonomy, yet they all share a growing sense of interdependence and awareness that in order to meet their aggressive performance targets they will need to learn both from and with each-other. In short, the focus is on working smarter - to quote the vision from the Knowledge Management team: "BP knows what it knows, learns what it needs to learn, and uses its knowledge more productively than any other company."

Making the Vision a Reality

"By the end of 1997, we want to deliver a demonstrable increase in our ability to manage knowledge. We want to enhance our knowledge assets, assess our ability to manage these assets, and to look at what the critical areas of knowledge are for us."

The team has three broad areas of focus for their approach to helping BP become that smarter company.

Getting the Organization Ready

The Knowledge Management team plan to talk with every BP business unit world-wide during 1997 to carry out what they describe as "engagement" - to create awareness and develop expectations across the company. An engagement typically consists of a powerful presentation and discussion with key staff, focusing on the importance of knowledge as a strategic asset and highlighting where knowledge management is already being successfully applied in the organization. The intent is that 80% of those engaged do something more than they are already doing to manage their knowledge.

After each engagement, the Knowledge Management team uses the feedback and ideas generated to evolve the way forward for BP's Knowledge Management strategy and implementation. To support this awareness activity, BP is building up a "showcase" of examples of knowledge management in action, drawing on best practice case histories. To further embed this thinking into the organization, the team are working with BP's Organizational Development staff to build aspects of knowledge management into the formal graduate induction and leadership development programs, so that delegates experience accessing BP's knowledge infrastructure, and broaden their networks to access key expertise from diverse parts of the company.

More ambitiously, Greenes is passionate about developing the appropriate leadership and knowledge management competencies in all staff, and further legitimizing sharing and learning processes in the company. Larry Prusak (IBM Consulting), who has regularly helped stimulate BP's thinking on knowledge management, summarized well the challenge that BP, or any other company, faces in a recent article: "I call my field 'knowledge management' but you can't manage knowledge. Nobody can. What you do - what a company does - is manage the environment that optimizes knowledge."

Virtual Teamworking in British Petroleum

One thousand staff in BP, together with over 30 of its key partners and suppliers, share extensive desktop collaboration, video-conferencing and information sharing tools, as part of a major program to support the creation of virtual teams. The technology element is augmented by the provision of coaching in new ways of working, aiming for sustainable changes in work patterns and behaviours. In addition to stimulating totally new ways of working, this capability enables a degree of tacit knowledge transfer between key staff throughout BP's federation of business units, and has already contributed tens of millions of dollars of value to the company.

Managing our Knowledge Assets

Managing knowledge assets involves making knowledge visible and accessible where it already exists - whether in the form of "packaged knowledge" on the Intranet, or as knowledge resident in people, accessible via a corporate yellow pages. It also involves understanding what BP's critical knowledge assets are, both for the present and the future. Once this is known, a programatic approach to "fill in the gaps" and seek new knowledge can be put into action.

BP's current track record in the oil industry is an indication of its ability to mobilize knowledge in real time - to bring key expertise to bear on a particular business problem or opportunity. Now the focus is on how this mobility can be supplemented with a systematic approach to the capture and transfer of knowledge. As a result of exposure to research by Prof. John Henderson (Boston University) on the US Army's Centre for Army Lessons Learned, BP is learning to apply a learning process known as an After Action Review.

This team-based process is applicable to any event where there is a desire to capture and apply lessons learned, whether to refinery maintenance, drilling optimization or even to senior management meetings. To gain first-hand exposure to the technique, BP has even flown in retired ex-US Army Col. Ed Guthrie to coach the staff in several of its operations.

As the capture of knowledge becomes a mainstream activity in BP, new roles are emerging in business units - the role of a "knowledge guardian", who proactively seeks out and codifies lessons and better practices from their part of the company. Often this "packaged knowledge" takes the form of a multimedia-rich resource on BP's rapidly growing intranet, where it can be easily showcased and linked to related people and information.

In managing its own knowledge assets, the company regularly looks to others as a source of best practice and creative ideas. BP, along with other organizations such as Ford, GlaxoWellcome, GM, Xerox, Kraft, the US Army and Coca Cola is currently a member of two cross-industry working groups, facilitated by the APQC and Boston University respectively. "We certainly don't have all the answers", says Greenes "we have a tremendous amount to learn from others in this field, and find great value in sharing both our strengths and weaknesses with fellow-travellers."

After Action Reviews (AARs)

Developed by the U.S. Army to enable its transformation from a late "Industrial Age" Army to an "Information Age" Army for the 21st Century, the After Action Review is a simple mechanism for individuals and teams to learn and capture knowledge immediately from successes and failures with just four questions:

1. What was supposed to happen?
2. What actually happened?
3. Why were there differences?
4. What can we learn?

The AAR process has been adopted by companies such as Motorola and General Electric - and now British Petroleum.

Leveraging our Expertise

Striving to make better use of the expertise already resident in the organization has lead BP into some pioneering work with new tools and technologies. The Virtual Teamwork Program is a good example of a holistic approach to the support of tacit knowledge transfer. Initiated in 1995 as a visionary experiment, but now accepted as "business as usual", the program brought together desktop video-conferencing and collaboration technologies with behaviour change "coaching". Almost 1,000 staff in BP, over 30 of its key partners and suppliers now regularly use this capability to transfer knowledge face-to-face.

The Peer Assist process is a less ad hoc approach to knowledge transfer and creative problem solving. Business units are encouraged to request assistance from their peers to address key problems or opportunities. The Peer Assist process also legitimizes the time and cost required to bring together a diverse group of professionals from around the world, who will spend several days working together as a transient team to identify new approaches, thereby stimulating existing and new networks across the company. It is accepted practice that Peer Assists are uncharged activities and, moreover, they illustrate the sort of federal behaviour that BP is pursuing to complement its organization.

To enable people to leverage the expertise across the group, several different learning projects and pilots are underway, adopting a variety of approaches: exploiting multimedia and video technology; creating electronic yellow pages that can be searched in a variety of ways; and encouraging people to list their interests, expertise and experiences that they are willing to share with anyone wishing to contact them, via face-to-face or even virtual meetings.

In summary, BP's overall approach can be characterized by these three threads - Getting the organization ready, Managing its knowledge assets and Leveraging its expertise - together with a holistic consideration of people, process and technology-related issues.

Finally, Kent Greenes is in no doubt as to the lasting relevance of knowledge management within BP: "Knowledge Management is not a fad for BP - it is high on the operational and strategic agenda of the company.

The question is not 'is Knowledge Management critical to our success?', but rather, 'how do we make it happen in a way that it becomes part of our day-to-day business?'"

How Oil Drilling Works

In 2008 alone, the United States produced an estimated 4.9 million barrels of crude oil per day and imported 9.8 million barrels per day from other countries [source: U.S. Energy Information Administration]. This oil gets refined into gasoline, kerosene, heating oil and other products. To keep up with our consumption, oil companies must constantly look for new sources of petroleum, as well as improve the production of existing wells.

How does a company go about finding oil and pumping it from the ground? You may have seen images of black crude oil gushing out of the ground, or seen an oil well in movies and television shows like "Giant," "Oklahoma Crude," "Armageddon" and "Beverly Hillbillies." But modern oil production is quite different from the way it's portrayed in the movies.

In this article, we'll examine how modern oil exploration and drilling works. We'll discuss how oil is formed, found and extracted from the ground. Oil is a fossil fuel found in many countries around the world. On the next page, we'll discuss how oil is formed and how geologists find it.

Forming Oil

Oil comes from the remains of tiny plants and animals (plankton) that died in ancient seas between 10 million and 600 million years ago. After the organisms died, they sank into the sand and mud at the bottom of the sea. Over the years, the organisms decayed in the sedimentary layers. In these layers, there was little or no oxygen present. So microorganisms broke the remains into carbon-rich compounds that formed organic layers. The organic material mixed with the sediments, forming fine-grained shale, or source rock. As new sedimentary layers were deposited, they exerted intense pressure and heat on the source rock. The heat and pressure distilled the organic material into crude oil and natural gas. The oil flowed from the source rock and accumulated in thicker, more porous limestone or sandstone, called reservoir rock. Movements in the Earth trapped the oil and natural gas in the reservoir rocks between layers of impermeable rock, or cap rock, such as granite or marble.

These movements of the Earth include:

Folding - Horizontal movements press inward and move the rock layers upward into a fold or anticline.

Faulting - The layers of rock crack, and one side shifts upward or downward.

Pinching out - A layer of impermeable rock is squeezed upward into the reservoir rock.

Locating Oil

Whether employed directly by an oil company or under contract from a private firm, geologists are the ones responsible for finding oil. Their task is to find the right conditions for an oil trap — the right source rock, reservoir rock and entrapment. Many years ago, geologists interpreted surface features, surface rock and soil types, and perhaps some small core samples obtained by shallow drilling. Modern oil geologists also examine surface rocks and terrain, with the additional help of satellite images.

However, they also use a variety of other methods to find oil. They can use sensitive gravity meters to measure tiny changes in the Earth's gravitational field that could indicate flowing oil, as well as sensitive magnetometers to measure tiny changes in the Earth's magnetic field caused by flowing oil. They can detect the smell of hydrocarbons using sensitive electronic noses called sniffers. Finally, and most commonly, they use seismology, creating shock waves that pass through hidden rock layers and interpreting the waves that are reflected back to the surface.

In seismic surveys, a shock wave is created by the following:

- Compressed-air gun - shoots pulses of air into the water (for exploration over water)
- Thumper truck - slams heavy plates into the ground (for exploration over land)
- Explosives - detonated after being drilled into the ground (for exploration over land) or thrown overboard (for exploration over water).

The shock waves travel beneath the surface of the Earth and are reflected back by the various rock layers. The reflections travel at different speeds depending upon the type or density of rock layers through which they must pass. Sensitive microphones or vibration detectors detect the reflections of the shock waves — hydrophones over water, seismometers over land. Seismologists interpret the readings for signs of oil and gas traps. Once geologists find a prospective oil strike, they mark the location Using GPS coordinates on land or by marker buoys on water.

Typical Gasoline Prices Around the World

The German Technical Cooperation (GTZ) has published a list of worldwide gasoline prices by country every year since 1991. The results for 2008 can be seen in this document. Two week updates for European countries can be consulted at the website of the Touring Club Switzerland.

Protests

India

At present petrol price hiked again by 3 rupees and now price varies from 65-75 rupees in various parts of India (16-September-2011). Protests against a hike in fuel prices shut down markets, schools, airports and businesses across India on 5 July 2010, and thousands of people were arrested as violence flared in some cities.

Brazil

The gas price reached 3 reais and over and some states, from April to May people made a creative kind of protest, they put only 0,50 cent of reais and asked for a quality test, and fiscal note. The gas prices rose since 2000s from about 1,90 R$ in 2000s to 2,70 in 2011.

History of Oil Disputes

1967 Oil Embargo

The 1967 Oil Embargo began on June 6, 1967, one day after the beginning of the Six-Day War, with a joint Arab decision to deter any countries from supporting Israel militarily. Several Middle Eastern countries eventually limited their oil shipments, some embargoing only the United States and the United Kingdom, while others placed a total ban on oil exports. The Oil Embargo did not significantly decrease the amount of oil available in the United States or any affected European countries due mainly to a lack of solidarity and uniformity in embargoing specific countries. The embargo was effectively ended on September 1 with the issuance of the Khartoum Resolution.

Oil Ministers' Conference

During the June 9-18 Oil Ministers' Conference in Baghdad several Arab countries issued a communiqué that two resolutions were unanimously passed:

1. *"Arab oil shall be denied to and shall not be allowed to reach directly or indirectly countries committing aggression or participating in aggression on sovereignty of any Arab state or its territories or its territorial waters, particularly the Gulf of Aqaba"*
2. *"The involvement of any country, directly or indirectly in armed aggression against Arab states will make assets of its companies and nationals inside the territories of Arab countries subject to the laws of war. This includes the assets of oil companies."*

Invitees included the United Arab Republic, Syria, Kuwait, Libya, Saudi Arabia, Algeria, Bahrain, Abu Dhabi, and Qatar. Iraq sent copies of the Council resolution to the Embassies of Iran and Indonesia, and sought the support of Venezuela.

Oil Embargo

The Baghdad Resolution is important because Egypt broadcast claims of US aircraft support on June 6. Iraq was the first country to limit their oil shipments, embargoing the United States and the United Kingdom on June 6. Iraq, Kuwait, Algeria, Bahrain eventually embargoed the United States and the United Kingdom. Syria stopped all oil exports, rather than just embargoing specific countries in order to avoid declaring specific nations as aggressors.

The United States advocated emergency measures in OECD meetings and supported the establishment of an International Industry Advisory Board.

The Advisory Board was critical in efficiently apportioning limited tanker resources and managing the distribution of the limited oil resources.

This was an effective measure to negate the oil embargo as there was no consensus on what countries to embargo, and more importantly, oil shipped to a European country could then be shipped to any of the embargoed countries. Some Arab countries encouraged the oil companies to circumvent the embargo, as the Amir of Kuwait even proposed to the US ambassador that companies simply tamper with shipping manifests to allow shipment of oil to prohibited countries.

Egypt sought to bend not only international political policy but also the policies of more moderate governments. and sought to export the socialist revolution to neighboring moderate (i.e. conservative) countries. The embargo resulted in public pressure on Middle Eastern leaders to support Arab solidarity. Nasser effectively limited moderate countries' political options lest they risk a revolution.

Khartoum Resolution

The Khartoum Resolution issued on September 1 allowed the moderate oil producing nations (Kuwait, Saudi Arabia, and Libya) to resume oil exports and regain this critical source of revenue without risking disquiet or even overthrow from their more radical citizens. In exchange, they agreed to give annual aid to "victims of Zionist aggression" namely Egypt and Jordan ($266 million and $112 million respectively). A full discussion as well as the text is available in the Khartoum Resolution article. The oil embargo was the main reason for the formation of OAPEC which would provide a forum for the discussion of using oil politically.

1973 Oil Crisis

The 1973 oil crisis started in October 1973, when the members of Organization of Arab Petroleum Exporting Countries or the OAPEC (consisting of the Arab members of OPEC, plus Egypt, Syria and Tunisia) proclaimed an oil embargo.

This was "in response to the U.S. decision to re-supply the Israeli military" during the Yom Kippur war. It lasted until March 1974. With the U.S. actions seen as initiating the oil embargo and the long term possibility of high oil prices, disrupted supply and recession, a strong rift was created within NATO. Additionally, some European nations and Japan sought to disassociate themselves from the U.S. Middle East policy.

Arab oil producers had also linked the end of the embargo with successful U.S. efforts to create peace in the Middle East, which complicated the situation. To address these developments, the Nixon Administration began parallel negotiations with both Arab oil producers to end the embargo, and with Egypt, Syria, and Israel to arrange an Israeli pull back from the Sinai and the Golan Heights after the fighting stopped.

By January 18, 1974, Secretary of State Henry Kissinger had negotiated an Israeli troop withdrawal from parts of the Sinai. The promise of a negotiated settlement between Israel and Syria was sufficient to convince Arab oil producers to lift the embargo in March 1974. By May, Israel agreed to withdraw from some parts of the Golan Heights.

Independently, the OPEAC members agreed to use their leverage over the world price setting mechanism for oil to stabilize their real incomes by raising world oil prices. This action followed several years of steep income declines after the recent failure of negotiations with the major Western oil companies earlier in the month.

Industrialized economies relied on crude oil, and OPEC was their predominant supplier. Because of the dramatic inflation experienced during this period, a popular economic theory has been that these price increases were to blame, as being suppressive of economic activity. A minority dissenting opinion questions the causal relationship described by this theory. The targeted countries responded with a wide variety of new, and mostly permanent, initiatives to contain their further dependency. The 1973 "oil price shock", along with the 1973–1974 stock market crash, have been regarded as the first event since the Great Depression to have a persistent economic effect.

Founding of OPEC

The Organization of the Petroleum Exporting Countries (OPEC), which then consisted of twelve countries, including Iran, seven Arab countries (Iraq, Kuwait, Libya, Qatar, Saudi Arabia, the United Arab Emirates), plus Venezuela, Indonesia, Nigeria, and Ecuador, had been formed at a Baghdad conference on September 14, 1960. OPEC was organized to resist pressure by the "Seven Sisters" (mostly owned by U.S., British and Dutch nationals) to reduce oil prices and payments to producing countries. At first OPEC had operated as an informal bargaining unit for the sale of oil by resource-rich Third World nations. OPEC confined its activities to gaining a larger share of the profits generated by the Western oil companies and greater control over the members' levels of production. As a result of this and other events in the early 1970s, it began to exert its economic and political strength; the major Western oil conglomerates, as well as the importing nations, suddenly faced a unified bloc of exporters.

End of Bretton Woods

On August 15, 1971, the United States pulled out of the Bretton Woods Accord taking the US off the Gold Exchange Standard (whereby only the value of the US dollar had been pegged to the price of gold and all other currencies were pegged to the US dollar), allowing the dollar to "float". Shortly thereafter, Britain followed, floating the pound sterling. The industrialized nations followed suit with their respective currencies. In anticipation of the fluctuation of currencies as they stabilized against each other, the industrialized nations also increased their reserves (printing money) in amounts far greater than ever before. The result was a depreciation of the value of the US dollar, as well as the other currencies of the world. Because oil was priced in dollars, this meant that oil producers were receiving less real income for the same price. The OPEC cartel issued a joint communique stating that, from then on, they would price a barrel of oil against gold.

This led to the "Oil Shock" of the mid-seventies. In the years after 1971, OPEC was slow to readjust prices to reflect this depreciation. From 1947-1967 the price of oil in U.S. dollars had risen by less than two percent per year. Until the Oil Shock, the price remained fairly stable versus other currencies and commodities, but suddenly became extremely volatile thereafter. OPEC ministers had not developed the institutional mechanisms to update prices rapidly enough to keep up with changing market conditions, so their real incomes lagged for several years. The substantial price increases of 1973-74 largely caught up their incomes to Bretton Woods levels in terms of other commodities such as gold.

Yom Kippur War

On October 6, 1973, Syria and Egypt launched a surprise attack on Israel. This new round in the Arab-Israeli conflict triggered a crisis already in the making; the price of oil was going to rise. The West could not continue to increase its energy consumption 5% annually, while also paying low oil prices, and selling inflation-priced goods to the petroleum producers in the developing Third World. This was stressed by the Shah of Iran, whose nation was the world's second-largest exporter of oil and a close ally of the United States in the Middle East at the time. "Of course [the world price of oil] is going to rise", the Shah told *The New York Times* in 1973. "Certainly! And how...; You [Western nations] increased the price of wheat you sell us by 300%, and the same for sugar and cement...; You buy our crude oil and sell it back to us, refined as petrochemicals, at a hundred times the price you've paid to us...; It's only fair that, from now on, you should pay more for oil. Let's say ten times more."

On October 12, 1973, President Richard Nixon authorized Operation Nickel Grass, an overt strategic airlift to deliver weapons and supplies to Israel, after the Soviet Union began sending arms to Syria and Egypt.

Arab Oil Embargo

On October 16, 1973, OPEC announced a decision to raise the posted price of oil by 70%, to $5.11 a barrel. The following day, oil ministers agreed to the embargo, a cut in production by five percent from September's output, and to continue to cut production over time in five percent increments until their economic and political objectives were met. October 19, US President Richard Nixon requested Congress to appropriate $2.2 billion in emergency aid to Israel, including $1.5 billion in out-right grants. George Lenczowski notes, "Military supplies did not exhaust Nixon's eagerness to prevent Israel's collapse.... This [$2.2B] decision triggered a collective OPEC response." Libya announced it would embargo all oil shipments to the United States. Saudi Arabia and the other OPEC states quickly followed suit, joining the embargo on October 20, 1973. At their meeting in Kuwait the OPEC oil-producing countries, proclaimed the oil boycott that provided for curbs on their oil exports to various consumer countries and a total embargo on oil deliveries to the United States as a "principal hostile country". The embargo was thus variously extended to Western Europe and Japan.

Though United States was the initial target of the embargo, it was later expanded to the Netherlands. Price increases were also imposed. Since short term oil demand is inelastic, demand falls little when the price is raised. Thus, oil prices had to be raised dramatically to reduce demand to the new lower level of supply. Anticipating this, the market price for oil immediately rose substantially, from $3 a barrel to $12. The world financial system, which was already under pressure from the breakdown of the Bretton Woods agreement, was set on a path of recessions and high inflation that persisted until the early 1980s, with oil prices continuing to rise until 1986.

Over the long term, the oil embargo changed the nature of policy in the West towards increased exploration, energy conservation, and more restrictive monetary policy to better fight inflation.

Chronology

- January 1973—The 1973–1974 stock market crash begins, as a result of inflation pressure, the Nixon Shock and the collapsing monetary system.
- August 23, 1973—In preparation for the Yom Kippur War, Saudi King Faisal and Egyptian president Anwar Sadat meet in Riyadh and secretly negotiate an accord whereby the Arabs will use the "oil weapon" as part of the upcoming military conflict.

- October 6 - Egypt and Syria attack Israeli occupied lands in Sinai and Golan Heights on Yom Kippur, starting the fourth Arab-Israeli War.
- October 8–October 10—OPEC negotiations with major oil companies to revise the 1971 Tehran price agreement fail.
- October 12— The United States initiates Operation Nickel Grass, an overt strategic airlift operation to provide replacement weapons and supplies to Israel during the Yom Kippur War. This followed similar Soviet moves to supply the Arab side.
- October 16 - Saudi Arabia, Iran, Iraq, Abu Dhabi, Kuwait, and Qatar unilaterally raise posted prices by 17% to $3.65 per barrel and announce production cuts.
- October 17—OPEC oil ministers agree to use oil as a weapon to influence the West's support of Israel in the Yom Kippur war. They recommend an embargo against non-complying states and mandate a cut in exports.
- October 19—US President Richard Nixon requests Congress to appropriate $2.2billion in emergency aid to Israel. This decision triggered a collective Arab response. Libya proclaims an embargo on oil exports to the United States; Saudi Arabia and other Arab states follow.
- October 23–October 28—The Arab oil embargo is extended to the Netherlands.
- October 26—The Yom Kippur War ends.
- November 5—Arab producers announce a 25% output cut. A further 5% cut is threatened.
- November 23—The Arab embargo is extended to Portugal, Rhodesia, and South Africa.
- November 27—U.S. President Richard Nixon signs the Emergency Petroleum Allocation Act authorizing price, production, allocation and marketing controls.
- December 9—Arab oil ministers agree to another five percent cut for non-friendly countries for January 1974.
- December 25—Arab oil ministers cancel the five percent output cut for January. Saudi oil minister Ahmed Zaki Yamani promises a ten percent OPEC production rise.
- January 7–January 9, 1974—OPEC decides to freeze prices until April 1.

- January 18—Israel signs a withdrawal agreement to pull back to the east side of the Suez Canal.
- February 11 - United States Secretary of State Henry Kissinger unveils the Project Independence plan to make U.S. energy independent.
- February 12–February 14—Progress in Arab-Israeli disengagement brings discussion of oil strategy among the heads of state of Algeria, Egypt, Syria and Saudi Arabia.
- March 5—Israel withdraws the last of its troops from the west side of the Suez Canal.
- March 17—Arab oil ministers, with the exception of Libya, announce the end of the embargo against the United States.
- May 31—Diplomacy by Henry Kissinger produces a disengagement agreement on the Syrian front.
- December 1974—The 1973–1974 stock market crash ends.

Immediate Economic Effects

The effects of the embargo were immediate. OPEC forced the oil companies to increase payments drastically. The price of oil quadrupled by 1974 to nearly US$12 per barrel (75 US$/m^3).

This increase in the price of oil had a dramatic effect on oil exporting nations, for the countries of the Middle East who had long been dominated by the industrial powers were seen to have acquired control of a vital commodity. The traditional flow of capital reversed as the oil exporting nations accumulated vast wealth. Some of the income was dispensed in the form of aid to other underdeveloped nations whose economies had been caught between higher prices of oil and lower prices for their own export commodities and raw materials amid shrinking Western demand for their goods. Much was absorbed in massive arms purchases that exacerbated political tensions, particularly in the Middle East.

This control of a vital commodity became known as the "oil weapon," which came in the form of an embargo and cutbacks in oil production from the Arab states to select industrial governments of the world to pressure Israel during the fourth Arab-Israeli War in October 1973. These target industrial governments included the United States, Great Britain, Canada, Japan, and the Netherlands. In retrospect, the purpose of the embargo, as perceived by these target governments, was to sway their foreign policies concerning Israel towards a more pro-Arab position by threatening to cut off exports of Arab oil, and that in altering their policies the Arab states would respond by again allowing their purchase of more oil. The Arab states selected their target governments to emplace their embargo, mostly affecting the European Common Market countries and Japan with a eventual 25% oil cut in production. However, in all five cases there did not appear to be the dramatic change in policy making as envisioned by the Arab states.

In the case of the United States, scholars argue that there already existed a negotiated settlement based on equality between both parties prior to 1973. Second, Soviet involvement in the Middle East as a threat to becoming another superpower confrontation was of more concern to the United States than the oil weapon.

A third reason, the interest groups and other government agencies that were more concerned with the implications of the oil weapon held little influential power concerning foreign policy in the Arab-Israeli conflict because of Kissinger's total dominance over this process. Also within the United States concerning the economic impact at the macro level, direct correlations have been drawn between the rise in oil prices and economic recessions. "Oil price shocks", referring to disruptions in the production and distribution of oil, that result in the increase of oil prices "have been held responsible for recessions, periods of excessive inflation, reduced productivity, and lower economic growth"

The effect of the Arab embargo had a negative influence on the U.S economy through causing immediate demands to address the threats to U.S energy security. On an international level, the price increases of petroleum disrupted market systems in changing competitive positions. At the macro level, economic problems consisted of both inflationary and deflationary impacts of domestic economies. The Arab embargo left many U.S companies searching for new ways to develop expensive oil, even in the elements of rugged terrain such as in hostile arctic environments. The problem that many of these companies faced is that finding oil and developing new oil fields usually require a time lag of 5 to 10 years between the planning process and significant oil production.

OPEC-member states in the developing world withheld the prospect of nationalization of the companies' holdings in their countries. Most notably, the Saudis acquired operating control of Aramco, fully nationalizing it in 1980 under the leadership of Ahmed Zaki Yamani. As other OPEC nations followed suit, the cartel's income soared. Saudi Arabia, awash with profits, undertook a series of ambitious five-year development plans, of which the most ambitious, begun in 1980, called for the expenditure of $250 billion. Other cartel members also undertook major economic development programs.

Meanwhile, the shock produced chaos in the West. In the United States, the retail price of a gallon of gasoline (petrol) rose from a national average of 38.5 cents in May 1973 to 55.1 cents in June 1974. State governments requested citizens not put up Christmas lights, with Oregon banning Christmas as well as commercial lighting altogether. Politicians called for a national gas rationing program. Nixon requested gasoline stations to voluntarily not sell gasoline on Saturday nights or Sundays; 90% of owners complied, which resulted in lines on weekdays.

The embargo was not uniform across Europe. Of the nine members of the European Economic Community (EEC), the Netherlands faced a complete embargo, the United Kingdom and France received almost uninterrupted supplies (having refused to allow America to use their airfields and embargoed arms and supplies to both the Arabs and the Israelis), whilst the other six faced only partial cutbacks. The UK had traditionally been an ally of Israel, and Harold Wilson's government had supported the Israelis during the Six Day War, but his successor, Ted Heath, had reversed this policy in 1970, calling for Israel to withdraw to its pre-1967 borders.

The members of the EEC had been unable to achieve a common policy during the first month of the Yom Kippur War. The Community finally issued a statement on November 6, after the embargo and price rises had begun; widely seen as pro-Arab, this statement supported the Franco-British line on the war, and OPEC duly lifted its embargo from all members of the EEC. The price rises had a much greater impact in Europe than the embargo, particularly in the UK (where they combined with strikes by coal miners and railroad workers to cause an energy crisis over the winter of 1973-74, a major factor in the change of government). The UK, Germany, Italy, Switzerland, and Norway banned flying, driving and boating on Sundays. Sweden rationed gasoline and heating oil. The Netherlands imposed prison sentences for those who used more than their given ration of electricity. Ted Heath asked the British to heat only one room in their houses over the winter.

A few months later, the crisis eased. The embargo was lifted in March 1974 after negotiations at the Washington Oil Summit, but the effects of the energy crisis lingered on throughout the 1970s. The price of energy continued increasing in the following year, amid the weakening competitive position of the dollar in world markets.

Price Controls and Rationing

Government price controls further exacerbated the crisis in the United States, which limited the price of "old oil" (that already discovered) while allowing newly discovered oil to be sold at a higher price, resulting in a withdrawal of old oil from the market and the creation of artificial scarcity. The rule also discouraged alternative energies or more efficient fuels or technologies from being developed. The rule had been intended to promote oil exploration. This scarcity was dealt with by rationing of gasoline (which occurred in many countries), with motorists facing long lines at gas stations beginning in summer 1972 and increasing by summer 1973.

In 1973, U.S. President Richard Nixon named William E. Simon as the first Administrator of the Federal Energy Office, or the "Energy Czar". Simon allocated states the same amount of domestic oil for 1974 that each consumed in 1972, which worked well for states whose populations were not increasing. In states with increased populations, lines at gasoline stations were common. The American Automobile Association reported that in the last week of February 1974, 20% of American gasoline stations had no fuel at all.

In the U.S., odd-even rationing was implemented; drivers of vehicles with license plates having an odd number as the last digit (or a vanity license plate) were allowed to purchase gasoline for their cars only on odd-numbered days of the month, while drivers of vehicles with even-numbered license plates were allowed to purchase fuel only on even-numbered days. The rule did not apply on the 31st day of those months containing 31 days, or on February 29 in leap years— the latter never came into play, since the restrictions had been abolished by 1976.

In some U.S. states, a three-colour flag system was used to denote gasoline availability at service stations — a green flag denoted unrationed sale of gasoline, a yellow flag denoted restricted and rationed sales, and a red flag denoted that no gasoline was available but the service station was open for other services. Additionally, coupons for gasoline rationing were ordered in 1974 and 1975 for Federal Energy Administration, but were never actually used for this crisis or the 1979 energy crisis.

The rationing led to incidents of violence, after truck drivers nationwide chose to strike for two days in December 1973 because they objected to the supplies Simon had rationed for their industry. In Pennsylvania and Ohio, non-striking truckers were shot at by striking truckers, and in Arkansas, trucks of non-strikers were attacked with bombs. America had controlled the price of natural gas since the 1950s, and with the inflation of the 1970s, the market price of natural gas was not encouraging the search for new reserves. America's natural gas reserves dwindled from 237 trillion in 1974 to 203 trillion in 1978, and the price controls were not changed despite President Gerald Ford's repeated requests to Congress.

Conservation and Reduction in Demand

To help reduce consumption, in 1974 a national maximum speed limit of 55 mph (about 88 km/h) was imposed through the Emergency Highway Energy Conservation Act. Development of the United States Strategic Petroleum Reserve began in 1975, and in 1977, the cabinet-level Department of Energy was created, followed by the National Energy Act of 1978.

Year-round daylight saving time was implemented from January 6, 1974 to February 23, 1975. The move spawned significant criticism because it forced many children to commute to school before sunrise. The pre-existing daylight-saving rules, calling for the clocks to be advanced one hour on the last Sunday in April, were restored in 1976.

The crisis also prompted a call for individuals and businesses to conserve energy, most notably a campaign by the Advertising Council using the tag line "Don't Be Fuelish." Many newspapers carried full-page advertisements that featured cut-outs which could be attached to light switches, reading "Last Out, Lights Out: Don't Be Fuelish."

By 1980, there were no longer full-size luxury cars with a 130-inch (3.3 m) wheelbase and gross weights averaging 4,500 pounds (2,041 kg). The automakers began phasing out the traditional front engine/rear wheel drive layout in favour of more efficient front engine/front wheel drive designs. Though not regulated by the new legislation, auto racing groups voluntarily began conserving as well. In 1974 the 24 Hours of Daytona was canceled and NASCAR reduced all race distances by 10%. The 12 Hours of Sebring race was cancelled.

In 1976, the U.S. Congress created the Weatherization Assistance Program to help low-income homeowners and renters deal with rising heating costs by reducing their demand through advanced insulation.

Secondary Effects

Various secondary effects occurred, notably toilet paper panics in Japan and the United States; these were unfounded panics which became self-fulfilling prophesies, and are classic examples of the Thomas theorem. Price rises and unfounded rumors of a toilet paper shortage – based on oil being used in paper manufacturing – caused a panic and hoarding of toilet paper in late October and early November in Osaka and Kobe, among other cities. In the US, Johnny Carson inadvertently caused a three-week panic when, on December 19, 1973, he read a news item regarding the US government falling behind on bids for toilet paper and quipping that the nation faced a toilet paper shortage on the *Tonight Show*.

Search for Alternatives

The energy crisis led to greater interest in renewable energy and spurred research in solar power and wind power. It also led to greater pressure to exploit North American oil sources, and increased the West's dependence on coal and nuclear power. This included increased interest in mass transit. In Australia, heating oil ceased being considered an appropriate winter heating fuel. This often meant that a lot of oil-fired room heaters that were popular from the late-1950s to the early-1970s were considered outdated. Gas-conversion kits that let the heaters burn natural gas or propane were introduced.

For the handful of industrialized nations that were net energy exporters, the effects of the oil crisis were very different. In Canada the industrial east suffered many of the same problems of the United States. In oil rich Alberta, however, there was a sudden and massive influx of money that quickly made it the richest province in the country. The federal government attempted to correct this imbalance through the creation of the government-owned Petro-Canada and later the National Energy Program. These efforts produced a great deal of anger in the west producing a sentiment of alienation that has remained a central element of Canadian politics to this day. Overall the oil embargo had a sharply negative effect on the Canadian economy. The economic malaise in the United States easily crossed the border and increases in unemployment, and stagflation hit Canada as hard as the United States despite Canadian fuel reserves.

The Brazilian government implemented a very large project called "Proálcool" (pro-alcohol) that mixed ethanol with gasoline for automotive fuel. To supplement Israel's over-taxed power grid, Harry Zvi Tabor, the father of Israel's solar industry, developed the prototype for a solar water heater now used in over 90% of Israeli homes.

Macroeconomic Effects

The 1973 oil crisis was a major factor in Japan's economy shifting from oil-intensive industries, and resulted in huge Japanese investments in industries such as electronics. The Japanese auto makers also took advantage of this embargo. After they realized what fuel costs were in the United States, they started producing small, more fuel efficient models, which began selling as an alternative to "gas-guzzling" American vehicles of the time. This triggered a drop in American auto sales that lasted into the 1980s.

The Western nations' central banks decided to sharply cut interest rates to encourage growth, deciding that inflation was a secondary concern. Although this was the orthodox macroeconomic prescription at the time, the resulting stagflation surprised economists and central bankers, and the policy is now considered by some to have deepened and lengthened the adverse effects of the embargo.

Long-term effects of the embargo are still felt. Many in the public remain suspicious of oil companies, believing they profiteered, or even colluded with OPEC. In 1974, seven of the fifteen top Fortune 500 companies were oil companies.

Effects on International Relations

The Cold War policies of the Nixon administration also suffered a major blow in the aftermath of the oil embargo. They had focused on China and the Soviet Union, but the latent challenge to U.S. hegemony coming from the Third World became evident. U.S. power was under attack even in Latin America.

The oil embargo was announced roughly one month after a right-wing military coup in Chile led by General Augusto Pinochet Chilean coup of 1973 toppled socialist president Salvador Allende on September 11, 1973. The United States' subsequent assistance to this government did little to curb the activities of socialist guerrillas in the region. The response of the Nixon administration was to propose doubling of the amount of military arms sold by the United States. As a consequence, a Latin American bloc was organized and financed in part by Venezuela and its oil revenues, which quadrupled between 1970 and 1975.

In addition, Western Europe and Japan began switching from pro-Israel to more pro-Arab policies. This change further strained the Western alliance system, for the United States, which imported only 12% of its oil from the Middle East (compared with 80% for the Europeans and over 90% for Japan), remained staunchly committed to backing Israel. The percentage of U.S. oil which comes from the nations bordering the Persian Gulf has remained steady over the years, with a figure of a little more than 10% in 2008.

Although historically having no connections to the Middle East, Japan was the most heavily dependent on its oil from this region, making up 71% of its imported oil from the Middle East in 1970. However, on November 7, 1973, the Saudi and Kuwaiti governments declared Japan a "nonfriendly" country directed towards changing its policy of noninvolvement in the Arab-Israeli conflict, placing a 5 percent production cut in December to Japan. The December production cut to the Japanese government caused somewhat of a panic, where on November 22 Japan issued a statement "asserting that Israel should withdraw from all of the 1967 territories, advocating Palestinian self-determination, and threatening to reconsider its policy toward Israel if Israel refused to accept these preconditions" By December 25, Japan was considered a friendly state.

With the oil embargo in place, the industrial governments of the world in some way altered their foreign policy regarding the Arab-Israeli conflict and after the use of the Arab oil weapon. These included European countries such as the UK who decided to refuse to allow the United States to use British bases in the UK and in Cyprus to airlift resupplies to Israel along with the rest of the members of the European Community. It also included the Japanese restatement on November 22, to "reconsider" their relations with Israel if Israel did not acknowledge their avocations to return to their pre-1967 territorial state, although this was never acted upon. Canada shifted towards a more pro-Arab position after displeasure was expressed by many Arab governments towards Canada's Middle Eastern position as one of being mostly neutral. "On the other hand, after the embargo the Canadian government moved quickly indeed toward the Arab position, despite its low dependence on Middle Eastern oil"

A year after the start of the 1973 oil embargo, the nonaligned bloc in the United Nations passed a resolution demanding the creation of a "new international economic order" in which resources, trade, and markets would be distributed more equitably, with the local populations of nations within the global South receiving a greater share of benefits derived from the exploitation of southern resources, and greater respect for the right to self-directed development in the South be afforded by the North.

In the post-Cold War era, Israel continues to serve the U.S.A. as a strategically important non-NATO ally in the Middle East. According to the American military journalist and commentator William M. Arkin in his book *Code Names*, the U.S. has prepositioned munitions, vehicles, and military equipment, and even a 500-bed hospital for use by US Marines, Special Forces, and Air Force fighter and bomber aircraft in a wartime contingency at least six sites in Israel. Late Republican

Senator Jesse Helms used to call Israel "America's aircraft carrier in the Middle East", when explaining why the US viewed Israel as such a strategic ally, saying that the military foothold in the region offered by the Jewish State alone justified the military aid that the US grants Israel every year. Israel is not the only country in the Middle East to host US military bases, though. There are American military facilities in Egypt, Jordan, Saudi Arabia, Oman, and the Persian Gulf states of Kuwait, Bahrain (headquarters of the United States Fifth Fleet), and Qatar.

Decline of OPEC

Since 1973, OPEC failed to hold on to its preeminent position, and by 1981, its production was surpassed by that of other countries. Additionally, its own member nations were divided among themselves. Saudi Arabia, trying to gain back market share, increased production and caused downward pressure on prices, making high-cost oil production facilities less profitable or even unprofitable. The world price of oil, which had reached a peak in 1979 during the 1979 energy crisis, at more than US$80 per barrel, decreased during the early 1980s to US$38 per barrel (239 US$/m^3). In real prices, oil briefly fell back to pre-1973 levels. Overall, the reduction in price was a windfall for the oil-consuming nations: United States, Japan, Europe, and especially the Third World.

Part of the decline in prices and economic and geopolitical power of OPEC comes from the move away from oil consumption to alternate energy sources. OPEC had relied on the famously limited price inelasticity of oil demand to maintain high consumption but had underestimated the extent to which other sources of supply would become profitable as the price increased. Electricity generation from nuclear power and natural gas, home heating from natural gas and ethanol blended gasoline all reduced the demand for oil.

At the same time, the drop in prices represented a serious problem for oil-producing countries in northern Europe and the Persian Gulf region. For a handful of heavily populated, impoverished countries, whose economies were largely dependent on oil — including Mexico, Nigeria, Algeria, and Libya — governments and business leaders failed to prepare for a market reversal, the price drop placed them in wrenching, sometimes desperate situations. When reduced demand and over-production produced a glut on the world market in the mid-1980s, oil prices plummeted and the cartel lost its unity. Oil exporters such as Mexico, Nigeria, and Venezuela, whose economies had expanded in the 1970s, were plunged into near-bankruptcy, and even Saudi Arabian economic power was significantly weakened. The divisions within OPEC made subsequent concerted action more difficult.

Nevertheless, the 1973 oil shock provided dramatic evidence of the potential power of Third World resource suppliers in dealing with the developed world. The vast reserves of the leading Middle East producers guaranteed the region its strategic importance, but the politics of oil still proves dangerous for all concerned to this day.

Long-term Effects

Prior to the embargo, the geo-political competition between the Soviet Union and the United States, in combination with low oil prices that hindered the necessity and feasibility for the West to seek alternative energy sources, presented the Arab States with financial security, moderate economic growth, and disproportionate international bargaining power. Following the embargo, higher oil prices instigated new avenues for energy exploration or expansion including Alaska, the North Sea, the Caspian Sea, and Caucasus.

Soviet Reaction

Prior to the ascendancy of Anwar Sadat to president of Egypt in 1970, the Middle East had been an important arena in the global superpower competition, most lucidly displayed in the arms sales and cooperation between the American and Soviet governments with Israel, Saudi Arabia, and Iran allied to The United States, and Egypt, Syria, and Iraq allied with the Soviet Union. Although none of these states entered into any formal alliances comparative to the North Atlantic Treaty Organization, they did benefit greatly from the geo-political competition in the region and vacillations in alignment often resulted in greater gains of assistance.

This competitive environment, beneficial to the regional states involved, was mitigated sharply after 1970. Sadat's dismissal of Soviet specialists in Egypt and the dramatic price increases in hydrocarbons hardened relations with all of the Middle East and created new opportunities for the export of Soviet oil. Exploration in the Caspian Basin and Siberia became more cost effective. Former cooperation evolved into a far more adversarial relationship as the Soviet Union increased oil production and export (by 1980 the Soviet Union was the world's largest producer of oil) to take advantage of the supply problems in the West created by OPEC's production reductions. This growing economic competition turned into genuine fears of military aggression after the 1979 Soviet invasion of Afghanistan, leaving the Persian Gulf states to look to the United States for the type of security guarantees against Soviet military action in the Persian Gulf that the Israelis had exclusively received only a decade earlier.

Growing Security Concerns

The Soviet invasion of Afghanistan was only part of the growing security destabilization in the Middle East, most obviously seen in the increased sale of American weapons, technology, and outright military presence. Saudi Arabia and Iran became increasingly dependent on bi-lateral American security assurances to combat both external and internal threats, including increased military competition between these states because of the increased oil revenues. Both states were seemingly competing for preeminence in the Persian Gulf and using increased revenues on disproportionately powerful military forces. By 1979, Saudi weapon purchases from the United States were in excess of five times the amount that Israel was purchasing annually.

Following the failure of the Shah during January 1979 to maintain control of Iran, the Saudis were forced to deal with the prospect of internal destabilization via Islamic fundamentalism, a reality which would quickly be revealed in the seizure of the Grand Mosque in Mecca by Wahhabi extremists during November and a Shia revolt in al-Hasa during December. Growing fears about eventual Western energy independence, various security threats, and the absence of a Western rival in the geo-political competition over the Middle-East led the Arab states in a more dependent relationship with the West. This is most explicit in Saudi Arabia's consistent policy of price and production moderation in an effort to reduce the chances of Western alienation and the opportunity costs for alternative energy production. The exchange for Western moderation in Arab-Israeli affairs ultimately led to a reshaping of the Middle-Eastern geo-political landscape that was significantly less advantageous than prior to 1973.

Impact on Motor Industry

West Europe

The motor industry was one of Western Europe's most affected industries in the wake of the 1973 oil crisis. After the Second World War most West European countries applied heavy taxes to motor fuel because it was imported, and as a result most cars made in Europe were small and economical. However by the late sixties as wealth increased car sizes were rising despite heavy fuel taxes, although some of the more upmarket brands were building cars that could take lead-free fuel, and there were still a number of "economy" cars in production at this time. But the oil crisis gradually saw many West European car buyers move away from larger, less economical cars. The most notable result of this transition in the car market was the rise in popularity of compact hatchbacks.

The only notable small hatchbacks built in Western Europe at the time of the oil crisis were the Peugeot 104, Renault 5 and Fiat 127. By the end of the decade, the market had massively expanded with the introduction of the Ford Fiesta, Opel Kadett (sold as the Vauxhall Astra in Great Britain), Chrysler Sunbeam and Citroën Visa.

Buyers looking for larger cars were increasingly drawn to medium sized hatchbacks that were virtually unknown in Europe in 1973, but by the end of the decade were gradually replacing saloons as the mainstay of this sector. Between 1973 and 1980, the following medium sized hatchbacks were launched across Europe: the Chrysler/Simca Horizon, Fiat Ritmo (Strada in the UK), Ford Escort MK3, Renault 14, Volvo 340/360, Opel Kadett and Volkswagen Golf. These cars offered new standard of fuel economy, which were much needed in the aftermath of the oil crisis.

The new cars launched in the wake of the oil crisis were considerably more economical than the traditional saloons they were taking the place of, and even attracted a considerable number of buyers who would have otherwise chosen cars in the next sector. Their success continued into the 1980s and by the later part of the decade, some 15 years after the oil crisis, hatchbacks almost monopolised most European small and medium car markets, and had gained a substantial share of the large family car market.

U.S.

As in Western Europe, U.S. automakers were significantly impacted by the 1973 oil embargo and energy crisis. Before the energy crisis, large, heavy, and powerful cars were the standard in the U.S. By 1971, the standard engine in a Chevrolet Caprice was a 400-cubic inch (6.5 liter) V8. The wheelbase of this car was 121.5 inches (3,090 mm), and *Motor Trend*'s 1972 road test of the similar Chevrolet Impala logged no more than 15 miles per gallon on the highway.

After the energy crisis, however, gasoline cost more and reduced the demand for large cars. The Toyota Corona, the Toyota Corolla, the Datsun B210, the Datsun 510, the Honda Civic, the Mitsubishi Galant (a captive import from Chrysler sold as the Dodge Colt), the Subaru DL, and later the Honda Accord all had four cylinder engines that were more fuel efficient in comparison to the typical V8 and six cylinder engines found in North American vehicles. From Europe, the Volkswagen Beetle, the Volkswagen Fastback, the Renault 8, the Renault LeCar, and the Fiat Brava were also offered. As buyers began exchanging large cars for the smaller imported ones, Detroit responded with the Ford Pinto, the Ford Maverick, the Chevrolet Vega, the Chevrolet Nova, the Plymouth Valliant, and the Plymouth Volaré.

Some buyers lamented the small size of the first compacts that came from Japan, and both Toyota and Nissan (known as Datsun during the 1970s) introduced larger cars called the Toyota Corona Mark II, replaced by the Toyota Cressida, the Mazda 616, and Datsun 810 which gave buyers increased passenger space and some luxury amenities, such as air conditioning, power steering, AM-FM radios, and even power windows and central locking without increasing the price of the vehicle. These larger compacts were at the very limit of Japanese government regulations concerning size and engine displacement so that they could still be affordable in the Japanese Domestic Market, yet offer export buyers larger cars that sacrificed fuel economy for passenger accommodation and a higher price. Toyota also sold the Toyota Crown from 1965 to 1974 with very limited amount of sales. Compact trucks were also introduced to the USA, with the Toyota Hilux and the Datsun Truck, followed by the Mazda Truck also sold as the Ford Courier, with Isuzu selling their compact truck as the Chevrolet LUV.

An increase in imported cars into North America forced the Big Three (General Motors, Ford, and Chrysler) to introduce smaller and fuel-efficient models for domestic sales. The Dodge Omni/Plymouth Horizon from Chrysler, the Ford Fiesta, and the Chevrolet Chevette all had four-cylinder engines and room for at least four passengers by the late '70s. By 1985, the average American vehicle received 17.4 miles per gallon, compared to 13.5 miles per gallon in 1970. The improvements stayed even though the price of a barrel of oil remained constant at $12 from 1974 to 1979.

While at the same time these new imports were major inroads in the American market, sales of large sedans for most makes (except Chrysler products) recovered within two model years of the 73' Oil Crisis. Sales of models such as the Cadillac DeVille, Buick Electra, Oldsmobile 98, Lincoln Continental, Mercury Marquis, and various other luxury oriented sedans became popular again in the mid-70s. The only full-size models to see permanent reductions in sales were the lower price models; such as the Chevrolet Impala, and Ford Galaxie 500. At the same time, slightly smaller, if not entirely more fuel efficient mid-size models such as the Oldsmobile Cutlass, Chevrolet Monte Carlo, Ford Thunderbird and various other models sold well.

This led to the somewhat odd juxtaposition of small economical imports introducing themselves as major elements of the market, while at the same time heavy, expensive, largely impractical vehicles (with 7 mpg; Lincoln sold 80,321 Mark Vs in 77) selling alongside the new imports in equally impressive numbers. In 1976; Toyota, with an average weight around 2,100 lbs sold 346,920 cars in the United States, while Cadillac with an average weight around 5,000 lbs sold 309,139 cars.

Federal safety standards, such as NHTSA Federal Motor Vehicle Safety Standard 215 (pertaining to safety bumpers), and compacts like the 1974 Mustang II were a prelude to the DOT "downsize" revision of vehicle categories. By 1977, GM's full-sized cars reflected on the 1973 oil crisis and preceded later DOT downsizing. By 1979, virtually all the big "full size" American cars were "downsized", featuring smaller engines and smaller dimensions outside. Chrysler Corporation ended production of their full-sized luxury sedans at the end of the 1981 model year, moving instead to a full front wheel drive lineup for 1982 (except for the M-body Dodge Diplomat/Plymouth Gran Fury and Chrysler New Yorker Fifth Avenue sedans).

It has been suggested that if mass production of overdrive transmissions had been introduced, there would not have actually been any vehicle downsizing. But since this has actually happened it turns out not to be true.

1979 Energy Crisis

The 1979 (or second) oil crisis in the United States occurred in the wake of the Iranian Revolution. Amid massive protests, the Shah of Iran, Mohammad Reza Pahlavi, fled his country in early 1979 and the Ayatollah Khomeini soon became the new leader of Iran. Protests severely disrupted the Iranian oil sector, with production being greatly curtailed and exports suspended. When oil exports were later resumed under the new regime, they were inconsistent and at a lower volume, which pushed prices up. Saudi Arabia and other OPEC nations, under the presidency of Dr. Mana Alotaiba increased production to offset the decline, and the overall loss in production was about 4 percent. However, a widespread panic resulted, added to by the decision of U.S. President Jimmy Carter to order the cessation of Iranian imports, driving the price far higher than would be expected under normal circumstances. In April of the same year, President Carter began a phased deregulation of oil prices. At the time, the average price of crude oil was $15.85 per barrel (42 US gallons (160 L)). Deregulating domestic oil price controls allowed U.S. oil output to rise sharply from the Prudhoe Bay fields, although oil imports fell sharply. Long lines once again appeared at gas stations and convenience stores, just as they did in 1973.

In 1980, following the outbreak of the Iran–Iraq War, oil production in Iran nearly stopped, and Iraq's oil production was severely cut as well. After 1980, oil prices began a 20-year decline down to a 60 percent price drop in the 1990s. Oil exporters such as Mexico, Nigeria, and Venezuela expanded production ; USSR became the first world producer, and North Sea and Alaskan oil flooded onto the market.

Iran

In November 1978, a strike by 37,000 workers at Iran's nationalized oil refineries initially reduced production from 6 million barrels (950,000 m^3) per day to about 1.5 million barrels (240,000 m^3). Foreign workers (including skilled oil workers) fled the country. On January 16, 1979, Shah of Iran, Mohammad Reza Pahlavi and his wife left Iran at the behest of Prime Minister Shapour Bakhtiar (a long time opposition leader himself), who sought to calm down the situation.

Effects

Other OPEC Members

The rise in oil price benefited other OPEC members, which made record profits.

United States

The oil crisis had mixed effects in the United States, due to some parts of the country being oil-producing regions and other parts being oil-consuming regions.

Richard Nixon had imposed price controls on domestic oil, which had helped cause shortages that led to gasoline lines during the 1973 Oil Crisis. Gasoline controls were repealed, but controls on domestic US oil remained.

The Jimmy Carter administration began a phased deregulation of oil prices on April 5, 1979, when the average price of crude oil was US$15.85 per barrel (42 US gallons (160 L)). Starting with the Iranian revolution, the price of crude oil rose to $39.50 per barrel over the next 12 months (its all time highest real price until March 7, 2008.) Deregulating domestic oil price controls allowed domestic U.S. oil output to rise sharply from the large Prudhoe Bay fields, while oil imports fell sharply. Due to memories of oil shortage in 1973, motorists soon began panic buying, and long lines appeared at gas stations, as they had six years earlier during the 1973 oil crisis.

As the average vehicle of the time consumed between two to three liters (about 0.5-0.8 gallons) of gasoline (petrol) an hour while idling, it was estimated that Americans wasted up to 150,000 barrels (24,000 m^3) of oil per day idling their engines in the lines at gas stations.

During the period, many people believed the oil companies artificially created oil shortages to drive up prices, rather than factors beyond human control or the US' own price controls. The amount of oil sold in the United States in 1979 was only 3.5 percent less than the record set for oil sold the year previously.

Many politicians proposed gas rationing; one such proponent was Harry Hughes, Governor of Maryland, who proposed odd-even rationing (only people with an odd-numbered license plate could purchase gas on an odd-numbered day), as was used during the 1973 Oil Crisis. Several states actually implemented odd-even gas rationing, including Pennsylvania, New York, New Jersey, and Texas. Coupons for gasoline rationing were printed but were never actually used during the 1979 crisis.

On July 15, 1979, President Jimmy Carter outlined his plans to reduce oil imports and improve energy efficiency in his "Crisis of Confidence" speech (sometimes known as the "malaise" speech). It is often said that during the speech, Carter wore a cardigan (he actually wore a blue suit) and encouraged citizens to do what they could to reduce their use of energy.

He had already installed solar power panels on the roof of the White House and a wood-burning stove in the living quarters. However, the panels were removed in 1986, reportedly for roof maintenance, during the administration of his successor, Ronald Reagan.

Carter's speech argued the oil crisis was "the moral equivalent of war". Several months later, in January 1980, Carter issued the Carter Doctrine, which declared that any interference with U.S. oil interests in the Persian Gulf would be considered an attack on the vital interests of the United States.

Additionally, as part of his administration's efforts at deregulation, Carter proposed removing price controls that had been imposed in the administration of Richard Nixon before the 1973 crisis. Carter agreed to remove price controls in phases; they were finally dismantled in 1981 under Reagan. Carter also said he would impose a windfall profit tax on oil companies. While the regulated price of domestic oil was kept to $6 a barrel, the world market price was $30.

In 1980, the U.S. Government established the Synthetic Fuels Corporation to produce an alternative to imported fossil fuels.

Oil Patch

When the price of West Texas Intermediate crude oil increased 250 percent between 1978 and 1980, the oil-producing areas of Texas, Oklahoma, Louisiana, Colorado, Wyoming, and Alaska began experiencing an economic boom and population inflows.

Automobile Fuel Economy

At the same time, Detroit's then-Big Three automakers (Ford, Chrysler, GM) were marketing downsized full-sized automobiles like the Chevrolet Caprice, the Ford LTD Crown Victoria and the Dodge St. Regis which met the CAFE fuel economy mandates passed in 1978. Detroit's response to the growing popularity of imported compacts like the Toyota Corolla and the Volkswagen Rabbit were the Chevrolet Citation, and the Ford Fairmont; Ford replaced the Ford Pinto with the Ford Escort and Chrysler, on the verge of bankruptcy, introduced the Dodge Aries K. GM was having unfavorable market reactions to the Citation, and introduced the Chevrolet Corsica and Chevrolet Beretta in 1987 which did sell better. GM also replaced the Chevrolet Monza, introducing the 1982 Chevrolet Cavalier which was better received. Ford experienced a similar market rejection of the Fairmont, and introduced the front wheel drive Ford Tempo in 1984.

Detroit was not well prepared for the sudden rise in fuel prices, and imported brands were now more widely available in North America and had developed a loyal customer base. Many imported brands utilized fuel saving technologies such as fuel injection and multi-valve engines over the common use of carburetors. GM's Cadillac division experimented with their V8-6-4 power plant (the ancestor of the modern-day Active Fuel Management and/or variable displacement), which was a market failure. Nonetheless, overall fuel economy increased, which was one factor leading to the subsequent 1980s oil glut.

1980s Oil Glut

The 1980s oil glut was a serious surplus of crude oil caused by falling demand following the 1970s Energy Crisis. The world price of oil, which had peaked in 1980 at over US$35 per barrel ($93 per barrel today), fell in 1986 from $27 to below $10 ($54 to $20 today). The glut began in the early 1980s as a result of slowed economic activity in industrial countries (due to the crises of the 1970s, especially in 1973 and 1979) and the energy conservation spurred by high fuel prices. The inflation adjusted real 2004 dollar value of oil fell from an average of $78.2 in 1981 to an average of $26.8 per barrel in 1986.

In June 1981, *The New York Times* stated an "Oil glut!... is here" and *Time Magazine* stated: "the world temporarily floats in a glut of oil," though the next week an article in *The New York Times* warned that the word "glut" was misleading, and that in reality, while temporary surpluses had brought down prices somewhat, prices were still well above pre-energy crisis levels.

This sentiment was echoed in November 1981, when the CEO of Exxon Corp also characterized the glut as a temporary surplus, and that the word "glut" was an example of "our American penchant for exaggerated language." He wrote that the main cause of the glut was declining consumption. In the United States, Europe and Japan, oil consumption had fallen 13% from 1979 to 1981, due to "in part, in reaction to the very large increases in oil prices by the Organization of Petroleum Exporting Countries and other oil exporters," continuing a trend begun during the 1973 price increases.

After 1980, reduced demand and overproduction produced a glut on the world market, causing a six-year-long decline in oil prices culminating with a 46 percent price drop in 1986.

The 1973 oil crisis and the 1979 oil crisis turned oil from a cheap to a very expensive energy source. During the 1973 energy crisis, the price of oil quadrupled. Oil never returned to pre-1973 levels, either in real or nominal terms, even during the 1980s glut.

The nominal price continued its slow increase after the crisis ended. Six years later, the price more than doubled during the 1979 energy crisis. OPEC and Saudi Arabia artificially raised the price of oil several times in 1979 and 1980. Also during this time, several OPEC members significantly lowered their production levels, the Iran hostage crisis occurred, and the Iran–Iraq War began.

There was fear that the world's oil market supply was tenuous, causing the price of oil to escalate and that OPEC would dictate very high prices in a shortage.

Production

OPEC, Non-OPEC, & World oil production, 1973-2004

Non-OPEC

During the 1980s, non-OPEC production increased worldwide.

US

In April 1979, Jimmy Carter signed an executive order which was to remove market controls from petroleum products by October 1981, so that prices would be wholly determined by the free market. Ronald Reagan signed an executive order on January 28, 1981 which enacted this reform immediately, allowing the free market to adjust oil prices in the US.

This ended the withdrawal of old oil from the market and artificial scarcity, encouraging increased oil production. The US Oil Windfall profits tax was lowered in August 1981 and removed in 1988, ending disincentives to US oil producers. Additionally, the Alaskan Prudhoe Bay Oil Field entered peak production, supplying the US West Coast with up to 2 million bpd of crude oil.

OPEC

From 1980 to 1986, OPEC decreased oil production several times and nearly in half to maintain oil's high prices. However, it failed to hold on to its preeminent position, and by 1981, its production was surpassed by Non-OPEC countries.

OPEC had seen its share of the world market drop to less than a third in 1985, from nearly half during the 1970s. In Feb 1982, the *Boston Globe* reported that OPEC's production, which had previously peaked in 1977, was at its lowest level since 1969. Non-OPEC nations were at that time supplying most of the West's imports.

OPEC's membership began to have divided opinions over what actions to take. In September 1985, Saudi Arabia tried to gain market share by increasing production, creating a "huge surplus that angered many of their colleagues in OPEC". High-cost oil production facilities became less or even not profitable.

US Imports

The US imported 28 percent of its oil in 1982 and 1983, down from 46.5 percent in 1977, due to lower consumption. Reliance on Middle East sources dwindled even further as Britain, Mexico, Nigeria and Norway joined Canada in the forefront of American suppliers.

Imported crude oil from Libya was banned in the United States on March 10, 1982.

Reduced Demand

OPEC had relied on the price elasticity of demand of oil to maintain high consumption, but underestimated the extent to which other sources of supply would become profitable as prices increased. Electricity generation from nuclear power and natural gas; home heating from natural gas; and ethanol blended gasoline all reduced the demand for oil. New passenger car fuel economy rose from 17 mpg in 1978 to more than 22 mpg in 1982, an increase of more than 30 percent.

Impact

The 1986 oil price collapse benefited oil-consuming countries such as the United States, Japan, Europe, and Third World nations, but represented a serious loss in revenue for oil-producing countries in northern Europe, the Soviet Union, and OPEC.

In 1981, before the brunt of the glut, *Time Magazine* wrote that in general, "A glut of crude causes tighter development budgets" in some oil-exporting nations. In a handful of heavily populated impoverished countries whose economies were largely dependent on oil production — including Mexico, Nigeria, Algeria, and Libya — government and business leaders failed to prepare for a market reversal. With the drop in oil prices, OPEC lost its unity. Oil exporters such as Mexico, Nigeria, and Venezuela, whose economies had expanded in the 1970s, were plunged into near-bankruptcy. Even Saudi Arabian economic power was significantly weakened.

Iraq had fought a long and costly war against Iran, and had particularly weak revenues. It was upset by Kuwait contributing to the glut and allegedly pumping oil from the Rumaila field below their common border. Iraq invaded Kuwait territory in 1990, planning to increase reserves and revenues and cancel the debt, resulting in the first Gulf War.

The USSR had become a major oil producer before the glut. The drop of oil prices contributed to the nation's final collapse.

In the US, domestic exploration declined dramatically, and the number of active drilling rigs was nearly halved in 1982." Oil producers held back on the search for new oilfields for fear of losing on their investments. In May 2007, companies like ExxonMobil were not making nearly the investment in finding new oil today that they did in 1981. Cities that had experienced tremendous growth when oil prices were high, most notably Houston and New Orleans, endured severe local recessions as prices collapsed.

2000s Energy Crisis

From the mid-1980s to September 2003, the inflation-adjusted price of a barrel of crude oil on NYMEX was generally under $25/barrel. During 2003, the price rose above $30, reached $60 by August 11, 2005, and peaked at $147.30 in July 2008. Commentators attributed these price increases to many factors, including reports from the United States Department of Energy and others showing a decline in petroleum reserves, worries over peak oil, Middle East tension, and oil price speculation.

For a time, geo-political events and natural disasters indirectly related to the global oil market had strong short-term effects on oil prices, such as North Korean missile tests, the 2006 conflict between Israel and Lebanon, worries over Iranian nuclear plans in 2006, Hurricane Katrina, and various other factors. By 2008, such pressures appeared to have an insignificant impact on oil prices given the onset of the global recession. The recession caused demand for energy to shrink in late 2008, with oil prices falling from the July 2008 high of $147 to a December 2008 low of $32. Oil prices stabilized by October 2009 and established a trading range between $60 and $80.

New Inflation-adjusted Records

The price of crude oil in 2003 traded in a range between $20–$30/bbl. Between 2003 and July 2008, prices steadily rose, reaching $100/bbl in late 2007, tying the previous all time inflation-adjusted record set in 1980. A steep rise in the price of oil in 2008 - also mirrored by other commodities - culminated in an all time high of $147.27 during trading on July 11, 2008, more than a third above the previous inflation-adjusted high. High oil prices and economic weakness contributed to a demand contraction in 2007-2008. In the United States, gasoline consumption declined by 0.4% in 2007, then fell by 0.5% in the first two months of 2008 alone. Record-setting oil prices in the first half of 2008 and economic weakness in the second half of the year prompted a 1.2 Mbbl (190,000 m^3)/day contraction in US consumption of petroleum products, representing 5.5% of total US consumption, the largest decline since 1980 at the climax of the 1979 energy crisis.

Possible Causes

Demand

World crude oil demand grew an average of 1.76% per year from 1994 to 2006, with a high of 3.4% in 2003-2004. World demand for oil is projected to increase 37% over 2006 levels by 2030, according to the 2007 U.S. Energy Information Administration's (EIA) annual report. In 2007, the EIA expected demand to reach an ultimate high of 118 million barrels per day (18.8×10^6 m^3/d), from 2006's 86 million barrels (13.7×10^6 m^3), driven in large part by the transportation sector. A 2008 report from the International Energy Agency (IEA) predicted that although drops in petroleum demand due to high prices have been observed in developed countries and are expected to continue, a 3.7 percent rise in demand by 2013 is predicted in developing countries.

This is projected to cause a net rise in global petroleum demand during that period. Transportation consumes the largest proportion of energy, and has seen the largest growth in demand in recent decades. This growth has largely come from new demand for personal-use vehicles powered by internal combustion engines. This sector also has the highest consumption rates, accounting for approximately 55% of oil use worldwide as documented in the Hirsch report and 68.9% of the oil used in the United States in 2006. Cars and trucks are predicted to cause almost 75% of the increase in oil consumption by India and China between 2001 and 2025. In 2008, auto sales in China have been expected to grow by as much as 15-20 percent, resulting in part from economic growth rates of over 10 percent for 5 years in a row.

Demand growth is highest in the developing world, but the United States is the world's largest consumer of petroleum. Between 1995 and 2005, US consumption grew from 17.7 million barrels (2,810,000 m^3) a day to 20.7 million barrels (3,290,000 m^3) a day, a 3-million-barrel (480,000 m^3) a day increase. China, by comparison, increased consumption from 3.4 million barrels (540,000 m^3) a day to 7 million barrels (1,100,000 m^3) a day, an increase of 3.6 million barrels (570,000 m^3) a day, in the same time frame. Per capita, annual consumption by people in the US is 24.85 barrels (3.951 m^3), 1.79 barrels (0.285 m^3) in China, and 0.79 barrels (0.126 m^3) in India.

As countries develop, industry, rapid urbanization and higher living standards drive up energy use, most often of oil. Thriving economies such as China and India are quickly becoming large oil consumers. China has seen oil consumption grow by 8% yearly since 2002, doubling from 1996-2006. Although swift continued growth in China is often predicted, others predict that China's export dominated economy will not continue such growth trends due to wage and price inflation and reduced demand from the US. India's oil imports are expected to more than triple from 2005 levels by 2020, rising to 5 million barrels per day (790×10^3 m^3/d).

Another large factor on petroleum demand has been human population growth. Because world population grew faster than oil production, production per capita peaked in 1979 (preceded by a plateau during the period of 1973-1979). The world's population in 2030 is expected to be double that of 1980.

The Role of Fuel Subsidies

State fuel subsidies have shielded consumers in many nations from the price rises, but many of these subsidies are being reduced or removed as the cost to governments of subsidization increases.

In June 2008, AFP reported that: "China became the latest Asian nation to curb energy subsidies last week after hiking retail petrol and diesel prices as much as 18 percent... Elsewhere in Asia, Malaysia has hiked fuel prices by 41 percent and Indonesia by around 29 percent, while Taiwan and India have also raised their energy costs."

In the same month, Reuters reported that:

"Countries like China and India, along with Gulf nations whose retail oil prices are kept below global prices, contributed 61 percent of the increase in global consumption of crude oil from 2000 to 2006, according to JPMorgan.

Other than Japan, Hong Kong, Singapore and South Korea, most Asian nations subsidize domestic fuel prices. The more countries subsidize them, the less likely high oil prices will have any affect [*sic*] in reducing overall demand, forcing governments in weaker financial situations to surrender first and stop their subsidies.

That is what happened over the past two weeks. Indonesia, Taiwan, Sri Lanka, Bangladesh, India, and Malaysia have either raised regulated fuel prices or pledged that they will. "

The Economist reported: "Half of the world's population enjoys fuel subsidies. This estimate, from Morgan Stanley, implies that almost a quarter of the world's petrol is sold at less than the market price." U.S. Secretary of Energy Samuel Bodman stated that around 30 million barrels per day (4,800,000 m^3/d) of oil consumption (over a third of the global total) is subsidized. But energy analyst Jeff Vail warned that cutting subsidies would do little to reduce global prices.

Supply

An important contributor to price increases has been the slow down in oil supply growth, which has continued since oil production surpassed new discoveries in 1980. The fact that global oil production will decline at some point, leading to lower supply is the main long-term fundamental cause of rising prices. Although there is contention about the exact time at which global production will peak, there are now very few parties who do not acknowledge that the concept of a production peak is valid. However, before the record oil prices of 2008, some commentators argued that global warming awareness and new energy sources would limit demand before the effects of supply could, suggesting that reserve depletion would be a non-issue.

A large factor in the lower supply growth of petroleum has been that oil's historically high ratio of Energy Returned on Energy Invested is in significant decline. Petroleum is a limited resource, and the remaining accessible reserves are consumed more rapidly each year. Remaining reserves are increasingly more technically difficult to extract and therefore more expensive.

Eventually, reserves will only be economically feasible to extract at extremely high prices. Even if total oil supply does not decline, increasing numbers of experts believe the easily accessible sources of light sweet crude are almost exhausted and in the future the world will depend on more expensive unconventional oil reserves and heavy oil, as well as renewable energy sources. It is thought by many, including energy economists such as Matthew Simmons, that prices could continue to rise indefinitely until a new market equilibrium is reached at which point supply satisfies worldwide demand.

A prominent example of investment in non-conventional sources is seen in the Canadian tar sands. They are a far less cost-efficient source of heavy, low-grade oil than conventional crude, but when oil trades above $60/bbl, the tar sands become attractive to exploration and production companies. While Canada's tar sands region is estimated to contain as much "heavy" oil as all the world's reserves of "conventional" oil, efforts to economically exploit these resources lag behind the increasing demand of recent years.

Until 2008, CERA (a consulting company wholly owned by energy consultants IHS Energy) did not believe this would be such an immediate problem. However, in an interview with *The Wall Street Journal,* Daniel Yergin, previously known for his quotes that the price of oil would soon return down to "normal", amended the company's position on May 7, 2008 to predict that oil would reach $150 during 2008, due to tightness of supply This reversal of opinion was significant, as CERA, among other consultancies, provided price projections that were used by many official bodies to plan long term strategy in respect of energy mix and price.

Other major energy organisations, such as the International Energy Agency (IEA), had already been much less optimistic in their assessments for some time. In 2008, the IEA drastically reduced its prediction of production decline from 3.7% a year to 6.7% a year, based largely on better accounting methods, including actual research of individual oil field production throughout the world.

Terrorist and insurgent groups have increasingly targeted oil and gas installations.. Sometimes, such attacks are perpetrated by militias in regions where oil wealth has produced few tangible benefits for the local citizenry, as is the case in the Niger Delta. Many factors have resulted in possible and/or actual concerns about reduced supply of oil. The post-9/11 war on terror, Labour strikes, hurricane threats to oil platforms, fires and terrorist threats at refineries, and other short-lived problems are not solely responsible for the higher prices. Such problems do push prices higher temporarily, but have not historically been fundamental to long-term price increases.

Investment Demand

Investment demand for oil occurs when investors purchase *futures contracts* to buy a commodity at a set price for future delivery. "Speculators are not buying any actual crude.... When [the] contracts mature, they either settle them with a cash payment or sell them on to genuine consumers."

Several claims have been made implicating financial speculation as a major cause of the price increases. In May 2008 the transport chief for Germany's Social Democrats estimated that 25 percent of the rise to $135 a barrel had nothing to do with underlying supply and demand. Testimony was given to a U.S. Senate committee in May indicating that "demand shock" from "Institutional Investors" had increased by 848 million barrels (134,800,000 m^3) over the last five years, similar to increases in demand from China (920 million barrels (146,000,000 m^3)).

The influence of Institutional Investors, such as sovereign-wealth funds, was also discussed in June 2008, when Lehman Brothers suggested that price increases were related to increases in exposure to commodities by such investors. It claimed that "for every $100 million in new inflows, the price of West Texas Intermediate, the U.S. benchmark, increased by 1.6%." Also in May 2008, an article in *The Economist* pointed out that oil futures transactions on the New York Mercantile Exchange (NYMEX), nearly mirrored the price of oil increases for a several year period, however the article conceded that the increased investment might be following rising prices, rather than causing them, and that the nickel commodity market had halved in value between May 2007 and May 2008 despite significant speculative interest.

It also reminds readers "Investment can flood into the oil market without driving up prices because speculators are not buying any actual crude... no oil is hoarded or somehow kept off the market," and that prices of some commodities which are not openly traded have actually risen faster than oil prices. In June 2008, OPEC's Secretary General Abdullah al-Badri stated that current world consumption of oil at 87 Mbbl/d (13,800,000 m^3/d) was far exceeded by the "paper market" for oil, which equals about 1.36 billion bpd, or more than 15 times the actual market demand.

In response to the possibility that financial speculators artificially inflated the oil market, the U.S. Congress began hearings in June 2008 to discover if actions to "tighten restrictions on pension funds, investment banks and other investors that they say are driving up fuel prices" were necessary.

An interagency task force on commodities markets was formed in the U.S. government to investigate the claims of speculators influence on the petroleum market concluded in July 2008 that "market fundamentals" such as supply and demand provide the best explanations for oil price increases, and that increased speculation was not statistically correlated with the increases.

The report also noted that increased prices with an elastic supply would cause increases in petroleum inventories. As inventories have actually declined, the task force concluded market pressures are most likely to blame. Similarly, other commodities which are not subject to market speculation (such as coal, steel, and onions) have seen similar price increases over the same time period. In June 2008 U.S. energy secretary Samuel Bodman had said that insufficient oil production, not financial speculation, was driving rising crude prices. He said that oil production has not kept pace with growing demand. "In the absence of any additional crude supply, for every 1% of crude demand, we will expect a 20% increase in price in order to balance the market," Bodman said. This contradicts earlier statements by Iranian OPEC governor Mohammad-Ali Khatibi indicating that the oil market is saturated and that an increase in production announced by Saudi Arabia was "wrong". OPEC itself had also previously stated that the oil market was well supplied and that high prices were a result of speculation and a weak U.S. dollar.

In September 2008, a study of the oil market by Masters Capital Management was released which claimed that speculation did significantly impact the market. The study stated that over $60 billion was invested in oil during the first 6 months of 2008, helping drive the price per barrel from $95 to $147 per barrel, and that by the beginning of September, $39 billion had been withdrawn by speculators, causing prices to fall.

Monetary Inflation and the Value of the US Dollar

The Austrian School of economics holds that price inflation derives from monetary inflation, and its advocates, such as the Ludwig von Mises Institute and congressman Ron Paul, argue that loose monetary policy from the Federal Reserve and other central banks is a major contributor to the increase in oil prices, and the cause of both commodity speculation and dollar devaluation.

Oil is quoted and traded in US Dollars. Therefore by definition the price or value of oil fluctuates based on investors' assessment of the value of oil and US Dollars. This has led to concern among some economists that the principal earned from the sale of oil may lose value in the long run if the U.S. dollar loses real value. Some analysts believe that as much as $25 of the June 2008 prices around $140 were due to dollar devaluation.

The US Dollar price of oil demonstrated a strong positive correlation with the EUR/USD exchange rate from 2006 to 2010.

Effects

There is debate over what the effects of the 2000s energy crisis will be over the long term. Some speculate that an oil-price spike could create a recession comparable to those that followed the 1973 and 1979 energy crises or a potentially worse situation such as a global oil crash. Increased petroleum prices are however reflected in a vast number of products derived from petroleum, as well as those transported using petroleum fuels.

Political scientist George Friedman has postulated that if high prices for oil and food persist, they will define the fourth distinct geopolitical regime since the end of World War II, the previous three being the Cold War, the 1989-2001 period in which economic globalization was primary, and the post-9/11 "war on terror".

In addition to high oil prices, from year 2000 volatility in the price of oil has increased notably and this volatility has been suggested to be a factor in the ongoing financial crisis which began in 2008.

Forecasted Prices and Trends

According to informed observers, OPEC, meeting in early December, 2007, seemed to desire a high but stable price that would deliver substantial needed income to the oil producing states, but avoid prices so high that they would negatively impact the economies of the oil consuming nations. A range of 70–80 dollars a barrel was suggested by some analysts to be OPEC's goal.

Some analysts point out that major oil exporting countries are rapidly developing; and because they are using more oil domestically, less oil may be available on the international market. This effect, outlined in the export land economic model, could significantly reduce the oil available for trade and cause prices to continue to rise. Particularly significant are Indonesia (which is now a net importer of oil), Mexico and Iran (where demand is projected to exceed production in about 5 years), and Russia (whose domestic petroleum demand is growing rapidly).

In May 2008, T. Boone Pickens, an influential oil investor who believes the world's oil output is about to peak, predicted oil prices would hit $150 a barrel by the end of the year. "Eighty-five million barrels of oil a day is all the world can produce, and the demand is 87 m," Mr Pickens said in an interview with CNBC. "It's just that simple."

In June 2008, Alexei Miller, head of Russian energy giant Gazprom, warned that the price of oil is likely to hit $250 a barrel sometime in 2009. Miller said that while speculation had played a role in oil prices, "this influence was not decisive." Bloomberg reported that, as of mid-June, "At least 3,008 options contracts have been purchased giving holders the right to buy oil at $250 a barrel in December". Also in June 2008, Shukri Ghanem, head of Libya's National Oil Corporation, said: "I think it [the oil price] will go higher. That is a trend that will continue for some time. The easy, cheap oil is over, peak oil is looming."

On June 26, 2008, OPEC President Chakib Khelil said in an interview: "I forecast prices probably between $150-170 during this summer. That will perhaps ease towards the end of the year." Iran's OPEC governor Mohammad-Ali Khatibi predicts that the price of oil would reach $150 a barrel by the end of this summer.

Near-term peak oil proponent Matthew Simmons predicts a rise to $300 a barrel or higher by 2013 as sweet crude petroleum becomes more scarce and major producers begin failing to meet demand.

In November, as prices fell below $60 a barrel, the IEA warned that falling prices may create both a lack of investment in new sources of oil and a fall in production of more expensive unconventional reserves such as the tar sands of Canada. The IEA's chief economist warned, "Oil supplies in the future will come more and more from smaller and more difficult fields," meaning that future production requires more investment every year.

A lack of new investment in such projects, which had already been observed, could eventually cause new and more severe supply issues than had been experienced in the early 2000s according to the IEA. Because the sharpest production declines had been seen in developed countries, the IEA warned that the greatest growth in production was expected to come from smaller projects in OPEC states, raising their world production share from 44% in 2008 to a projected 51% in 2030. The IEA also pointed out that demand from the developed world may have also peaked, so that future demand growth was likely to come from developing nations such as China, contributing 43%, and India and the Middle East, each about 20%).

Timothy Kailing argued against the IEA's earlier predictions in a 2008 Journal of Energy Security article. He pointed out the difficulty of increasing production even with vastly increased investment in exploration and production in mature petroleum regions. By looking at the historical response of production to variation in drilling effort, this analysis claimed that very little increase of production could be attributed to increased drilling. This was due to a tight the quantitative relationship of diminishing returns with increasing drilling effort: as drilling effort increased, the energy obtained per active drill rig was reduced according to a severely diminishing power law. This fact means that even an enormous increase of drilling effort is unlikely to lead to significantly increased oil and gas production in a mature petroleum region like the United States.

In its 2008 World Energy Outlook, the International Energy Agency (IEA) predicted a rate of decline in output from the world's existing oilfields of 6.7% a year.

The End of the Crisis

By the beginning of September 2008, prices had fallen to $110. OPEC secretary Abdalla El-Badri said that it intended to cut output by about 500,000 barrels (79,000 m^3) a day, which he saw as correcting a "huge oversupply" due to declining economies and a stronger U.S. dollar. On September 10, the International Energy Agency (IEA) lowered its 2009 demand forecast by 140,000 barrels (22,000 m^3) to 87.6 million barrels (13,930,000 m^3) a day.

As many countries throughout the world entered an economic recession in the third quarter of 2008, prices continued to slide. In November and December, global demand growth fell, and U.S. demand fell 10% overall from early October to early November 2008 (accompanying a significant drop in auto sales).

In their December meeting, OPEC planned to reduce their production by 2.2 million barrels (350,000 m^3) per day, though they admitted their resolution to reduce production in October had only an 85% compliance rate.

Petroleum prices had fallen to below $35 in February 2009, but on May 6, 2009 had risen back to mid-November 2008 levels at about $56. The global economic downturn left oil storage facilities with more oil than in any year since 1990, when Iraq's invasion of Kuwait upset the market.

As of May 2011, the price of U.S. WTI crude reached $113, while Brent crude, more indicative of world price due to a supply glut at Cushing Oklahoma, reached $127 a barrel. After several weeks of fluctuating between rising and falling prices, protests in the Middle East and North Africa drove prices up. Although prices were beginning to ease with the calming of the revolution in Egypt, prices spiked to $100 for the first time since September 2008 with the protests in Libya.

Bibliography

Anthony H.: *The Gulf and the West: Strategic Relations and Military Realities*, Westview Press, Boulder, Colo., 1988.

Armistead, George: *Safety in Petroleum Refining and Related Industries*, New York: John G. Simmons & Co., 1950.

Barua, Lohit: *Natural Gas Measurement and Control: A Guide for Operators and Engineers*, McGraw-Hill Professional Book Group, London, 1991.

Bromley, Simon: *American Hegemony and World Oil: The Industry, the State System, and the World Economy*. University Park, Pa., 1991.

Chowdhary, L.R. : *Petroleum Geology of the Cambay Basin, Gujarat, India*, Indian Petroleum, Delhi, 2004.

Christopher J. Moody: *Experimental Organic Chemistry: Principles and Practice*, WileyBlackwell, Oxford, 1989.

Davis, John: *Oil and Canada-United States Relations*, National Planning Association, New York, 1959.

Devereux, Steve: *Drilling for Oil & Gas: A Nontechnical Guide,* PennWell, Tulsa, OK, 1999.

Edward W.: *United States Oil Policy and Diplomacy: A Twentieth-Century Overview*. West-port, Conn.: Greenwood Press, 1983.

Edward, John : *History of Oil Well Drilling*, Book Division, Gulf Pub. Co., Houston, 1971.

Feis, Herbert: *Petroleum and American Foreign Policy*. Stanford: Food Research Institute, 1944.

Frank, Alison Fleig: *Oil Empire: Visions of Prosperity in Austrian Galicia,* Harvard University Press, 2005.

Garverick, Linda: *Corrosion in the Petrochemical Industry*. Materials Park, Ohio: ASM International, 2000.

Ghalambor, Ali : *Petroleum Production Engineering: A Computer-assisted Approach,* Gulf Professional Pub., Burlington, MA, 2007.

Hannum, M.B.: *Late Quaternary Evolution of the Kennebec and Damariscotta River Estuaries*, Geological Sciences, Univ. Maine, Orono, 1997.

Henley, E. J. and J. D. Seader: *Equilibrium Stage Operations in Chemical Engineering,* John Wiley and Sons, New York, 1981.

Jiang, R. : *Atlas for Coal Petrography of China*, China University of Mining and Technology Press, Beijing, 1996.

Kent, Marian: *Oil and Empire: British Policy and Mesopotamian Oil, 1900-1920*. London: Macmillan, 1976.

Klare, Michael: *Resource Wars: The New Landscape of Global Conflict*. Metropolitan Books / Henry Holt, 2001.

Langran, G.: *Time in Geographic Information Systems,* Taylor & Francis, Bristol, 1992.

Leopold, L.B. : *Water in Environmental Planning*, W.H. Freeman and Co., San Francisco, CA, 1978.

Macko, S. : *Organic Geochemistry; Principles and Applications*, Plenum Press, New York, 1993.

Maddox, R. M. : *Mass Transfer: Fundamentals and Applications*, Prentice-Hall PTR, Upper Saddle River, NJ, 1985.

Norman J.: *Nontechnical Guide to Petroleum Geology, Exploration, Drilling, and Production.* PennWell Corporation, Delhi, 2001.

Odell, Peter R.: *Oil and World Power: Background of the Oil Crisis,* New York: Viking Penguin, 1986.

Peuquet, D.: *Representations of Space and Time*. New York: Guilford Press, 2002.

Rabek, J.: *Experimental Methods in Physical Chemistry and Photophysics*, New York: Oxford University Press, 1989.

Saferstein, Richard: *Criminalistics: An Introduction to Forensic Science*. Upper Saddle River, NJ: Prentice Hall, 1998.

Thomas, L.: *Handbook of Practical Coal Geology*: John Wiley & Sons, Chichester, 1992.

Torben Smith Sørensen: *Surface Chemistry and Electrochemistry of Membranes*, CRC Press, NY, 1999.

Underhill, J. R., Lappin M.: *3D Seismic Technology: Application to the Exploration of Sedimentary Basins*, Geological Society, London, Memoir, 2003.

Vervalin, Charles H.: *Fire Protection Manual for Hydrocarbon Processing Plants*. Houston: Gulf Publishing Co, 1985.

Walton, H. E. : *The Chronological History of the Petroleum and Natural Gas Industries,* Clark Book Co., Houston, 1963.

William L.: *The Oil Business As I Saw It: Half a Century with Sinclair*. Norman: University of Oklahoma Press, 1954.

Yergin, Daniel: *The Prize: The Epic Quest for Oil, Money, and Power*. New York: Simon and Schuster, 1991.

Index

J

K

L

M

N

O

P

R

S

T

V

W

❑❑❑